AFGHANISTAN
A HISTORY OF CONFLICT

Other Books by the Author:

Non Fiction

Afghanistan
Afghanistan: Key to a Continent
Fathercare: a handbook for single fathers
Imperial Call
Modern Iceland
Nimbus
The Science of Winning Squash
The Third Man: a biography of William Murdoch
Three Tomorrows

Fiction

The Queen of Spades, an Afghan adventure
The Survivors

AFGHANISTAN

A HISTORY OF CONFLICT

JOHN C. GRIFFITHS

ANDRE
DEUTSCH

First published in 1981 by André Deutsch Ltd

This updated edition published in 2001 by André Deutsch
An imprint of the Carlton Publishing Group
20 Mortimer Street
London
W1T 3JW

A CIP catalogue record for this book is available from the British
Library.

ISBN 0 233 05053 1

Printed and bound in Great Britain by Mackays of Chatham.

For the poor, bloodied Afghans, Peace Be Upon Them.

list of maps

Contents

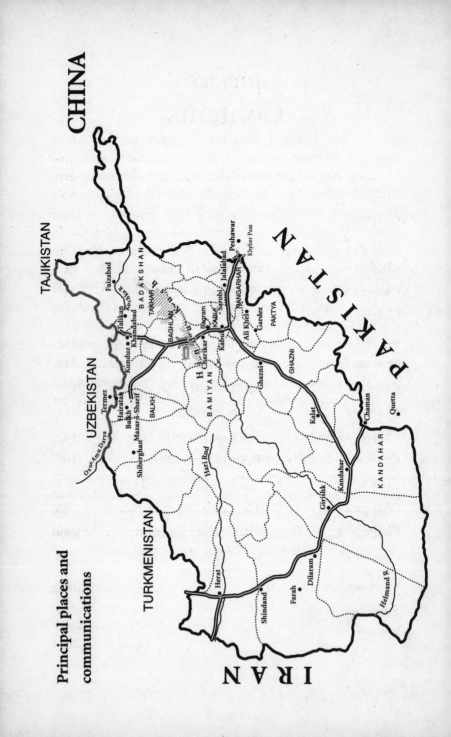

Principal places and communications

preface

When André Deutsch asked me to update this book in a month I accepted because I felt a reasonably accessible background to the present conflict in Afghanistan would serve a useful purpose. I also felt I owed a debt to the Afghan people accumulated over the years which could be repaid in some small way by telling their story. I have not attempted to catalogue the fluid and constantly changing events in Afghanistan since the World Trade Center attack, but have confined myself to observations on general trends. While able to utilise much of the material from my last Afghan book for Deutsch (*Afghanistan: Key to a Continent*) for the early part of this one I am also much indebted to the scholars and specialists on whose comprehensive and more detailed studies I have since drawn. Some of these are referred to in the short reading list and I hope they will excuse any errors and infelicities that remain in the text as a result of my haste.

I am grateful to the librarians and others who have helped me obtain information and documentation at very short notice among them Mary Bone, Sherri Carnson, Peter Colvin, Karen Davis, Catherine Hume, Christian Purefoy, and the ladies of Monmouth library. My final thanks must go to my editor, Nick Brock for patient and painstaking improvement of my text and my publisher Claire Richardson for her encouragement.

John Griffiths

White Rocks House
October 25, 2001

INTRODUCTION

On a clear night in June 1747, the army of Nadir Shah of Persia, whose conquests had ranged from Turkey to India, lay encamped not far from Meshed* in northern Persia. Its royal commander had decided to punish a rebellious Kurdish tribe which had attacked his stud farm at Radkan. For this rebellion – and it was but one of many at the time – Nadir Shah had only his own increasing mental derangement to blame, for it was leading him into cruelties horrifying even by the standards of a cruel age. A French priest who accompanied the Shah records that "wherever he had halted he had many people tortured and put to death, and had towers of their heads erected".

Ahmad Khan, an Afghan noble in his early twenties, sat outside his tent in the Shah's encampment, reflecting on the circumstances that had brought him, the son of one of Nadir's defeated opponents, into the Persian monarch's personal staff at the age of 16 to become, now, the commander of that Afghan contingent, four thousand strong, which had been at the core of so many of the Shah's campaigns.

An excited messenger from Nadir broke into his meditations. Ahmad was to arm his Afghans, arrest all the officers of the Shah's personal bodyguard in the morning, and take over the guard duties himself. His master – always suspecting plots, some real, some imagined – had that day learned of yet another conspiracy against him. He had tried to flee the camp, but the guards had dissuaded him with

*There are numerous English spellings extant of this as of many other Persian, Pushtu and Arabic terms that appear in this text. My preferences are chosen fairly arbitrarily, but in quotations I retain those used in the original.

protestations of loyalty. Yet it was the commander of the guard who was the chief instigator of the plot, and the Shah was taking no chances. The conspirators were to be put in irons.

Unfortunately for the Shah, his instructions to Ahmad were overheard by an agent of the conspirators; they realized that their only hope lay in immediate action in anticipation of the counterplot. Many of them backed out of the crisis, but a handful made their way into Nadir's tent past the acquiescent guard. One conspirator slashed off the hand that the Shah raised in self-defence, another then struck off his head. The murder – perhaps tyrannicide would be a more accurate description – had to be kept secret from the Afghan and Uzbeg troops so that these could be taken unawares in the morning. But Ahmad Khan was to benefit from having a friend in the right place. One of Nadir Shah's widows was able to get a message to him about the attack. Such a thing seemed incredible; even so, Ahmad stood his men to arms all night and at first light ordered them to the Shah's tent to establish the accuracy of the report. At the women's quarters further advance was barred by the Turkmen guards who were plundering the camp indiscriminately, but the Afghans fought their way through to learn for themselves that they had been told the truth.

By now, the disparate tribal contingents were seizing the chance to settle old scores. A dozen minor battles flared throughout the camp. In the confusion of Nadir Shah's instantly disintegrating empire, Ahmad and his followers hacked their way out of the camp and began their march home – taking the fabulous Koh-i-Noor diamond with them. By the time they neared their destination, Kandahar, the members of the Afghan force, drawn from a variety of tribes, had come to the conclusion that they now owed no allegiance to a Persian suzerain and should claim independence under their own elected chief. But who was this chief to be?

The story has it that for eight long sessions they debated the matter, during all of which time Ahmad Khan said not a word. Then, in the ninth session, as the argument slackened through sheer weariness, the darvesh Sabir Shah jumped to his feet to advance Ahmad Khan's claims. "Why all this verbosity? God has created Ahmad Khan, a much greater man than any of you. His is the most noble of all the Afghan families. Maintain, therefore, God's work, for His wrath will weigh heavily on you if you destroy it." While this account may seem an unlikely tale, clearly Ahmad Khan – or Ahmad Shah Durr-i-Durran (Pearl of Pearls), as he now became – had already made a great impression on his fellow Afghans by virtue of his ability and personality. This impression he was quickly to enhance by his subsequent actions.

No sooner had Ahmad entered Kandahar than he managed to seize a treasure caravan of tribute bound for Nadir Shah. This he generously and shrewdly distributed among the Afghan chiefs. It was also psychologically astute of him to give the new name of Durrani to his own tribe, the Abdali, thus identifying them with himself and not with past feuds, quarrels and jealousies. In the course of the next 26 years, his military and political genius was to create an Afghanistan that was, for the first time, a distinct political entity in Central Asia, and a clearly recognizable progenitor of present-day Afghanistan.

To begin an account of present-day Afghanistan with a description of the events and outcome of a single night may seem a little odd. But that June night in 1747 is much more than a dramatic adventure in the life of a tribal chief. It not only typifies the treachery, brutality and intrigue that have been commonplace in so much Afghan history; it also marks a watershed in Afghanistan's development. On the one side, there are two thousand years and more in which the country was washed over by the sedimentary ethnic tides of invasion after invasion, and during which it – or various parts of it – formed only provinces of extensive empires. On the other side, there is the simultaneous expansion of the European powers in Asia and the growth, albeit gradual, of some sort of national consciousness in Afghanistan itself.

The problems which faced Ahmad Shah – the judicious and equitable distribution of limited wealth, the unification of naturally heterogeneous peoples, the balance between local freedom and an overall stable central rule, subservience to suzerain powers – have been, in various forms, the major problems of Afghanistan during the two-and-a-half centuries since the start of his reign. It is with the evolution of those problems and their consequences for today that this book is concerned.

1

FULCRUM OF EMPIRES

The peaks and passes of the Hindu Kush have been the fulcrum by which ambitious powers have tried to lever an empire into their grasp for over two thousand years, long before there was such a country as Afghanistan.

Afghans* are first referred to as a people in the tenth century AD, but as the tribal inhabitants of certain parts of the country now known as Afghanistan, rather than as "nationals" of the whole country. In the eighteenth and nineteenth centuries Afghans themselves would have talked of their own regions by tribal names, and any references to the larger area would probably have been to "Pushtun". It was only through Persian and English writers that the term "Afghanistan", and indeed "Afghans", first came into general usage, due to the fact that the ruling house was Afghan. Throughout this book, the people of Afghan race are denoted by the Indian word "Pathans". To call them "Pushtuns" would imply that they all speak Pushtu, which is not the case. The term "Afghans" is here made to refer to all citizens of modern Afghanistan, not solely to that racial group to which the term strictly applies. It must be borne in mind, however, that in earlier times no members of the other racial groups would have dreamed of calling themselves Afghans.

The country of the Afghans is one of sharp contrasts in climate, terrain and people. There are deserts of every kind, in

*G.Michanovsky suggests that the name derives from the Sanskrit Avagana' which in turn goes back to the Sumerian (c.3000BC) word for the mountainous region of Badakshan "Ab-bar-Gan" or "High Country".

the midst of which the traveller comes with eye-catching suddenness on green and fertile valleys or a confetti of purple flowers scattered across seemingly arid soil. In summer they may encounter a heat that seems to make the very flesh singe, while in winter a scimitar wind guards the snow-blocked passes of the mountains that cover so much of the country.

The people vary greatly in stature, colour, race and feature, the ethnic sediment deposited in the tidal wake of at least two thousand years of invasions, sweeping by along the breakwater of the Hindu Kush mountains and towards India. The Hindu Kush cuts Afghanistan virtually in half, running from the thin strip of inaccessible mountains in the north-east that barely separates Russia, China and Pakistan, almost to the empty desert sands of the western border with Iran. South and south-east lie Kandahar, Ghazni and Kabul, to the north and north-east Mazar-i-Sharif, and Faizabad, to the west Herat. Northward of these towns, the river Oxus forms much of the border with Russia. In the south of the country, the people are mainly Pathans; in the north, Tajiks, Turkmen, Kirghiz and Uzbegs; and in the central mountains, Hazaras.

Every landward invasion of the subcontinent – save for that of the Arabs, in the eighth century of our era, through the then much more fertile Makran – has pivoted on the south-western end of the Hindu Kush or has filtered, in season, through its high passes. This has given a continental strategic significance to Herat, Kandahar and Kabul. The pattern of invasion and empire has been markedly repetitive. The impulse of the first irresistible thrust south or east; a pivot on the south-western flank of the Hindu Kush; a brief pause to conquer and consolidate some such vantage point as Ghazni or Kabul; a sweep down into India and a battle in the first open country beyond the Indus, to establish a seat in northern India itself;

and then the gradual softening of the conquerors in the enervating climate until they can no longer resist new invaders pressing behind them or are overthrown for a brief interregnum by a locally nurtured dynasty – for two millennia, this has been the oft-repeated experience of those over whom the endless armies swept.

In his history of the Pathans, Sir Olaf Caroe lists no less than 25 dynasties ruling over all or part of what is now Afghanistan – from the Achaemenian dominion of Cyrus and Darius the Great in the sixth century BC to the last of the ruling house of the Barakzai, Prince Daoud, overthrown by the Russian-backed coup of 1978. In turn, Daoud was to be followed in swift succession by half-a-dozen other heads of government. In the first two millennia of this period Persian influence was not merely dominant but well-nigh exclusive – even most of those invaders who were not themselves Persian had undergone the transmutation of contact with Persian culture through either submission or conquest. This Persian influence still pervades Afghan life today.

Of all the conquests of the land of the Afghans, none can match – in military genius, at least – that of Alexander the Great who, in the four years between the battle of Gaugamela in 331 BC and the onset of his India campaign from its base at Alexandria Arachosia (Charikar), conquered the peoples of Khurasan, Transoxiana, and what we now call Afghanistan. He left behind him Greek-garrisoned cities, many bearing his name, which he hoped would be centres of civilized and ordered dominion. Alexander's hopes were not to be fulfilled. He conquered but could not subdue these Central Asian peoples, and no sooner had he died than his lieutenants, the new Hellenistic rulers of the old Persian satrapies, fell out among themselves. None of them was strong enough to achieve an overall control, although Hellenistic kingdoms –

such as that of the Seleucids and Graeco-Bactrians – were to survive in small parts of the area for a few more decades.

The significance of Alexander's invasion lies not so much in its military accomplishments, nor even in the social influence which, superficially at least, it appears to have had, as in its reversal, for the first time, of the common flow of conquest from the East to the West. Although the sweeping invasions of the hordes of Central Asia were still to come, from now on the peoples of the Mediterranean and mainland Europe could turn their eyes eastward, not just to watch for the dust clouds of invasion, but to dream of plunder, profit and glory for themselves.

The Macedonians were ousted by the only empire in this first millennium of our Afghan story to owe nothing to the Persians: the Maurya empire of Chandragupta in India. Under his grandson Asoka, Maurya rule in the second century BC spread the influence of Buddhism throughout this part of Asia. Today, however, little evidence of that faith remains in Afghanistan. Sadly, even the great rock-carvings of Bamiyan, which the ravages of Genghis Khan could not destroy, have now been smashed by the artillery of the fanatical Taliban.

Two other dynasties are worth noting prior to the coming of Islam. Though enduring for less than a hundred years, the Graeco-Bactrian empire of Demetrius and Menander, centred on Taxila (185–97BC), nurtured one of the great artistic flowerings of the ancient world – the sculptures of Gandhara. Although it now appears that many of the accomplishments of Gandharan art were achieved under the following Kushan dynasty, the impetus for this beautiful fusion of Greek and Buddhist artistic concepts stems from the earlier empire. Later, in the fifth century AD, Bactria was overrun by the White Huns: men of Turkic origin, tall and white-skinned. Checked momentarily by the Sassanid empire in Persia, by the end of the century the White Huns had not only made that empire tributary to their own, but had also mastered northern India, where their rule endured well into the sixth century of our era.

The breakdown of law and order following the invasion of the White Huns perhaps initiated that self-reliant parochialism which is at the root of the fierce tribal and microgeographical independence and mutual hostility which characterizes the structure of Afghan society in recent centuries. Even the unifying influence of Islam has been unable to break down this attitude.

Contrary to what some Afghan historians would have us believe, Afghanistan was not converted to Islam the moment the Prophet breathed the word. In fact, the first Muslim regime to control a considerable part of the country (and even then it was fully effective only south of the Hindu Kush) was the Ghaznavid kingdom. The town and province of Ghazni formed a part of the Persian Samanid empire and was governed for them by a series of Turkish mamluks. Sabuktagin, who served the last of these, overthrew his master in 977 and founded the dynasty which he named after the town. Under his son Mahmud it did, indeed, achieve considerable military and cultural renown, but, like so many others, it was short-lived. It was in Mahmud's reign, however, that Islam was forcibly made the religion of Afghanistan. Ghazni was sacked in 1150 by the otherwise undistinguished (if vainglorious) Tajik, Alauddjn Jahansoz – the World Burner, as he liked to be called. He compelled each of his captives to carry a heavy pack of the soil of Ghazni to his capital, Firoz-Koh in the mountains of Ghor. There he butchered his captives, mixed their blood with the soil of their native town, and built victory towers with the resultant mortar. It is hard to believe that such a barbarous tradition should lie behind the supposedly mild and peaceful Tajiks who farm the countryside north of Kabul, but that they still have the capacity for ferocious deeds is demonstrated by the seizure of the Afghan throne by a Tajik as recently as 1929, and their fierce resistance both to the Russian invaders and to the Taliban. For a brief period, then, rule over the Ghaznavid empire was borne by the forbears of the present Afghan Tajiks until they were brushed aside by the Mongol hordes of Genghis Khan, who again destroyed Ghazni some 70 years later.

Before reaching Ghazni in 1221–22, Genghis Khan had already razed cities and ravaged peoples over great swathes of Asia. Yet it was almost by accident that he came to establish his dreadful rule over so much of this part of Asia. His own home region firmly under his control, he was quite willing to live decently with his neighbour to the West, to whom he sent the following note:

> I am the sovereign of the sunrise, and thou the sovereign of sunset. Let there be between us a firm treaty of friendship, amity and peace, and let traders and caravans on both sides come and go, and let the precious products and ordinary commodities which may be in my territory be conveyed by them into thine, and those in thine to mine.

To give substance to his message he sent a treasure caravan of five hundred camels laden with gold, silver, silk, furs, sable and other "elegant and ingenious" rarities.

Unfortunately for the future of Central Asia, a greedy officer in command of the border seized Genghis Khan's treasure and butchered all but one member of the caravan. When, to add insult to injury, Genghis' messengers demanding recompense were returned with singed beards, he unleashed the devastation with which his name has come to be associated. As Juvaini wrote only 30 years later, "with one stroke a world which billowed with fertility was laid desolate, and the regions thereof became a desert". In his history of Afghanistan, Fraser-Tytler was only exaggerating slightly when he said "the Mongol invasions of Central Asia and Europe were, until the rise of the Nazis under Hitler, the greatest catastrophe which has befallen mankind". In 1220, Genghis Khan crossed the Oxus and sacked the city of Herat, which lies on an open road 50 miles from the border of the former Soviet Union. He then advanced on the ancient centre of arts and learning in Balkh, so completely devastating this area that when it was visited by the Moroccan traveller Ibn Batuta in 1333 he found only rubble and desolation where there had once been great cities. Ghazni itself fell to the lot of Genghis Khan's son Chagatai, but he never visited or took an interest in this outpost of his domain which had been destroyed as a cultural centre. There is perhaps some justice in the fact the Mongols were to leave even less trace of their achievements, if that is the right word, than did the kingdoms they laid waste. The only enduring, positive witnesses to their invasions are the colonies of Mongol Hazaras in west-central Afghanistan: a land of narrow valleys, rugged blocks of mountains and swift turbulent rivers, in keeping with the nature of the inhabitants who are aggressive and constantly at odds with the other peoples of the country.

Yet Afghanistan, reduced to an even more anarchic condition, had not yet done with the Mongols, or at least with a Turco-Iranian branch of them. In 1379 Tamerlane crossed the Oxus by a bridge of boats at Termez, one of the few practicable bridging points and the main port for the Soviet invading army exactly six hundred years later. In 1398 Tamerlane's cavalry crossed the Khawak Pass en route for India. In Afghanistan itself, he even mounted a campaign against the tribesmen in the wild and mountainous country north-east of Kabul. Termed "Kafirs" by the Muslim faithful, their land, "Kafiristan" – the Land of the Unbelievers – embraced Islam at sword point in 1895, and has since been more felicitously known as Nuristan – "the Land of Light". It was during this campaign that Tamerlane and his men tobogganed recklessly down a mountainside on their shields to attack the enemy! The empire of Tamerlane was very different from that of his Mongol predecessors, based as it was on the city of Samarkand – so richly and beautifully embellished by the buildings and works of art commissioned by the lame conqueror. Other cities, such as Herat, became flourishing centres of the arts under his immediate successors. It was the determination to regain Samarkand and restore its glories that obsessed Babur – descended from both Tamerlane and Genghis Khan – before he realized that the ambition was a hopeless one, and instead turned his attention to India. Although for many years after the loss of his kingdom in Ferghana, Babur still pursued his youthful dreams, in the end the relentless logic of the southward advance of the Uzbegs under Shaibani Khan forced him to seek a kingdom in Kabul and the lands beyond the Indus. Shaibani Khan bequeathed to Afghanistan the Uzbeg people still living in the northern part of the country, while Babur went on to found one of the world's most magnificent empires, that of the Mogul dynasty in India.

In October 1504, Kabul fell into a new ruler's hands without a fight.* "So, towards the end of [this] month", wrote Babur in his memoirs, "by the blessing of Almighty God I obtained and subjected Kabul and Ghazni with their provinces without effort or battle." (If Babur made history on the grand scale, he also wrote it with the delightful personal touch we find in his autobiographical *Baburnama*.) He clearly

---

*The fact that Babur's uncle, Ulugh Beg, had held the city for 32 years, until 1501, may account in part for the ease of its capture.

recognized the strategic advantages of Kabul. Successful raids on India might be made from any base in southern Afghanistan, but Kabul must be securely held for the permanent conquest of northern India. ("Indian" empires of the various Asiatic conquerors never had sufficient impetus to embrace the whole of southern India.) Yet for Babur the attractions of Kabul – which, as one legend has it, was founded by and named after Cain – extended far beyond mere strategic advantage. "From Kabul," wrote Babur, "you can go in a single day to a place where the snow never falls, and in two hours you can also reach a place where the snow never melts, except at times in a particularly hot summer." The qualification shows the typical realism of the man who saw that Kabul was "a land to be governed by the sword, not the pen".

That 21 years elapsed between Babur's capture of Kabul and his conquest of India in December 1525, with an army of less than 12,000 men, was due to the difficulty of consolidating his base along the line from Kandahar to Kabul. This proved a laborious task in the face of the hostility of the hill tribes: those men whom Ibn Batuta had described as "a tribe of Persians called Afghans. They hold mountains and defiles, possess considerable strength, and are mostly highwaymen". Indeed, it may be that the decision to turn his attention to building up an empire in India was influenced by his inability completely to subdue the Pathan tribesmen. These, he realized, he might contain but never control. The turbulent and independent spirit of these tribal peoples is one of the great constants of Afghanistan's history. Despite the many invasions, they have changed little since the time of Alexander.

Babur finally penetrated into northern India, and at much-embattled Panipat, site of so many contests for the mastery of the subcontinent, he gained the brilliant and decisive victory that gave him the throne of Delhi. By choosing this city as the

centre of his empire, he made Afghanistan once more the
northern outpost of an Indian empire, as in the days of the
Maurya dynasty, and with the inevitable debilitating
consequences. The Mogul succession in India was
dramatically, if only temporarily, interrupted by Sher Shah –
probably the most outstanding of the many Afghans to have
carved out kingdoms away from their native land. (Sher Shah
himself reigned in Delhi for only six years – from 1539 to 1545
– but his successors reigned for a further decade.) Although
the reign of Babur's son Humayun was shaken for only a few
years, he and his descendants were never able to establish
complete control over Afghanistan, much of which eventually
came once more under the influence of Persia. After another
two hundred years of petty tribal intrigue and conflict this
same Persian influence became indirectly responsible for the
creation of modern Afghanistan through the events described
in the introduction to this book.

Ahmad Shah's principal objective was to unite the various
Afghan peoples. He realized that this unity could only be
achieved by a loosely knit system – a sort of feudal federalism
by which the independent prerogatives of the tribal chiefs
would be guaranteed by the central power provided they gave
it military support. At the same time, it was at least partly to
guard against possible rivals that he appointed prominent
members of his family to important posts, which became
virtually hereditary – a practice not unknown in modern
Afghanistan. He went a step further, and constituted a Majlis
(or council) of nine chiefs which played a genuinely influential
part in policy-making. Though he could, and did, deal severely
with the more blatant and persistent offenders against his
regime, he also gained a reputation for remarkable clemency at
a time when this was rare.

The second major instrument of Ahmad Shah's policy of

unification was the age-old device of foreign conquest. This has been well described by Mountstuart Elphinstone in his perceptive *Account of the Kingdom of Caubul* (1815):

> For the consolidation of his power at home he relied in great measure on the effects of his foreign wars. If these were successful, his victories would raise his reputation, and his conquests would supply him with the means of maintaining an army, and of attaching the Afghan chiefs by favour and rewards; the hopes of plunder would induce many tribes to join him, whom he could not easily have compelled to submit; by carrying the great men with his army he would be able to prevent their increasing, or even preserving, their influence in their tribes; and the habits of military obedience would prepare them for a cheerful submission to his government at home; the troops also, having the King constantly before their eyes, and witnessing the submission of their hereditary chiefs, would learn to regard him as the head of the nation; and he might hope, as the event proved, that his popular manners, and the courage, activity, vigilance and other military virtues which he possessed, would impress all ranks with respect, and strongly attach his soldiers to his person.

Ahmad Shah's first step after taking power in Kandahar in 1747 was to subdue Kabul, and Ghazni en route. Before the end of the year, less than six months after coming to power, he had set out on the first of those eight invasions of India that were to fulfil so successfully the policy described by Elphinstone. However, fortunately for the future of his own country, and unlike so many previous invaders of the subcontinent, he had no ambition or desire to transfer his seat of government to Delhi and to rule India. Ahmad Shah's interest was in conquest, not empire, and after his campaigns he always returned to Kabul. It is doubtful whether he would have maintained his kingdom from a capital in Delhi.

Afghanistan at this time was fortunately relieved of external pressures by the disintegration earlier in the century of the Mogul and the Persian Safavid empires, and the Sikhs had not yet become established. Although Ahmad Shah generally defeated his Indian opponents (principally Sikhs and Marathas) in battle, they flowed in again like puddle water behind his wagon wheels as soon as he marched on. He could not maintain permanent lines of communication across territory still in the hands of such formidable opponents. He returned to his own country after each invasion to consolidate his domestic position and to extend the other frontiers of his empire. In the early years of his reign he extended his dominions northwards by adding Bamiyan and Badakshan, and, across the Oxus, Khurasan.

When Ahmad Shah died at the age of 50, from a particularly unpleasant combination of diabetes and an ulcerating nose wound, the old-style internecine struggle for power immediately broke out again among his sons, and gradually his empire crumbled.

In 1818, after a series of particularly barbaric plots and counterplots in which the blinding of opponents was commonplace, the successors of Ahmad Shah were ousted by the Muhammadzai Barakzai clan. The ancestor of this clan, a group within the Durrani tribe, had stood down in the leadership contest from which Ahmad Shah emerged as the chosen chief of the Afghans. It was during the disputes over the succession in the first quarter of the last century that the Punjab and Peshawar were finally lost to the Afghan kingdom.

The Barakzai, the second branch of whom provided the last monarch, had very strong emotional ties with Peshawar, the winter capital of its ancestors until wrested from them by Sikh arms. This close dynastic association with a "lost province" was possibly in the minds of those early Victorians, like Alexander Burnes, who believed that stability in this part of the world depended on the restoration of Peshawar to the Durrani kingdom. It was a contributory factor in the persistent irredentism in subsequent Afghan monarchs.

The kingdom which Ahmad Shah had carved out for himself did have certain elements of cohesion. Save for its tenuously held regions in Khurasan and east of the Khyber, in the Punjab and southwards in Baluchistan and Sind, Ahmad Shah's realm covered, broadly speaking, the area of present-day Afghanistan. That it required external compression, to be applied by the advancing empires of Britain and Russia, to make these elements coalesce to a degree is the next major part of Afghanistan's history.

2
THE GREAT GAME

With the founding of the Mogul empire by Babur, the centuries of pre-eminence of the horse-bowmen of Central Asia came to an end. Not until the Chinese incursion of 1962 would India again be invaded from Central Asia. But, if the great subcontinent was now secure from attack from the north, at the courts of the Great Mogul emperors there appeared – outwardly diffident and deferential, at heart observant, curious and ambitious – the outriders of a far more powerful invasion from a different direction and of a different kind.

By the mid-eighteenth century, at the time when the Afghans were forming their first independent kingdom under Ahmad Shah, the British were establishing themselves firmly, under the aegis of the East India Company, in substantial parts of India. As mercantile interests developed into political involvement, so the latter engendered a British military presence, first in conflict with the rival power of France and its Indian allies and then, after the defeat of France, with the native principalities themselves. Thus the British found themselves constantly obliged to extend the areas under their military control in order to maintain the stability necessary for prosperous trade. The British advance towards the frontiers of Afghanistan, both by means of diplomacy and war, culminated in the first and second Sikh wars (1845 and 1849). These, by breaking the power of Ranjit Singh's successors, brought British rule right up to the borders of Afghanistan.

Nor was Britain alone in extending its power towards Afghanistan, although Russia's expansion to its south-east did not get under way until almost a generation after the consolidation of the British presence in northern India. During the first half of the nineteenth century, the Russians were engaged in taking over the Kirghiz steppes, and were still a long way from their twentieth-century frontiers with Afghanistan. Their ventures in this part of the world had to be conducted at second hand. In 1838, they persuaded the Persians to lay siege to the strategically situated city of Herat. The implications of this seemed clear. As a British diplomat based with the Persian army observed: "The fall of Herat would destroy our position in Afghanistan and place nearly all that country under the influence or authority of Russia and Persia." However, the defence of Herat, courageously conducted under the leadership of a young British lieutenant* who had just arrived in the city, was stubborn and the city held out until Britain's threat of war forced the Shah to break off the operation and withdraw his army, thus temporarily thwarting Russian ambitions in the area.

Russia's aims at the time were mainly commercial, if a dispatch dated 20 October 1838, from Count Nesselrode, the Russian Foreign Minister, to his Ambassador in London is to be believed. It refers to the:

> indefatigable activity displayed by English travellers in spreading disquiet among the people of Central Asia, and in carrying agitation even into the heart of the countries bordering on our frontiers; while on our part we ask nothing but to be admitted to (share) in fair competition the commercial advantages of Asia. English industry, exclusive and jealous, would deprive us entirely of the benefits which it (claims) to reap alone; and would cause, if it could, the produce of our manufacturers to disappear from all the markets of Central Asia.

*Eldred Pottinger, whose exciting subsequent career, before dying young of a fever on the ship home, included survival of the retreat from Kabul in 1842 and – with one other man only – of the massacre at Charikar which immediately preceded it.

Dust Mohammed was the able ruler who had emerged from the anarchy of the first quarter of the nineteenth century to govern Afghanistan at this formative time. He ousted the Saddozai descendants of Ahmad Shah to become the first of the Barakzai clan to hold the throne. Anxious though he was to secure British friendship, he never met with the response he deserved from the Raj. Lord Auckland, the Governor-General of India during this period, misinterpreted the significance of events in Afghanistan and the importance of at least a prophylactic friendship with Dust Mohammed in countering Russian ambitions.

Auckland embarked on an intrigue with the Sikh leader, Ranjit Singh, to place a puppet ruler, Shah Shuja, on the Afghan throne. In taking these actions, he launched Britain on the first of the three Afghan wars that were to prove so disastrous for its relations with Afghanistan.

The pattern of these events is worth examining in some detail because its parallels with twentieth-century Russian policy are not just academic exercises for the historian, but were a source of inspiration for the mujehadin, the Afghan freedom fighters. Their confidence that the Russians could not impose a government on their country was derived in part from the fact that the great world power of the nineteenth and earlier twentieth centuries failed three times in such an attempt.

Shah Shuja briefly occupied the throne in Kabul in the opening decade of the century before fleeing to comfortable exile in India, whence he made one or two half-hearted attempts to regain his kingdom. It was from this retirement that the British and their temporary allies, the Sikhs, rescued him when Russian threats, through the instrument of Persia, appeared to imperil the security of the region. Dust Mohammed himself desired nothing so much as to remain independent of all the great powers. However, for appearance's sake, the British accused him of irredentism and "ambition injurious to the security and peace of the frontiers of India". Shah Shuja, eager to regain a throne by any means, readily forswore all such "ambition" and indeed agreed to pay tribute to the Sikhs as well. The British, like the Russians in the twentieth century, claimed that far from invading Afghanistan, they were actually supporting Shuja's troops "against foreign interference and factious opposition".

Shah Shuja was crowned with great pomp at Kandahar in April 1839, but, as Captain Havelock wrote at the time, "… unless I have been deceived all the national enthusiasm of the scene was entirely confined to his Majesty's immediate retainers. The people of Kandahar viewed the whole affair with the most mortifying indifference." The ceremony at Kabul later in the year had much the same hollow ring. Clearly the British would have to maintain their military presence after all if their protégé was to remain in power. They built cantonments in Kabul and Kandahar and supported garrisons at Girishk, Kalat-i-Ghilzai, Jalalabad, Ghazni, and Charikar, but beyond these towns Shuja's writ did not run. The countryside was in open rebellion and Dust Mohammed's victory at Charikar – though for some inexplicable reason he surrendered to the British after it – was herald of a "signal catastrophe" yet to come. After uprisings in Kabul and the provinces and the murder first of Sir Alexander Burnes, and then of the obtuse Sir William Macnaghten, the British forces beat a precipitate, ill-managed, and sometimes shameful retreat in the bitter January weather of 1842. In one of the worst disasters in British military history they lost an entire army, all but the handful of men and women held by local chiefs, and the subsequently celebrated Dr Brydon.

After their victory the tribes rapidly resumed their old rivalries, which often erupted into open fighting. The British were not slow to take ruthless advantage of these divisions. By the autumn of 1842, Kabul was retaken and Dust Mohammed had been quietly allowed to resume his throne. British retribution ranged from the senseless and rather petty burning of the old bazaar in Kabul to Major General Knott's butchering of "every man, woman and child within the village of Killah-Chuk", near Ghazni, in revenge for the wiping out of a detachment of his men. It is perhaps unsurprising that the heritage of hatred and distrust the British created for themselves in the nineteenth century was to last, to some extent, even to the present day.

With one significant difference, the pattern when the Soviets invaded was much the same – only the names had changed. The Russians seemed just as unlikely to suffer a major conventional military defeat at the hands of the Afghan freedom fighters, such was the disparity in weapons and resources. Nor, in reality, did they. But such was the similar debilitating effect of Afghan guerrilla tactics, honed over many centuries, that Russia lost her resolve to pursue her original objective, but we shall come to that in Chapter 10.

The first Afghan war was followed by 70 years of vacillation in British policy for, even in the high noon of expansionism in the latter half of the nineteenth century, there were strong differences of opinion regarding Afghanistan. Things looked very different from the respective vantage points of London and Delhi, while the changes of political power in England between half-hearted Imperialists and ill-informed Liberals made the pursuit of a consistent policy almost impossible.

Those, like Lord Roberts and the Duke of Cambridge, who favoured an active British presence in Afghanistan, supported what came to be known as the "forward policy", which accepted the logic of imperial necessity. The argument was that if India could not be defended along its existing frontiers, it was essential to push those frontiers forward to the natural barrier of the Hindu Kush. Only in this way could authority and jurisdiction over the wild frontier tribes be established, the Afghans be convinced of the advisability of throwing in their lot with the British, and the Indian Empire be secured. Had the "forward policy" been put fully into operation in an avowedly imperialist mood, it is at least arguable that the stability of the area would today be greater than it is. But Liberal opinion rejected this policy outright, chiefly because of its belief that aggressive wars were morally indefensible; and also, perhaps, in reaction to the secondary argument of the "forward school" – that control of the tribal areas would provide the British army with a new recruiting source of good fighting men, loyal cannon-fodder for the Raj.

On coming to power, the Liberals tried to reverse decisions and dispositions made in the name of the forward policy, some of them going so far as to suggest that, if a natural frontier were required for India, Britain would do well to withdraw to the Indus.* They did not perhaps fully appreciate the bloody consequences of such a withdrawal. The hill tribesmen, left to their own devices, would take their traditional road of plunder and depredation, and this in all probability would provoke the traditional response of brutal reprisals and punitive expeditions. Even so, it was Liberal opinion which, by promoting the concept of a buffer state, was to some extent responsible for the creation of modern Afghanistan – although one need not go so far as Sir Thomas Holdich who, at the turn of the century, wrote:

*In view of the criticism of this Liberal advocacy of the southerly "realistic" frontier on the Indus, it is only fair to note that this policy was not simply a notion dreamed up in remote London by what Imperialists call the "Perish India" school of radicals. First suggested by Sir James Outram, the celebrated Political Agent, in 1854, the Indus frontier line was also advocated by other men on the spot, including Sir John (later Lord) Lawrence, Governor-General, 1863–68 .

We have contributed much to give a national unity to that nebulous community which we call Afghanistan (but which Afghans never call by that name) by drawing a boundary all round it and elevating it into the position of a buffer state between ourselves and Russia. What is there about Afghanistan to guarantee its continued existence as a buffer state between England and Russia? No other country in the world is interested in its prolonged existence except these two. Afghanistan, as a national entity, can only exist by favour of military support of one or the other of them. We need hardly enquire on which side the burden will always lie.

There is a nice irony in this last remark. During the second half of the nineteenth century, the Russians moved inexorably southward into Central Asia under the leadership of such brilliant generals and administrators as Kaufman and Skobelev. The logic and justification of this advance was set out in a memorandum of the Russian Chancellor, Prince Gorchakov, in 1864; in a different geographical context, it might have come from the pen of a British minister:

The position of Russia in Central Asia is that of all civilized states which come into contact with half savage, wandering tribes possessing no fixed social organization.

It invariably happens in such cases that the interests of security on the frontier, and of commercial relations, compel the more civilized states to exercise a certain ascendancy over neighbours whose turbulence and nomad instincts render them difficult to live with. First we have incursions and pillage to repress. In order to stop these, we are compelled to reduce the tribes on our frontiers to a more or less complete submission. Once this result is attained they become less troublesome, but in their turn they are exposed to the aggression of more distant tribes. The state is obliged to defend them against these depredations and to chastise those who commit them. Hence the necessity of *distant and costly expeditions, repeated at frequent intervals, against an enemy whose whole social organization enables him to elude pursuit.* (My italics.) If we content ourselves with chastising the freebooters and then retire, the lesson is soon forgotten. Retreat is ascribed to weakness, for Asiatics respect only visible and palpable force; that arising from the exercise of reason and a regard for the interest of civilization has as yet no hold over them. The task has, therefore, to be performed over again. The United States in America, France in Algeria, Holland in her colonies, England in India – all have been inevitably drawn to a course wherein ambition plays a smaller part than imperious necessity and where the greatest difficulty is knowing where to stop.

Soon Britain was also to return full-bloodedly to the forward policy which had been in abeyance as a consequence of the Indian Mutiny of 1857 and of the prevalence of the Liberal attitudes at home. In 1876, Disraeli appointed Lord Lytton to be Viceroy of India, with a clear brief to reinstate the "forward policy". A memorandum of instructions clearly summarized the situation Lytton was sent to change, and he was asked to "consider the probable influence of that situation upon the uncertain character of an oriental chief whose ill-defined dominions are thus brought within a steadily narrowing circle between the conflicting pressures of two great military empires, one of which expostulates and remains passive, while the other apologizes and continues to move forward."

As a result of Lytton's close adherence to his instructions, Britain was soon embroiled in a second Afghan war (1878–79). This was successful militarily, a swiftly moving campaign leading to the capture of such key points as Kabul and Kandahar. Indeed, in 1879 or 1880, the British very likely could have taken over the control and administration of Afghanistan south of the Hindu Kush, thereby bringing the forward policy, of which Lytton was so staunch a supporter, to its logical conclusion. Yet Disraeli's Viceroy got cold feet and looked for a way out of assuming for Britain de facto responsibility for the area. Although an ardent forwardist, in the first three months of 1880 Lytton realized that his speculative plans for breaking up Afghanistan could only involve the same tragic disasters as those experienced in Lord Auckland's time, and would also place an intolerable burden on both Treasury and Army. He perhaps now recognized, as so many others had before him, the difference between defeating and controlling the Afghan tribes.

The change in policy was finally secured when Gladstone defeated Disraeli in the election of March 1880 and sent the Marquess of Ripon to replace Lytton as Viceroy. Indeed, British policy towards Afghanistan had been a major issue in the election, and the Liberal "regressive" view had been eloquently put by Gladstone in one of his Midlothian speeches:

> Remember, the sanctity of life in the hill villages of Afghanistan among the winter snows is as inviolable in the eye of almighty God as can be your own. Remember that He who has united you as human beings in the same flesh and blood, has bound you by the law of mutual love, is not limited by the shores of this island, is not limited by the bounds of Christian civilization; that it passes over the whole surface of the earth, and embraces the meanest along with the greatest in its unmeasured scope.

With the Conservative defeat, it was these impeccable – if rather generalized – sentiments which became the motivating force behind British policy in India and displaced the "forward policy". Writing to the new Viceroy in May 1880, Lord Hartington, Secretary of State for India in the new Gladstone administration, was terse and to the point in his estimate of what had been gained by the second Afghan war: "Thus it appears that as the result of two successful campaigns, of the employment of an enormous force, and of the expenditure of large sums of money, all that has yet been accomplished has been the disintegration of the state which it was desired to see strong, friendly and independent, the assumption of fresh and unwelcome liabilities in regard to one of its provinces, and a condition of anarchy throughout the remainder of the country."

It was fortunate for Britain that at this juncture there came to the Afghan throne perhaps its greatest occupant: Abdur Rahman, one of the few men who could have restored the measure of stability to Afghanistan so essential to British policy. By 1881, the policy of the buffer state was again in operation, applied by a Liberal government in the hope, rather than the assurance, that the Afghans would resist the Russians as vigorously as they had the British. Such conflict as there was between the great powers was still at second hand, as at Herat 40 years earlier, only now it was a British protégé who was worsted when the Russians, in 1885, after occupying the oasis of Merv in the previous year, soundly defeated a large Afghan army barring their final advance up to the River Oxus.

On the last day of March 1885, the Russians attacked and seized the Afghan-held Panjdeh oasis at the very time when London and St Petersburg were negotiating the precise demarcation of the new frontier between Russia and Afghanistan. That this was not intended to be the final Russian goal was made quite clear in the newspaper *Novosti* shortly afterwards. Herat lay within temptingly easy grasp, and *Novosti* urged that Russia must press on to occupy the city and so "pierce a window" looking south-eastwards, a convenient halting place for a still further advance towards the Indian Ocean in fulfilment of Russia's "historic destiny". The tsarist government may well have reckoned that, with the anti-imperialist Liberals in power in Britain, it could steal a march on the negotiations, and gain a useful strategic position, by a coup de force. If so, they were deceived. Gladstone sought for and obtained from Parliament a war credit of £11 million. For several weeks it seemed possible that Britain would go to war with Russia; but eventually the latter climbed down. The diplomats of the two countries returned to their task of defining the boundaries of the Amir of Afghanistan's dominions: a definition which, in fact, gave Panjdeh to the Russians in exchange for various salients of territory on the Amir's side of the Oxus.

Nothing gives a clearer indication of where the real sovereignty of Afghanistan lay at this time than these and later boundary negotiations between Britain and Russia. The Afghans were mere spectators, while the government of the Chinese empire refused to take part in the boundary demarcation discussions in 1895 over the small area of the Wakhan affecting its border. From 1889, the British and Chinese governments had been resisting Russian incursion into the Pamirs, a mountainous region (the "Roof of the World") where the two new empires in Asia met the oldest surviving empire of the continent at the north-western extension of the Tibetan tableland. The Pamir Convention of 1895 between Britain and Russia settled the Wakhan question to the satisfaction of London and St Petersburg, and official circles there felt small concern at the absence of an endorsement of the new demarcation by the government of the decaying Chinese empire. In November 1963 Peking finally recognized its frontier with Afghanistan as determined by the Pamir Convention. China thus surrendered the line of argument that the Chinese People's Republic had adhered to in regard to the Simla Convention of 1914 which defined the Indo-Tibetan frontier – that it was never formally ratified by the imperial government of China, and was therefore invalid. This Tibetan boundary question became a *casus belli* in 1962. It is unlikely, but not impossible, that the Afghan boundary, demarcated by the Pamir Convention, could become a source of conflict between China and Afghanistan.

In 1893 another troublesome boundary was demarcated, equally high-handedly, on the eastern and southern borders of Afghanistan. The Durand Line (named after the British administrator responsible for devising it) is a topographically convenient foothill boundary which cuts right across ethnic and tribal divisions. This political severance of the Pathan tribes on either side of it – a severance they have been inclined to ignore at will – not only gave rise to a whole genre of early twentieth-century schoolboy fiction, but has also since bitterly embroiled the governments of Pakistan and Afghanistan, between which countries the Durand Line now runs.

Sir Olaf Caroe has cogently argued that the Durand Line is far less arbitrary than it may appear. According to Caroe, the intention of the colonial officials who drew it up in 1893 was to divide the tribes which looked naturally south and east to Peshawar, Kohat, and Quetta, on what is now the Pakistan side of the border, from the Afghan tribes whose focus was on Kabul, Ghazni and Kandahar.

The planting of boundary posts on the northern frontier of Afghanistan by the joint Anglo–Russian commission was something more than a topographical exercise; it indicated the tacit if limited agreement of two mutually suspicious powers to recognize the confines of their respective spheres of influence. Thus Holdich could calmly note, having described Herat and Quetta as the two hinges of the gate to India: "these two doors are locked, there is nothing in this year of grace 1900 that need cause us any apprehension for the future safety of the country".

Although the opportunity for effective exercise of any forward policy was gone for good by the turn of the century, its advocates were still promoting it. The Hon. George Curzon (as he then was) waxed eloquent in *The Times* shortly before becoming Viceroy of India:

> Russia has, by the Pamir Convention concluded with Great Britain, just come into possession of three-fourths of the whole territory known as the Pamirs, and of a position which brings her down to the main stream of the Oxus. Locally, this involves a great extension of her military and political prestige. If at the very same moment that she is thus permitted to advance up to the Hindu Kush on the north, Great Britain voluntarily retires from a position which she has occupied for ten years on the south, but one interpretation will be placed upon this coincidence by the natives of those regions. They do not understand high diplomacy, and they do not read the letters of retired governors and generals in *The Times*. But with one alphabet they are perfectly familiar, and its two symbols are forward and backward. They will say that Russia is the winning and Britain the receding power.

Lord Roberts spoke as earnestly, if less eloquently, in the House of Lords:

> The forward policy, in other words the policy of endeavouring to extend our influence over, and establish law and order on, that part of the border where anarchy, murder and robbery up to the present time have reigned supreme, a policy which has been attended with the happiest results in Baluchistan and the

Gilgit frontier – is necessitated by the incontrovertible fact that a great military power is now within striking distance of our Indian possessions and in immediate contact with the state, for the integrity of which we have made ourselves responsible. Some forty years ago the policy of non-interference with the tribes, so long as they did not trouble us, may have been wise and prudent, though selfish and not altogether worthy of a great civilizing power.

But the necessities of European politics were changing and no longer sustained the same degree of confrontation on the frontiers of Central Asia. Indeed, Russia and Britain, sharing a common fear of the growing military strength of imperial Germany in Europe and a common uneasiness over its ambitious diplomatic and commercial forays into the Near East, became allies in 1907 in association with France. The two great Asian empires settled down to administer their respective territories round the frontiers of Afghanistan in ways that were sometimes very similar and sometimes exhibited revealing differences.

One common factor, giving each imperial regime an apparently perennial vigour, was the supply line to the home country for recruitment – in Britain's case by sea, in Russia's by the network of railways reaching to the remotest corners of its southern provinces. A revolution in communications had brought about what numerous revolutions in military technology and tactics had failed to achieve. For the first time, there were now empires in this part of Asia whose rulers did not go into an enervated decline within a few generations since they were constantly refreshed by transfusions of blood kept fresh in the climatic and moral refrigerators of northern Europe. Such empires would endure, or would pass away only through voluntary relinquishment.

In conception, the imperial ideals of Britain and Russia might seem very similar. For example, an enlightened Russian colonial administrator could write in his memoirs after the Russian annexation of Transcaspia:

The entry of Russia into Central Asia, followed by the introduction of European methods and civilization, brought a breath of fresh air to a land despoiled and impoverished by centuries of Asian despotic rule. The reader, accustomed to differentiate between what he has been taught to regard as Western civilization and conditions in Russia, may fail to appreciate the magnitude and effect of the changes wrought in the life of Central Asia by tzarist and autocratic Russia. Slavery was brought to an end; the arbitrary legislation of the Khans, Emirs, and their puppets, the Beks, who controlled a large part of their masters' wealth, such as their flocks, was superseded by Russian law, under which all the inhabitants, irrespective of their standing, were equal. Hitherto enslaved captives from every race in Asia, emancipated overnight, hastened home to spread the news of these wondrous changes, introduced by a humane administration, upheld by one universal writ, and enforced by Russian arms. Henceforth, the verdicts of the kadis (judges) in the local courts were based on the wise adaptation of the Shari'at (the holy law of Islam) to the Russian conception of justice.

Would a member of the Indian Civil Service have differed much from this in his description of what he believed British rule to be achieving in India?

In Russia, however, the disease of bureaucracy spread even more virulently than it did in British India. Moreover, into Russia's southern empire poured an influx of colonial settlers from the poorer and tougher sections of Russian society, and these were not going to allow any nice regard for native susceptibilities to hamper their determination to make good. Britain, in India at least, was not faced with the same problem, for there the empire-builders were in the main dedicated career-officers who returned to their own country on completing their service. The Russians tended to despise the British, in the first place for not putting their colonies to better commercial use, and secondly for not imposing outright their own laws and customs on the subject peoples. Russianize, not liberalize, was the formula for tsarist imperialism: a formula the Soviets were quick to adopt. (For example, in the 1980s it was estimated that 40 per cent of the Soviet Central Asian population was of Russian origin.)

By the beginning of the twentieth century, then, a military and diplomatic stalemate had been reached as if by a kind of Newtonian Third Law of politics. Between the two equal and opposite forces lay Afghanistan.It was probably fortunate for the great powers bickering over Afghanistan that, during the nineteenth and much of the twentieth century, the country's potential leaders were preoccupied with throne hunting.

The age-old pattern of clan, family and personal rivalry for power was aggravated by the attempts of outside powers, the British in particular, to manipulate Afghan rulers to their own ends. The importance of personal magnetism and leadership was, and is, greater in Afghanistan than in most countries. During the nineteenth century, Abdur Rahman (1880–1901) was the only man of sufficient stature to negotiate with the British the kind of independence the country enjoyed until the Soviet Invasion. But with Russia troubling Abdur Rahman's northern frontiers after the annexation of Panjdeh, he could not afford to dispense with Britain's patronage. Even so, he took good care to exclude from his kingdom, as far as possible, both British and Russian military and diplomatic representatives. He also secured the loyalty of his defeated

Pathan tribal opponents by resettling them in non-Pathan areas, where their dislike of their neighbours would outweigh the temptation to rebel against a Pathan ruler.

During the First World War, the Afghans, despite many temptations, kept their promise to remain neutral. Nevertheless, the war undermined the foundations of genuine imperial power for Britain and, after 1917, the new communist regime in Russia was wholly absorbed in the problems of consolidating its domestic control. Thus the Afghans found themselves free to aspire to greater independence.

To some extent, independence was achieved as a reaction to the very restraint exercised by the Amir of Afghanistan during the war. Neutrality was exceedingly irksome to a people that saw in the war an opportunity to throw off the foreign yoke, and particularly that of the British, who ruled over parts of the old Afghan kingdom in the north-west of India. Moreover, there was always the excuse of going to the aid of the Caliph under attack from infidels – although such an excuse would have carried less weight in early twentieth-century Afghanistan, then rather isolated from the rest of the Muslim world, than in other Islamic countries. Hence, when Amir Habibullah was murdered in 1919, it was not difficult for his younger son Amanullah, darling of the hotheads and nationalists, and in control at the crucial moment of the capital, Kabul, to seize power at the expense of his conservative elder brother. However, Amanullah had an almost unlimited capacity for arousing the antagonism of the powerful conservative elements in the country, particularly the mullahs – Muslim religious leaders. Within a very short time, he found his hold becoming precarious.

With considerable political astuteness, in May 1919 Amanullah launched the third Afghan war with the British under the double pretext of a struggle for independence and a jihad, or holy war. Although he was quickly defeated, his campaign achieved its objectives in a way that a rising between 1914 and 1918 would have failed to do. This was the psychological moment. A war-weary, and wiser, Britain accorded full independence to Afghanistan by releasing it from all the limitations on its freedom of action in foreign affairs that had been imposed in the past. The Treaty of Rawalpindi of 1919 was followed two years later by another confirming the position. In the latter year, the Russians likewise signed a rather more grandiose, if less fully honoured, treaty. Amanullah was temporarily assured of his throne.

His retention of it, however, depended not on the British or the Russians but on his own people. The intemperate reforming zeal – probably stimulated by the reforms of Reza Shah in Persia – of a young man of limited ability who was determined to drag his country into the twentieth century no matter how loud its protests, was too much for a society which was still living, quite contentedly, in the Middle Ages.

Resistance to Amanullah took active shape in 1924, when he introduced a sweeping programme for the emancipation of women. This would not only have educated them but, even more provocative to traditionalists, it would have freed them from complete domination by their menfolk. The mullahs raised the tribes in rebellion. One mullah was arrested for declaring the reforms to be against the law of Islam and that when they came in, Islam would go out. (This attitude still prevails today among most Afghan males and the Taliban in particular.) Although Amanullah's forces were eventually successful, the rebellion was brought to an end only when he agreed to allow the Loya Jirgah, the Great Assembly (a representative council of notables, not a body elected "democratically" in the Western sense), to repeal his measures. One cannot help wondering what became of those few women who went to Europe for education and were then called back to be reincarcerated in purdah, just as their great grand-daughters have been today.

Amanullah had neither the power nor the personality to create an acceptable system of modern government, greatly though this was needed. A countrywide trail of derelict and useless gadgetry, costing far more than Afghanistan's limited exchequer could bear, testified depressingly to the headlong and ill-informed way he had set about an essential task. He was encouraged to resume his reckless pursuit of wholesale reform and modernization when, late in 1927, he embarked on a splendid and extensive tour of Europe.

Inspired by what he saw in more advanced countries, on his return the following year Amanullah proclaimed again a programme of reforms. There was to be an assembly of 150 elected representatives legislating and supervising the executive under a constitutional monarch; monogamy was to be introduced, along with compulsory and secularized education for children of both sexes. Implicit in his policy was the creation of separate "church" and "state" on the lines of the system developed (at the cost of much social and political strife) in some of the European countries he had visited. But such a policy, based on a distinction between the sacred and secular, and threatening as it did the power base and consequent material privileges of the mullahs, was quite incomprehensibly alien in an Islamic state at that time. All this he proclaimed to an assembly of chiefs and other notables, not made any more amenable by the enforced and embarrassing discomfort of surrendering their flowing tribal costume for European formal dress. Sir Francis Humphrys, British Minister in Kabul at the time, reported back of the King that, "He violated the safe conduct which he had given to the mullahs and tribal leaders by a series of open and clandestine executions; he banished out of jealousy for their influence with the people, the best brains and most experienced noblemen in the state; he allowed his inveterate hatred of the mullahs to pass all reasonable bounds; and finally he alienated the sympathies of his army by persistently ignoring their interests and by the importation of foreign advisers."

Insurrection broke out again. This time, despite its fragmentary nature, it continued with growing intensity until, in the ensuing disintegration of order and central authority, the throne in Kabul was seized by a Tajik brigand, Bachha-i-Saqao – "son of the water carrier". Amanullah himself retreated by stages to exile in Italy.

Thus, in 1929, it looked as if Afghanistan was about to plunge yet again into one of its periods of anarchy. The Russians, who had been trying to exert influence at the Afghan court with only spasmodic success, were only too eager to exploit the situation. However, Britain, by declaring and following a policy of absolute neutrality in the struggle between the brigand usurper and his opponents, obliged Russia to do likewise. On this occasion the struggle for power in Afghanistan was undertaken solely by internal candidates, and it soon transpired that the most effective of these was Nadir Khan, Amanullah's kinsman and founder of the last royal dynasty. His main strength lay in the support given him by tribes of the frontier districts. It is significant that Nadir owed his success as much to the tribes on the British side of the Durand Line – despite the efforts of the North-West Frontier Agency to prevent his recruiting there – as to those from the Afghan side. Early in October 1929, these forces took Kabul and on the sixteenth of the month Nadir was proclaimed King with the title of Muhammad Nadir Shah.

Nadir Shah was a man of sufficiently strong personality to attract the support of the tribes. Although at first he had to rely on these turbulent and unruly followers, he was able in the next four years, by identifying himself with the conservatives and by appointing his brothers to major ministerial posts, to stabilize the country. To ensure this stability, he and his successors built up the armed services in size, efficiency and prestige. The consequent potential for a military coup in a country where, apart from the tribes, there were no other organized power complexes, seems to have been overlooked. Nadir also reconstituted the Loya Jirgah, making it a body of delegates from every tribe and province. In 1930, after the confirmation of his accession, 105 members were chosen – not, of course, elected – to form a nucleus, meeting more regularly to rubber-stamp the decisions of the executive. Such was Nadir Shah's conservative concession to "modernism", in contrast to Amanullah's sweepingly radical emulation of Western institutions.

The new regime succeeded in diminishing the influence of the great powers by limiting their opportunities for operations of any kind in Afghanistan itself – whether diplomatic, military or economic – and by carefully balancing a concession to one by a concession to another. At the start of Nadir Shah's reign, the Russians crossed the Oxus into the virtually lawless northern provinces and penetrated deep into Afghan territory in pursuit of a bandit who had been harassing the Russian side from an Afghan base and whom they thought the Afghans were too dilatory in bringing to justice. The incursion had the desired result of making the Afghans bring him to book themselves and, indeed, it accelerated the restoration of order and central control to the northern provinces. But soon Russian influence became as remote as British, and other Europeans – Germans in particular – began to play an increasing part in the technical development of Afghanistan.

When, four years after his succession, Nadir was

assassinated by a schoolboy,* the transition of power to his son through a family regency was perfectly smooth. Throughout the 1930s, enjoying a considerable measure of internal stability, Afghanistan made its first serious steps towards economic development, particularly in communications, irrigation and the search for mineral resources. At the same time, its government refrained from over-vigorous expression of its dislike for the country's imperial neighbours. Though abating in no way its reluctance in practice to recognize the Durand Line as its southern frontier with the British Empire in India, Afghanistan adhered to its declared neutrality throughout the Second World War. This neutrality was of critical importance in 1940 when Britain was stretched to its utmost and Germany was lavish in its blandishments in the hope that Afghanistan could be induced to create trouble on India's North-West Frontier.

As in 1919, a world war and its consequences were to have important repercussions for Afghanistan. The European imperial powers in Asia were everywhere in retreat after 1945. Their victory, the repossession of the lands lost to Japan and the retention of those they had successfully defended, was to be the farewell gesture of their power. Only in Soviet Asia were the imperialists not in retreat. Indeed, the German invasion of European Russia had accelerated the growth of industry and communications in Asiatic Russia, where the Soviet authorities built up the economic "masse de manoeuvre" to defeat the Germans. While Britain's withdrawal from India in 1947 removed any remaining threat from Afghanistan's southern border, there was, immediately beyond its northern

---

The youth was a natural son of Ghulam Nabi, executed by Nadir Shah as a prominent and disaffected adherent of Amanullah. But so isolated was the assassination from political action that it was certainly motivated by personal revenge, rather than political conspiracy.

border, a rapidly expanding economy and modern social organization among peoples ethnically similar to those on the Afghan side of the Oxus. To the west, only Britain and America's expressed determination to use force if necessary had secured the withdrawal of a Russian army of occupation from northern Persia. This situation was in marked contrast to that among Afghanistan's neighbours and cousins to the south and east, among whom confusion reigned as a result of the bloody transfer of power, and who were in any case totally absorbed in the problems of trying to create the new state of Pakistan out of nothing.

In many parts of Asia after the Second World War, the Americans tried to fill the vacuum left by the departure of the European powers. But, for a variety of reasons, in the Indian subcontinent they could not adequately replace the bulwark of the British Empire against a downward thrust from Central Asia towards India.

India itself gradually drifted from genuine neutrality in the 1950s into the pro-Soviet camp, largely as a reaction to US military support for the military regimes of an economically and politically unstable Pakistan. In 1965 and again in 1971, the successor states to the Raj were at war – the second time with disastrous consequences for both the morale and the economic stability of West Pakistan. In the December 1970 elections which ended 12 years of military rule, Zulfikar Ali Bhutto gained a clear majority in West Pakistan (but not, significantly, in Baluchistan or the North-West Frontier Province). However, Sheikh Mujibur Rahman's Awami League had swept the polls (achieving 90 per cent of the popular vote) in East Pakistan. A separate and independent Bangladesh, which had been a subject of bazaar speculation for years, became a real possibility and when Rahman could not get the virtual autonomy he demanded, insurrection broke out in the eastern half of the divided nation. The Pakistan army, mainly recruited from West Pakistan, a thousand miles from its supply base, was compelled by a hostile India to fly round, rather than over, that country's territory, so could not contain the Bengali insurrection. In a last desperate attempt to relieve pressure in the east, Pakistan opened up the western front against India itself and within a fortnight the war was over, 90,000 Pakistani prisoners were in Indian hands and some 3,000 square miles of its former territory had been lost. The traumatic effect of this defeat greatly influenced Pakistan's international attitudes, and in particular its suspicion of America and parallel reliance on China for military and economic assistance. (Conversely, the same mutual suspicion pushed Mrs Gandhi into a 20-year pact with the Soviet Union.)

For the next five years, as a result of natural disasters, political dissension and economic mismanagement, Pakistan struggled unsuccessfully to tackle its problems – none of which were more significant for the future of the whole region than its clashes with neighbouring Afghanistan over the allegiance of the Pathans living within the borders of the new state. An understanding of this conflict, which has come to be known as "the Pushtunistan issue", is essential to an appreciation of the tensions between Afghanistan and its southern neighbour.

3

PUSHTUNISTAN UNJAST

"Afghanistan Unjast, Pushtunistan Unjast! Afghanistan Unjast, Pushtunistan Unjast!" Hour after hour the shrill, monotonous cry of the lorry-driver's bacha* drove one slowly to the verge of frenzy on the long journey, during my first visit to Afghanistan in 1957, on the road from Kandahar to Kabul. "This is Afghanistan, this is Pushtunistan."

The Afghan slogan draws its inspiration from the Solomon-like arbitration which demarcated the border between Afghanistan and Pakistan that runs through the foothills which lead up to the Sulaiman mountains of Afghanistan itself. The "convenient" frontier sliced through many tribal areas despite efforts to relate it to the local bazaars to which the various tribes normally gravitated. But bazaars were not the only focii and British cartographical distinctions were largely ignored by the people living along what came to be known as the Durand Line. They crossed the boundary as if it did not exist, and were naturally indignant, in the usual forceful Pathan way, whenever they met with reprisals or obstructions for so doing. The restriction of an artificial frontier proved particularly irksome for nomads whose lives and movements were dictated by the location of traditional pastures from which they were now sometimes cut off.

*One of these agile youths, whose prehensile powers are quite amazing, is to be found clinging to the back of most Afghan lorries. His chief function is to leap perilously between the wheels whenever the vehicle stops on a slope and to thrust behind them the large wooden wedge that does service for the long-defunct brakes. He also helps the driver to collect the fares from the passengers. It is a kind of working apprenticeship.

While Amir Abdur Rahman, being a realist and bowing to superior force, accepted the Durand Line frontier, he did so grudgingly, for he was also a great patriotic leader and believed all the Pathan areas to be part of his kingdom. In his autobiography, Abdur Rahman declared that he did not regard the areas on the British side of the Durand Line as permanently ceded to the British, yet in that same volume he lists those very areas to which "I renounce my claims". Moreover, in the Treaty of Rawalpindi (1919), "the Afghan government accepts the Indo-Afghan frontiers accepted by the late Emir". The determination to regain these districts is a significant thread running through all subsequent Afghan history, and the opinion that they form a natural part of Afghanistan has been strongly held by all of Afghanistan's recent rulers. Only by understanding the intensity of feeling on both sides of the Durand Line can we appreciate the potential the Pushtunistan issue has to destroy stability in the two neighbouring states.

Lacking the relative strength which is the necessary ingredient of irredentism in the present climate of international opinion, Afghanistan has over the years modified its demand for the restoration of the whole of the old territory of the Durrani kingdom, superficially at least, to one for "Pushtunistan": an independent state for the Pushtu-speaking peoples south and east of the Durand Line on the Pakistan side, Pushtu being the language of most, but not all, of the Pathan tribesmen on both sides of this frontier. Such a state would naturally be expected to align itself closely with Afghanistan, but would not be a part of it. In the imagination of the Afghan cartographers, at least, this has already been accomplished, for the tourist guides that used to be issued to visitors in the 1960s and 1970s clearly marked Pakistan's tribal territories as "Pushtunistan". What Afghanistan claims as

Pushtunistan corresponds to the North-West Frontier Provinces of British India and of present-day Pakistan, the boundary of which ran from the border with China in the north to Baluchistan. (This latter area, it should be noted, is sometimes included in the proposed Pushtunistan.) It traverses every kind of scenery, from the great mountains and beautiful green valleys of Gilgit and Chitral to the Baluch desert – the dump, it is said, where Allah deposited the rubbish of creation.

On the North West Frontier Nature has conspired to create a backcloth appropriate to the character of the area's inhabitants, and which, despite the destructive power of modern warfare, remains fundamentally the same as it has always been. The scenic variety of the frontier districts on both sides of the Durand Line seems almost unlimited. Few experiences have had as great an impact on me as my first trip along the frontier which I describe here.

Leaving Kabul by the Lataband Pass as evening approaches, spiralling up the sinuous yellow road to 9,000 feet, you see the valley below and the hills around beginning to turn to a hard blue as the light fades. Then, as if nature is playing on a theatre organ, the sky's colour changes minute by minute. Just before the last streaks of purple, red and gold on the horizon darken into blackness, a storm breaks. There is no rain, and for a long time no thunder, and the lightning leaps nimbly from cloud to cloud, showing up the mountains like a huge cardboard cut-out. Here nature is so conscious of her power she disdains to bluster and threaten, and is content to dazzle. As you drive down the far side in the dark, the lightning projects a flickering photographic exhibition of small chai khanas, the tea houses that never seem to close, revealed to their very depths, the lightning flashes so bright that the glowing lanterns on their verandahs are extinguished to the sight. Hills, trees and shrubs leap into momentary life, faces blink for a second and are shut in darkness again. Moving on down the Khyber at dawn to Peshawar, you leave behind the narrow defile speckled with innumerable plaques commemorating the otherwise forgotten deeds of heroism of those who fought to take and hold the pass.

Turning around at neatly geometrical, Raj-redolent Peshawar, your road leads south and west again, this time on the Pakistan side of the frontier, until you reach Kohat where a local restaurateur pounces to lead you to the heart of the town. You are being conducted to the sanctum of a master magician, past the booths of lesser conjurors and quacks – only the magic on this occasion is solely culinary. Don't close your eyes in passing each stall or you may succumb to the temptation of their many smells: roasting corncobs, nuts and a variety of meats. With your eyes open the temptation will not seduce you, for their living coat of bulge-headed flies is enough to deter all but a starving or a Pathan stomach. The magician's cave itself is plunged in gloom, and against this background the long-bearded patron crouches over a row of gleaming bowls that catch the light prying through the open side of the shop. Raised on his dais, he deigns to give you a welcoming nod then, prince of devils, returns to gloat over and stir the vegetable afrits in his explosive cauldrons. A strong smell of spice hangs over them as they cook, although "cook" is a tame word to describe the process, for gouts of yellow liquid leap like shell splashes round the bright red tomatoes which eddy round lower in the bowl, while rich green chillies, newly added, slip furtively between them.

Continuing your journey beyond Kohat, you are treated to a geological extravaganza. The road plunges into a crazy, Neapolitan ice of clay and red and yellow sandstone. In many places, the terrain has been tilted through ninety degrees by the earth's movement, and yet the different strata are still sharply defined. Much of the softer layers has been worn away, leaving sharp fins of harder rock only a few feet thick but miles long and hundreds of feet high. The space between is occasionally cultivated, but more often it is just a bare hot strip of dust. From there you come to a region of harder rocks cut with gorges and passes, the road clinging to the lip of a ravine hundreds of feet above a marble-green river. Out of one pillar of rock a huge head, a hybrid of Greek and Asiatic, has been carved. From time to time you emerge from the gullies through the hills on to stretches of flat desert, or semi-desert, gravel and small stones, often crossed by wide, shallow watercourses left by the year's rain, which seems to fall, if at all, in a wasteful few days and swiftly disappear. At one point, the desert is broken by an incongruous ten-mile belt of cultivated jungle, after which it changes its nature yet again. The scenery is startlingly evocative of one of Hollywood's fanciful films about the Foreign Legion. The desert, with its outcrops of honeycombed sandstone, high temperature and Colorado atmosphere, is dotted with "legion" forts, manned by the North-West Frontier Force. The desert is home to a multitude of dust demons: spirals of sand thirty to a hundred feet high which swirl tortuously across the landscape, elastically changing shape as they go.

You may spend the night at one of the garrisons where the officers' mess seems more Sandhurst than Sandhurst, but where the entertainment is essentially Pathan: a display perhaps of tribal dancing and satire. The dance is rather like the Afghan atan, the dancers hopping about like birds and jerking their heads sharply from side to side, thus making a flying plumage of their long black hair. The music is without melody, the rhythm varying greatly, the dancers coming at moments almost to a standstill and at others jumping and stamping in a *sforzando* of frenzy punctuated by regular crashing breaks. The musicians, four in number, walk slowly round inside the circle of dancers, clapping on small tabors or playing on a wailing reed instrument. The purpose of the dance is to excite a battle frenzy; erotic dances, common to Western cultures, play but a small part in these predominantly male societies. By the glazed look of some of the dancers after forty minutes, the desired result seems to be achieved. The dance is followed by a pantomime which gives full scope to the Pathan's great gift for mimicry and comic gesture, and in which the ordinary soldier seizes the opportunity to satirize his officers.

The journey gets harder as you drive on south-west, this time in the cab of a bus bursting at the rivets with passengers; there are twelve in the driver's cab alone. The floor is heaped up with baskets; jammed tightly against them, you prop your feet on a stone water-jar, knees pushed up to the chin so that you can scarcely move in any direction and are forced into the meditative position of a more than usually masochistic fakir.

Your clothes stick in clammy swabs to those of your neighbours and mutual sweats mingle in one steady flow. On one side of you is a man with 'flu and on the other his pock-faced son who leans his head on your shoulder and sprawls over your legs. A third, clad in a loud check shirt, is jabbering and spitting like a human monkey, and all over you crawl two small children whose lips and faces are burst open by suppurating boils and festering sores. The heat, sweat, noise and stench is such that even the acrid smell of *biri*, the rolled tobacco leaves that make up a Pakistani cigarette, is a welcome anaesthetic.

At last you reach Dalbandin, the town everyone has been talking about in the bus. You feel an immense relief, but when you clamber out you realize that Dalbandin is only a small group of huts clustered around a few government offices, a fort and a railway station: a mere village surviving in a wilderness of sand that assaults it in tireless waves which appear to be sucking up its outposts inch by inch. Yet there is a gaunt beauty in its few blasted trees waving desperate, crazy fingers out of their graves of sand and in the simplicity of the white-fronted buildings defying the desert. On one edge of the village, next to the football pitch – just a patch of sand a little less soft than the rest – you find a resthouse that has somehow snatched a comparative paradise from the ground of this desert hell. There is a pool in the compound, and grass, and green trees, and clumps of a lovely bush which blossoms with warm pink and orange flowers.

On again, this time in the single-track train that runs like a lifeline through the Pakistan frontier provinces and Baluchistan. You are now out of the territories of the Pathans proper and well into Baluchistan. Here:

The desert singes, and the stubborn rock
Split to the centre sweats at every pore.

Your nostrils are suddenly assailed by the pungent odour of the earth's flesh on fire, scorching beneath the sun as unmistakably as that of any human body. For over two hundred miles there is no water at all, except that brought once a week in the wagons of the train. Nor is there any natural wildlife except the "sandfish": a small snake-like creature about the size of a blindworm and of a light sandy colour. There is apparently nothing for it to live on, yet it survives, and from its tail the natives extract a precious oil used in the making of perfume. Villages here exist only because of the treasures of the desert and the black hot hills that traverse it: manganese and other minerals or, as at Nok Kundi, the most beautiful marble in Asia. Perfume and marble; Eve's beauty from the serpent's tail and her palaces quarried and fetched from the very mouth of hell.

It is these varied territories and differing peoples of the southern frontier districts which Afghan governments dream of making into a single coherent state. The lorry-driver's bacha should be calling not "Pushtunistan Unjast" but "Pushtunistan Kujast?" – "Where is Pushtunistan?"

Apart from the sentimental attachments of the royal family, a mixture of gratitude and fear probably provided a subconscious motive for the desire of Afghanistan's autocratic monarchs from the time of Nadir Shah to the fall of Zahir Shah to see the Pathan areas as a whole come within a greater degree of Afghan control, however theoretically indirect. During the chaos that followed Amanullah's overthrow in 1929, the British carefully refrained from any involvement and, verbally at least, tried to dissociate the tribesmen on their side of the frontier from the subsequent struggle for power in Afghanistan. These British admonitions, however, were ineffective, and the bulk of the tribal forces which gave Nadir Shah the ultimate victory were, in fact, recruited south of the Durand Line. This was a common precedent from which the Taliban would benefit equally in the 1990s and that any anti-Taliban alliance that invades would certainly come to regret resurrecting.

Immediately after the Second World War the Afghans were enthusiastically endorsing every British precedent opinion which, by any stretch of the imagination, could be said to uphold the validity of their claim for an independent Pushtunistan in the new India. It must be remembered that at this time the constitutional plan envisaged that many of the Princely States would retain their autonomy, not that they would be militarily annexed by the "pacifist" government of India.

The Bray Committee's view that "if self-determination is to be allowed any play at all in India, it should surely be allowed to the Pathan race, whom providence has interposed between India and foreign aggression", was music to Afghan ears. From Mountbatten's remark that "agreements with the tribes on the North-West Frontiers of India would have to be negotiated with the appropriate successor authority", the Afghans inferred that Mountbatten favoured their claim. In my view, his reference was to any subsequent internal agreement there might be between the tribes and what subsequently became Pakistan. The last Viceroy made it quite clear that in his role as referee he could take no stance, but that it was for the two parties involved in the partition of India, Congress and the Muslim League, to decide whether or not the frontier would be an independent state. In fact the British government in India in 1944 sternly reminded the Afghans that the Durand Line was an established international boundary which should not concern them.

The referendum conducted in the North-West Frontier Province (NWFP) in 1947 thus only offered those Pathans south-east of the Durand Line the choice of joining India or Pakistan, a limitation about which the Afghans, with some justification, complained. Abdul Ghaffar Khan – the frontier Gandhi – and his brother campaigned hard for the boycott of the referendum, but had little impact, as the 55 per cent poll was only some 10 per cent down on previous polling levels. Inevitably 99 per cent of those voting preferred Pakistan and it became the position of the British government at independence, and has been since, that Pakistan became legal heir to all the treaty rights secured by the British in India.

The division of the Pathan tribes by the Durand Line led, after the partition of the Indian subcontinent in 1947, to an uneasy relationship between Afghanistan and Pakistan. The Afghans felt that their ambitions were now opposed by a weaker force; the Pakistanis, acutely conscious of their problems in welding together a new state from so many disparate entities, were determined that nothing should detract from strengthening the sense of national unity. Inevitably the two countries disagreed sharply over the issue of Pushtunistan.

In 1949 Pakistani air force planes operating on the frontier accidentally bombed a village on the Afghan side. Pakistan apologized and offered compensation. Afghanistan rejected all overtures. The Afghan Shura (a consultative Parliament with very limited executive power) – then appointed by the King, not elected – proclaimed that it recognized "neither the imaginary Durand nor any similar Line". In a speech the King, Zahir Shah, used a significant phrase. "Note also must be taken of the freedom-loving aspirations and the repeated protests of the *trans-Durand Afghans*." (My italics.)

The Afghan authorities encouraged the setting up of a so-called independent Pakhtun parliament in Pakistan itself. The Pakistanis responded by cutting off transit fuel supplies to Afghanistan and broadcasting demands to know whether Afghanistan proposed to grant independence to the Pathans on their side of the frontier – a challenge always calculated to provoke the fury of Afghan governments. On a more positive note, the Pakistan government made great efforts to make the tribes feel that they belonged to Pakistan and that their citizenship brought substantial material benefits. As a deliberate act of policy, expenditure in the tribal areas on education, health and rural development in the years following the creation of Pakistan was disproportionately high. Conversely, the transfer from tribal law and customs to the rule of national law was tactfully gradual. A steady recruitment of men from the tribal areas to the Pakistan regular army – among whose elite troops such North-West

Frontier Forces as the Waziristan Scouts stand supreme – also served initially to increase their attachment to Pakistan. When they are released from military service to return to their villages, they take with them not only the skills and literacy, but also the attitudes that they have acquired in the army. The number of military coups against what were seen as effete democratic governments and the loyalty of the military in the face of public unrest following the October 2001 US attacks on Afghanistan suggest that these attitudes still obtain.

For the first ten years of Pakistan's existence, the dispute fluctuated in intensity, though, as my experience recounted at the beginning of this chapter indicates, it remained an active myth in the popular mind and a useful rallying cry on the domestic political scene on both sides of the frontier. In 1960, however, it once again brought the two neighbours to the brink of outright war.

Diplomatic relations between Afghanistan and Pakistan had been resumed in 1957, after a two-year lapse following the merger of all the Western States of Pakistan, including the North-West Frontier Province, into a single West Pakistan. But, at the end of 1959, Pakistan felt compelled to protest against violations of its air space by Afghan aircraft and against provocative broadcasts on Kabul radio by the King and Premier in which both, in the name of Pushtunistan, repeated earlier claims to parts of Pakistan.

These incidents were the culmination of a persistent and increasingly tough attitude fostered by Daoud over the Pushtunistan question. In March 1960, Khrushchev publicly supported the Afghan claims. Pakistan riposted by proposing a referendum among Afghan Pathans to see if they would like to join Pakistan. The Afghans retorted by refusing to extend the visas of Pakistanis working in their country, expelling a number of them and making the life of those who remained virtually impossible. Pro-Pushtunistan propaganda was intensified by Afghan consular agencies, whose activities in this field had already aroused deep indignation in Pakistan.

It is difficult to decide exactly who started the fighting which broke out in the Bajaur area, north of the Khyber Pass, in September 1960 and again in May 1961. Pakistan claimed that it was repulsing incursions into its territory by armed groups backed by the Afghan army. The Afghans counter-claimed that Pakistan was in fact conducting a severe campaign of military reprisals and bombing against discontented Pathan tribesmen within its own borders. The Pakistanis admitted the bombing of one house, which they said was the headquarters of Afghan agents.

Afghan regular troops disguised as tribesmen were badly defeated by local Frontier Force soldiers and local villagers, but Punjabi units sent in by Ayub Khan, Pakistan's Pathan president, to support the local forces, received a scarcely less hostile reception. Apportioning blame in an area where the movements of population are considerable is not easy, although personally I feel that Pakistan probably had slightly the better case. Whatever the origins of the conflict, diplomatic relations were broken off in September 1961 and frontier traffic came to a standstill. By November, something like 200,000 Afghan nomads, who habitually leave their summer pastures in Afghanistan to cross over to Pakistan, found themselves stranded and near starvation in the mountain passes between the two countries, although a few managed to force their way over the border. The closure of the frontier was a sharp blow to the Afghan economy, and its consequences contributed to the resignation in March 1963, after ten years as virtual ruler of Afghanistan, of Prince Daoud. With Daoud gone, tension between the two countries began to ease and, through the good offices of the Shah of Persia, diplomatic relations were restored in May. Feelings remained strong, however, and, in 1966, Maiwandwal, then Prime Minister of Afghanistan, made it quite clear in conversation with me that he thought the Pushtunistan issue was as serious then as ever – perhaps even more serious, in that despite the expressed regret of both sides over the clash in 1960–61, there had been a complete failure to resolve the dispute to the satisfaction of all three parties: Pakistan, Afghanistan and the Pathans.

As a result, in its seemingly inevitable decennial cycle, the issue came to a head again in the mid-1970s. This time the problem was aggravated by two additional factors: increasing demands for greater regional independence in Pakistan and growing fears of the central Pakistan government that these might lead to the further disintegration of the state.

The secession of East Pakistan to become the sovereign state of Bangladesh has made subsequent Pakistan governments, whether civilian or military, almost paranoid about any hint of further separatism. Though Zulfikar Ali Bhutto's 1970 election victory was overwhelming in the rest of Pakistan, he was badly defeated in the NWFP and in Baluchistan he did not even win a single seat. The bulk of popular support was clearly for those parties, such as the National Awami Party, favouring if not outright independence, a very high degree of regional autonomy. In order to contain these pressures, the 1973 constitution devolved considerable federal powers to the regional governments which had been created in 1970. In response to local demand, there was also substantial investment in transport, medical services and education in these two regions, within the limit permissible in the precarious state of Pakistan's economy. The stabilizing effect of such measures was, however, diminished by the sudden return to power in Afghanistan of that ardent irredentist Daoud. Within a few days of taking over he was stirring up the old Pushtunistan issue which had played so large a part in his downfall a decade earlier. Though initially he spoke of "a peaceful and honourable settlement of the Pushtunistan problem" and "the hopes of the Baluch people", it was soon evident that his demands, and the tactics by which they were pursued, were no different from those of the late 1950s and early 1960s.

By 1975 Pakistan was bitterly, and on good evidence, accusing Afghanistan of stirring up trouble on the Pakistan side of the frontier, trouble which culminated in the assassination of H.M.K. Sherpao, a leading opponent of Pushtunistan in the NWFP government. The Pakistan Defence Minister denounced Afghanistan for training guerrillas, mounting sabotage and assassinations in Pakistan and for harbouring "absconders from justice". His view that the "sole aim of these activities is to create unrest and fear amongst the people of the NWFP and Baluchistan in advancement of Afghanistan's aggressive and irredentist aims" is hard to deny.

In February of that year, governor's rule was imposed in the NWFP as it was in Baluchistan in December, the National Awami Party was dissolved and its leader Wali Khan arrested – in effect for preaching the supreme heresy, secession.

General Zia's military coup in 1976, and ensuing events in Afghanistan itself, lowered the temperature slightly, but the fact that once again the tribal areas south of the Durand Line were being used by rebels against a Kabul regime to try to topple it by military means, made the situation potentially more dangerous than it had been for many years. To measure the validity of conflicting claims over Pushtunistan it is necessary to examine the moral, social and psychological basis of Afghanistan's claims, rather than their, in my view, shaky legal foundations.

The basis of the Afghan claim is that the Pushtu-speaking peoples are an artificially divided ethnic entity. That they are of the same race on both sides of the Durand Line cannot be in dispute, but that this border is the artificial and sole cause of division is open to argument. It is fallacious to assume that the Pathans are a naturally homogeneous whole. Their entire history is, rather, one of fierce and cruelly conducted inter-tribal disputes over everything from grazing grounds to kingdoms. Great tribes like the Yusufzai and the Durrani have been continually at skirmish with each other for centuries, and feelings of deep antagonism remain.

The essential characteristic of the Pathan tribe is a closely-knit and sharply defined pattern of family relationships that places everyone not of that group, and quite irrespective of his ethnic origins, among the world of potential enemies. At the same time, the Pathan – of whatever tribe – takes a strong pride in being a Pathan. The tribal group is the limit of the extent to which the Pathan is prepared to abate his jealously guarded individualism. Even within the family circle, rivalries and quarrels are often long and bitter, since the Pathan calls no man lord and admits his inferiority to nobody. To the world outside his tribal group, and apart from the demands of hospitality to wayfaring strangers, the Pathan's attitude alternates between a total indifference and a kind of tigerish contempt for the rest of the human animal kingdom, whose function is to provide, when necessary, individuals to satisfy the predator's appetite. Mountstuart Elphinstone, a most penetrating observer of Afghan life, graphically describes the character of the Pathan in his *Account of the Kingdom of Caubul*: "Their vices are revenge, envy, avarice, rapacity and obstinacy; on the other hand, they are fond of liberty, faithful to their friends, kind to their dependants, hospitable, brave, hardy, frugal, laborious and prudent; they are less disposed than the nations in their neighbourhood to falsehood, intrigue and deceit."

The Pathan character has changed little since the year 1814, when Elphinstone completed his account, although subsequent events have shown him to be wrong in his last claim. Even before the Soviet invasion one man in four still carried rifle, shotgun or pistol, and those that no longer strode gun in hand probably still had one at home – just in case. At the tribal arms factory near Kohat in Pakistan gaily decorated, near-perfect handmade imitations of the classic weapons of every nation were regularly manufactured. Since 1979 these have had to compete with the influx of industrially produced weapons of Soviet design dished out like kids' lollipops by the foreign powers stoking the conflict of the past 22 years. Examples could be seen bristling from the top of every market-bound bus or lorry. The occasional ornate *jezail* (one of those ancient muskets which seem more likely to destroy their owners than their targets) or the intricately decorated sheath of a triangular-bladed hunting-knife evoke memories of the stirring adventures vividly narrated by writers of the Edwardian boys' adventure-book school. Today the tribal smiths just as handily turn out copies of the small arms of the former Soviet empire which have been the common currency of destruction of every Afghan faction for the past twenty years.

Generosity and nobility of manner can yield to the most scathingly expressed form of contempt in the world: an ice-basilisk glance and a tiny gobbet of precision-planted spit at the despised one's feet. Moving with a springing stride, toes turned slightly inwards and rising at the heel, and with a tall, haughty carriage, the Pathan will flash at you from beneath stern black eyebrows a fierce look that can turn in an instant into a shy glance of soft brown eyes. Warlike spirit shares his soul with childish and delightful vanity, and a Pathan will lay down his rifle and cartridge belt, sit on a little peninsula of stones by the stream and pluck, paint and preen himself with shameless vanity in the mirror-shine of the lid of a boot-polish tin. A courteous and unembarrassed "good day" from him, striding past you as you attend to the call of nature in the desert; the care and protection of you, his guest, as an unquestioned obligation, even to death; his manly independence; his Rabelaisian humour – all this makes the Pathan a man to be liked and respected, to be treated tactfully and carefully; and a man rarely, if ever, to be organized within the impersonal conventions of a modern state.

It is highly unlikely that people of such a prickly and individualistic temperament, inheriting many inter-tribal enmities, antipathetic to the very idea of central rule, are going to agitate very forcefully for the creation of Pushtunistan – unless such agitation can serve as a means for satisfying their more parochial ambitions. Their outlook is, after all, little different now from the days when the Pushtu poet, Khushal Khan, trying vainly to unite the tribes against the Mogul Emperor Aurangzebe, bewailed: "Would that the Pushtuns could agree among themselves."

The real weakness of Afghan claims, to those more concerned with justice than law, lies in their lack of logical coherence, their internal contradictions. During an amiable, lengthy and courteous interview with me in 1966, Prime Minister Maiwandwal for just one brief instant sparked a flash of anger; it was when I asked him whether he thought any part of Afghanistan should become part of Pushtunistan. His sharp "never" and subsequent rebuke of my "irrelevant" question betrayed, not only strength of feeling, but perhaps also an awareness of the ambiguity and weakness of the arguments for an independent Pushtunistan. If there is a case to be made out for Pushtunistan on the grounds of natural ethnic affinity, assessed in terms of language, then all Pushtu-speaking peoples, from both sides of the border, should belong to it; which means that it should be created from territories belonging to Afghanistan no less than to Pakistan. If this case falls, partial groupings cutting across established states and boundaries make no sense in terms of securing stable and equitable territorial demarcation in this part of Asia. It may, however, seem to make sense in terms of other considerations. We shall see later, from the attitude of the Pathan ruling group in Afghanistan towards the minorities there, that the assumption by this group that Afghanistan is already a natural Pathan state has at least as much, and maybe more, significance for internal as for external interests.

One should not expect those involved to apply pure logic to the argument, in public at least. Pushtunistan, like the reunification of Germany, is one of those causes that no national leader or politician dare renounce, however little faith he may himself have in it; the cause has its own logic. In the 1950s and early 1960s the danger lay in an issue which, kept simmering for a variety of reasons, could suddenly be brought to the boil whenever the Soviet Union chose to apply more heat to the pot. It was an established axiom of Russian policy at the time that the Durand Line was part of a wicked imperialist plot which it was Afghanistan's duty to overthrow. In August 1951, for example, an article in the Soviet periodical *Literaturnaya Gazeta* declared:

As a direct result of the enforced division of the Afghan tribes, who are almost equally divided between Afghanistan and Pakistan and are carrying on a struggle for self-determination, and also as a result of the original traditions of the numerous nomad tribes, a situation is arising apparently of itself, apparently spontaneously, in which there could occur demarcation by bloodshed of the frontier that was originally plotted on the maps of the imperialists in London and Washington. Spontaneously rising tension, mutual enmity and incidents are exactly what the imperialists need in order to divide and rule.

It so happened that "tension" and the rest were also exactly what the Soviet imperialist philosophy of that time needed to facilitate its territorial expansion. But after the clash of 1960–61 between Afghanistan and Pakistan, the Soviet attitude changed. Having made a notable effort in 1965–66 to compose the quarrel between India and Pakistan over Kashmir, Russia did not want to see yet another frontier war flaring up in an area where the development of its interests required stability. Moscow seemed to recognize that such divisions in the Indian subcontinent were of benefit only to Peking. The main aim of Soviet diplomatic effort thus turned to persuading Afghanistan and Pakistan that they had mutual economic interests, for it was on this recognition that the unhampered flow of her own goods through these countries largely depended.

Although Afghan governments often include Baluchistan in the proposed Pushtunistan, the Baluch are not of the same stock and are no fonder of the Pathans than are the other minorities they dominate. Even before the fluctuating refugee crisis of the past 20 years the presence of some million Pathans in Pakistan Baluchistan itself, did not improve the relationship. In demographic terms the issue was of minor importance to Afghanistan, because only a very small proportion, probably less than 10 per cent, of the two million plus Baluch lived, or wandered, on the Afghan side of the border. The majority live either in Pakistan or in the south-east corner of Shi'a Iran where, as Sunni Muslims, they constitute an ill-regarded religious minority.

Baluchistan, however, for all the hostile aspect of its largely uninhabited desert, has a number of highly desirable economic features. The Sui gasfields are already well developed, and there are also considerable deposits of chrome, sulphur, coal and iron to be exploited. It also possessed that economic holy grail of Russian imperialism – access to the warm waters of the Arabian Sea. It is thus a desirable territory not only for its present rulers, Pakistan, and its covetous neighbour, but also for Russia and the land-locked successor republics of the Soviet Union that border northern Afghanistan. Nor could a stable and strong Iran afford to ignore its fate, as the Shah indicated in 1972 when he implied that in the event of the collapse of Pakistan he would occupy Baluchistan. In December 1979 sharp fighting with considerable casualties was reported from Iranian Baluchistan, when the regional capital Zahedan tried to assert its independence from Tehran.

The Baluch, however, are still a largely primitive, unsophisticated, and in many cases nomadic people, who do not have sufficient skilled citizens to develop their economic potential on their own. They do have a strong desire for a greater degree of control over their own destiny and bitterly resent the fact that their fierce opposition to central government was bloodily suppressed by military force three times in the 1970s. Political activity was in any case banned throughout Pakistan by President Zia shortly after he came to power, but perhaps more significant than the absence of a political outlet is the fact that early in 1979 the National Awami Party, which had expressed the desire for autonomy of both the Pathans and the Baluch, split into two wings. The division was on racial and political lines, with the Pakistani Pathans adopting a more moderate, less separatist stance, while the Baluch moved still further to the left.* The Baluch

*It is well to remember that whenever referring to Marxists in these countries we are dealing in terms of hundreds rather than thousands.

position was largely dictated by the fact that a number of its young men had been to Russia in recent years for training and had returned ardent Marxist revolutionaries. They had, for example, greeted the Taraki coup in Afghanistan with delight as being a step nearer their own independence. Their no less nationalist elders, however, as orthodox Muslims, were much less enthusiastic. Many of them were realistic enough to recognize that they would find it almost impossible to survive alone – even if any new independent state of Baluchistan were to embrace the Baluch in all three countries. Had the Soviet Union not disintegrated, the temptation offered by Soviet client-state status might have proved considerable as the Moscow-indoctrinated young men moved up into positions of power. An independent, but Soviet-dominated, Baluchistan would have sat astride the entrance to the Iranian Gulf as well as opening up the Arabian Sea for the direct outward flow of Russian goods. The gains, from the Soviet point of view, were much more attractive than those of any potential Pushtunistan.

In any case, the events of the past 20 years have rendered largely academic the legal, social and moral niceties of the Pushtunistan argument. The border, so carefully drawn by the British and so closely policed by Pakistan, has become a sieve whose interstices are now so porous as to render any attempt to filter what passes through it largely ineffective. The influx of some three-and-a-half million refugees, mostly Pathans, in one direction, the Pakistan-sponsored flow of mujehadin and munitions in the other, and the constant crossing and recrossing of drug smugglers and the transport mafia have virtually created a de facto Pushtunistan with the potential to destabilize Pakistan itself.

If the traditional concept of Afghanistan as a buffer state had held true in the post-war world, Russia might have been expected to move in as soon as the counter-pressure of the

British Empire was removed. That it did not was a clear indication that the policy-makers in the Kremlin believed that they were moving successfully at second hand towards their economic and political goals in the region. So what kind of society were they trying to manage, and how did they succeed in penetrating it.

4

WHO ARE THE AFGHANS?

Though often the most dramatic, relations with other countries are not the most critical of Afghanistan's problems. The real tasks facing its governments are internal: the problems of unity and minorities; the conflicting pressures, social and economic, of traditionalism and modernization (particularly in regard to the status of women and to Islam); and the difficulties of imposing sophisticated political methods and institutions on old tribal loyalties and attitudes.

In this chapter and the two following, I shall try to trace the main features of Afghan society and to explain the factors that conditioned its political and economic development in the years preceding the Soviet invasion. It is probably still too early to assess the long-term impact on Afghan society of that invasion and the subsequent civil war, but some consideration of prior trends may point to how it might develop if peace and stability were to be restored.

Moreover, to be seen in perspective, the appalling events of the past 22 years have to be set against a benchmark of Afghan normality. But first a word of warning should be given. It is pointless to put too much trust in Afghan statistics. Public enterprises seldom kept meaningful accounts even before 1978 and governments tended to substitute forecasts and wishful thinking for actual measurement of past accomplishment. It also seemed pointless to include figures after the Taraki coup in 1978 because the disruption of the economy and the even more than usually strident demands of propaganda made them meaningless in any long-term context.

The most challenging of the problems facing Afghanistan

has always been the creation of a sense of genuine national unity in a country whose constituent races have as little natural affinity as those in the Balkans. As mentioned in earlier chapters, when most foreigners use the word "Afghan" they are usually thinking of the Pathans, forgetting that among the country's inhabitants are very substantial minorities of Uzbegs, Hazaras, Turkmen and Tajiks, not to speak of many smaller groups, such as Aimaq, Kirghiz and Nuristani.

A reasonably accurate population survey carried out by AID in 1973 gave the settled population as a little over ten million, growing at just under 2 per cent a year. There were probably a further two million nomads, whose numbers remain fairly constant. Louis Dupree, on whose work the ethnic map on page 76 is based, made a 1973 estimate of 14 million. A 1978 Afghan government survey gave a figure of 15.5 million (then a little high in my view). These official surveys avoided breaking the numbers down by race for political reasons. Estimates of the proportion of Pathans vary from Dupree's 50 per cent to 75 per cent. Personally I think the figure is more likely to be between 45 and 50 per cent. The largest minority is that of the Tajiks, at between three and four million. Then there are about a million Uzbegs, and a million Hazaras, and almost as many Aimaq and Nuristanis, before we come down to the innumerable minor groups. Though the World Bank predicted a population explosion shortly before the Soviet invasion and a recent UN estimate put the figure at 20.1 million, a discount has to be calculated for the effects of two decades of war and the consequent disruption of family life. Estimates of the number who have died directly or indirectly vary from 1.5 to 2.5 million. Overall the present population, including some four million refugees, is probably between 15 and 18 million.

Though the main races dominate particular areas, as a result of calculated policies of dispersal by various rulers in the

Main ethnic areas of
Afghanistan and borders

Legend:
- AIMAQ
- BALUCH
- HAZARA
- KIRGHIZ
- NURISTANI
- PATHAN
- SETTLEMENTS
- TAJIK
- TURKMEN
- UZBEG
- uninhabited

CHINA

TAJIKISTAN

KIRGHIZ

TAJIK

TAJIK

Faizabad

TAJIK

NURISTANI

Kabul

PAKISTAN

UZBEKISTAN

UZBEG

Mazar-i-Sharif

UZBEG

HAZARA

TAJIK

Kandahar

AIMAQ

PATHAN

TURKMENISTAN

TURKMEN

uninhabited

Herat

uninhabited

BALUCHISTAN

uninhabited

IRAN

twentieth century, there are pockets of racially different settlements in most of the main regions. Usually these consist of Pathans in non-Pathan areas. A significant indication of the respective status of the different races is that in these mixed areas while Pathan immigrant males quite often marry local girls, the reverse is seldom true. A glance at the map will also show that, with the exception of the almost psychotically independent Hazaras and Nuristanis, all of the main racial groups in Afghanistan are part of ethnic areas which straddle Afghanistan's borders – a fact as likely to be significant to that country's future as it has been in the past.

The picture is further complicated by the existence and movement of the main nomad groups in the south-east, in Baluchistan, and in Badakshan in the north. By far the largest and most important of these groups is the Ghilzai, the most numerous of the true Afghan tribes, and with a reputation among foreigners for fanaticism and savagery unequalled even in Afghanistan. At one time the Ghilzai (or Ghalji) conquered much of Persia.

The nomads had an important function in the commercial and financial life of the villages on their route, often bringing and selling goods, lending money and even owning land and collecting rent. They also serve as an uncontrollable (and therefore, in Kabul's eyes, unacceptable) means of disseminating news of what is happening in other parts of the country. Increasingly often, even in the 1960s and 1970s, they either found their communal grazing land permanently occupied by pioneering farmers backed by the army, or barred to them by the political closure of frontiers they had never recognized. Perhaps unsurprisingly, the nomads looked on the farmers with contempt and usually managed to find an alternative grazing area. But the conflict of the past twenty years has severely disrupted these migratory patterns.

While placing great official emphasis on the need for national unity, successive governments of Afghanistan have done little to foster it in practice. Prime Minister Maiwandwal, for example, optimistically declared to me in 1966: "We do not think in terms of ethnic entities. We consider everybody in Afghanistan as Afghans." This was an admirable goal at which to strive, but most of the minority groups would claim that it has never been seriously pursued.

No democratic administration has ever had more than two non-Pathans in cabinets which have usually numbered between 15 and 20 people – Dr Yusuf's in 1963, for example, contained none. An even larger underprivileged group, women, who constitute about 55 per cent of the Afghan population, have been still less well represented. There have only ever been three women in the cabinet, never more than one at a time, and never in any post outside what might be considered the "feminine" posts of health and social welfare.

Babrak Karmal's PDPA cabinet, formed in February 1980, did contain four non-Pathans (out of 16), but this was not so surprising in view of the fact that the revolutionary cause was bound to attract support from among the minority groups who resented the apparently perpetual Pathan dominance. His cabinet had only one woman in it, Dr Ratebzad.

The minorities have always felt that Afghanistan is a country run by Pathans for Pathans and that the other groups are, in a sense, the victims of an internal colonialism. This is an impression, which must be shared by the foreign visitor. It is strengthened by past governments' preoccupation with exclusively Pathan issues, such as Pushtunistan, the status and use of Pushtu and the dominance of the "Pathan" capital, Kabul. Gestures, such as making Turki – the language of the Turkmen – an official language, did little to convince the minorities otherwise. A form of Persian known as Dari is the language common to the Afghan ethnic groups (not necessarily as the first language), except that many uneducated Pathans speak only Pushtu and the second language of most of them along the border with Pakistan is Urdu.

The government of this volatile mixture has always been firmly in the hands of the Pathans. Even in peacetime Pathan governors were to be found in most of the provinces, even where the population was predominantly of another ethnic group, but not – partly, it is true, because of the problem of the Pushtu language – a non-Pathan governor of a Pathan province. The overwhelming majority of administrators were also Pathans. It must be admitted that the Pathans do have a flair for administration and that even in an openly competitive society, without ethnic bias, they would probably occupy more than their share of key government and administrative posts.

The favoured position of the Pathans in pre-invasion Afghanistan was symbolized by the way in which Kabul thrived, apparently at the expense of the provinces. In amenities and services, Kabul was in many ways a typical modern metropolis. New blocks of offices and houses sprang up among the old mud dwellings; cars, restaurants and well-stocked shops were plentiful, as one would expect in a capital city. But its array of amenities and services was out of proportion when the city's peacetime population of around 750,000 is compared with that of the whole country.

For example, some 80 per cent of Afghanistan's sorely needed doctors practised in Kabul, where the prospects of augmenting their meagre government salaries by private practice were best, and where there were at least some hospital facilities. This gave Kabul a ratio of about one doctor per thousand people, as opposed to a national figure of one per 13,000. In one of the remote northern districts I visited, I met a doctor who had 200,000 patients on his list, no hospital, no assistants, no nurses and not even a local dispensary for drugs. His was the only car in the district and he worked for little better than a skilled labourer's wage. Sixty per cent of hospital beds were in the capital, which also enjoyed the same proportion of the country's domestic electricity supply and piped water.

Similarly, the capital had a near-monopoly of the best educational facilities. Almost all institutions of higher education, universities and technical colleges were centred in Kabul, although during the 1970s new ones were established in Jalalabad, Herat, Kunduz and Mazar, and the technical college in Kandahar grew considerably. A student who had once been to Kabul did everything in his power, or more often in his family's power, to avoid being sent back to the provinces. This was particularly true of the few women students. The provinces were deprived of the very people needed to demand and create the missing amenities and services, thus perpetuating a vicious circle.

While it is true that members of other ethnic groups in Kabul did benefit from its growth, the capital was and is essentially a Pathan-dominated city, and its growing modernity was viewed enviously by the ambitious provincial Uzbeg or Tajik. That this once-thriving metropolis is now little better than a series of loosely connected heaps of rubble is a poignant reminder of the transience of human structures from the days of Balkh, "Mother of Cities", to the present.

Even those improvements that did take place in the provinces were concentrated in the Pathan areas to the south and south-east of the Hindu Kush. The great schemes of agricultural development in Khost and the Helmand Valley, of forestry at Ali Khel, of hydroelectric power and agricultural irrigation in Nangarhar – these are all in Pathan provinces. Even where development was taking place in regions where other groups predominate, as with cotton ginning and processing in the north at Kunduz and along the Oxus, it was often in a place with a Pathan settler population dating from the government's deliberate shifting of Pathans to these areas before the Second World War. The resentments aroused by these disparities only added to the innate antipathy of the minorities towards a Pathan-dominated central government.

In the main, the Pathans live south of the great barrier of the Hindu Kush, and the bulk of the minority groups live to its north or in the south-west. Until the Salang Tunnel was opened in 1964, the mountains sealed off one-half of the country from the other in winter, except by the most circuitous route.

During the 1960s and 1970s, communications between Kabul and the main provincial cities were improved considerably, both by road and air, although such important centres as Faizabad and Farah were still linked to the capital by dirt roads whose monstrous potholes and fist-sized stones seemed to provide a free breaker's yard for any car I drove over them. Communications between the provinces themselves were virtually non-existent. To travel between Mazar-i-Sharif and Kunduz – the capital of the important neighbouring province of that name – you took your choice of the various tyre tracks of those who had passed across the desert before, and at the same time tried to follow the meandering line of dilapidated wooden beanposts bearing the single telephone line. To reach Kunduz from some of its outlying districts, you had to cross the river by a wooden ferry whose ballast system, a masterpiece of ingenious simplicity, consisted of bailing water from one of the two catamaran-style hulls to its equally rickety partner, while motive power was achieved by hauling on a rope. The 180-kilometre journey between the two towns in the 1950s took nine or ten hours' with time off for digging a two-wheel-drive vehicle out of the sand. Nor was there likely to be more than a single vehicle travelling in the opposite direction – which on those narrow switchback tracks was just as well.

In the late 1950s the 900 miles from Herat to Kabul via Kandahar could take ten days on the back of a lorry; ten years later it could be done by car in a day. Military road-building teams, backed by both Soviet and American finance and know-how, were not only rapidly creating a network of highways between the major cities, but were also hacking good roads out of mere narrow tracks in provinces such as Paktya. Even so, the bulk of transport was still by camel and donkey, horse and bullock cart, and great baulks of cedar wood found their way to Pakistan, two or four at a time, strapped to the sides of a camel.

Fifty years ago wheels of any kind, even on bicycles, were unknown in many Afghan villages. Yet, in terms of creating a sense of national unity, the establishment of good communications from province to province, as distinct from the direct links with Kabul – a permanent reminder of provincial dependence – was essential. The almost total destruction of the road network and of 3,500 of its bridges by mines, bombing and shelling has put things back to the camel-and-donkey age in almost all of Afghanistan.

Any humanitarian programme aimed at reuniting the country will have to give rebuilding the road system a high priority. The difficulties and expense of such road-building programmes should not be underestimated when grand speeches are made about aid to any post-Taliban Afghanistan. These roads have to cross deserts of shifting sand and stark black granite outcrops, go over rivers whose spring floods can wash away a solid stone bridge in a few minutes, and pierce mountains which climb to 18,000 feet. Money spent on fostering a sense of unity, however, is a sound investment, even if it brings in its wake still greater pressures from the provinces for a larger share of national expenditure.

The imbalance in favour of the Pathans, and the government's preoccupation with Pathan nationalism, served only to alienate the minorities completely. This was particularly true of the Uzbegs: a sophisticated and capable people who provided a large proportion of the country's professional men and entrepreneurs. The amount of private capital reinvested in the national economy even before the uncertainties of war was pitifully small. Desperately short of capital, Afghanistan could not afford so to neglect the private wealth of the Uzbegs as an internal resource.

If excessive emphasis is placed on ethnic affinities, and if it is legitimate in official circles for Pathan ambitions and interests to be projected southwards over the Pakistan border, then it can hardly be less legitimate for the Afghan Uzbegs to turn their eyes northwards to Uzbekistan, with which they have such close racial and cultural ties. One has only to witness their almost magical performance on horseback in their sport of *buzkashi* (which combines mounted mayhem with rugby football played with a beheaded goat) to realize that, in ethnic terms at least, their ties are with the horsemen of Soviet Central Asia.

In the early days of post-war economic penetration, the Soviet Union was not slow to exploit this affinity through the extensive use of Soviet Uzbegs in development projects in northern areas of Afghanistan; and, of course, those with radios are within reach of the ordinary domestic broadcasts of Uzbekistan and Tajikistan. Clearly, divided loyalties among such powerful and capable minorities would be fatal to any hopes of Afghan unity. Significantly the Soviet invading army soon reversed its initial policy of relying heavily on ethnic minority troops, particularly Uzbegs.

The Hazaras, whose Mongoloid features and apparent truculence of manner betray their descent from the hordes of

Genghis Khan,* do not require the support of outside influences to strengthen their intransigence. Living in the central mountain area known as the Hazarajat (an extension of the Hindu Kush), they are almost literally inaccessible to all forms of central government or authority, from tax collection to police. The extent of their isolation can be judged by the fact that it was only in the mid-twentieth century that a large, beautiful and historically important minaret was discovered near Jam, and the traveller trying to reach it could still enquire in vain at a village less than ten miles away.

The isolation of the Hazaras is further aggravated by the fact that they alone of any major group of Afghans belong to the Shi'a sect of Islam, and are consequently despised by their Sunni fellow citizens. There are practically no employment possibilities in the Hazarajat; and, since the area is largely barren, this aggravates the discontent of the Hazaras. If peace were restored, the presence of very high-grade iron-ore deposits at Hajigak near Bamiyan might go some way to solve the employment problem and so bring the Hazaras within the conventional pattern of a modern state.

The largest of the principal minority groups, the Tajiks, were by tradition and inclination a peaceful people – poets, dreamers, intellectuals – who earned their living by farming in the regions round Kabul, Kandahar and Herat. They are proud of being Tajik in an unassertive way, and showed a quiet and tactful courtesy towards strangers. Although they, like the Uzbegs, have links with their kindred across the Oxus, many of them emigrated to Afghanistan to escape from the persecution they were suffering during Stalin's forced collectivization of agriculture in the 1930s. If they had little love for the Pathans, and even founded a movement, Setem-i-Melli, against Pathan

---

The exact nature of this descent is much disputed by ethnologists, but that the Hazaras are of Mongol origin is not in question.

domination, they had no more for the Russians, as their fierce resistance to both indicates. Across all these groupings, like a restless and repetitive air plucked on the metal-stringed rebab, runs the life of the nomads. Those dust clouds on the horizon, when you come closer, are seen to be living acres of sheep and goats, or a long line of camels piled high with tents and utensils with mother and child perched atop, for once enjoying a rarely experienced ease. The women, in their rich greens, veil themselves a little at the sight of strangers, although purdah is not their domestic practice since it inhibits their role as the family workers. The camels, gaily decked out with bridles of fine blue, white and red beads, are preceded at a jaunty trot by the dogs. Boys and men, each with a stout stick, ride their fine horses or walk around their flocks, since the dogs seem to have little herding skill.

Soon they merge into the yellow haze again on their way to the high cool pastures of Badakshan. These are the nomads of the north. In the south, donkeys are perhaps more common than camels, rifles than knobbly sticks, women on foot than those riding. The colours are brighter and more varied, the column a little less orderly. North and south, the countryside is dotted with the nomads' flat tents which stand out like black blisters on the hot red flesh of the desert or merge into the background of dark hills; or perhaps they live in the round and carefully decorated felt huts of the more permanent settlements, into whose shadowy recesses the women disappear behind growling dogs at the first glimpse of a camera-bearing stranger.

It was not only on the frontiers with Pakistan that these nomads presented problems to any central government. Since they are highly suspicious of any attempt to record their numbers or movements, for fear of making themselves more liable to government interference and control, such social advances as education, medical services, agricultural improvement and parliamentary representation are rendered largely ineffectual in their case. They feel little loyalty to such an abstract concept as the state of Afghanistan or to its symbol of power, the Kabul-centred government. There is, in addition, a fierce rivalry of long standing between the largely nomadic Ghilzai and the ruling Durrani tribes.

If it is simplistic to attribute all of Afghanistan's ills to what some choose to call Islamic fundamentalism, it is no less naïve to imagine that they are capable of some purely ethnocentric solution. While it is true that the majority of rural Afghans in particular feel much greater affinity with their ethnic group than with any central government in Kabul, whatever its racial composition, the divisions go much deeper than that.

It was made clearly apparent during the fight of the mujehadin against the Russians and then amongst themselves that centuries of local conflict based on inter-tribal, inter-faction and even inter-village rivalry remained the dominant pattern. Pathan tribes, such as the Ghilzai and the Durrani, have always fought bitterly among themselves and the constant turning of coats during the Soviet invasion was partly a resurgence of such enmities. Among the supposedly homogeneous Hazara Shi'a, no less than eight contending factions were only temporarily and with difficulty brought into the single Wahdat coalition. Even the Tajiks and the Uzbegs had and have their factions and mutual betrayals, conflicting objectives and shifting alliances with other groups.

It is these divisions that make any post-Taliban state structure so difficult to devise. Should it perhaps be acknowledged rather than resisted and the main areas be allowed to accede to their ethnic neighbours?

But those neighbours might not wish to open the doors of their national homes for fear of finding they have been burgled by their guests. If large numbers of Tajik, Uzbeg, Pathan and even Ismaili ex-mujehadin, toughened and trained in war and well armed, were to join the already substantial numbers of their rebellious co-religionists and ethnic cousins in contiguous states, the stability of those neighbouring states would be threatened. The leaders of these multi-racial states, it must be remembered, are throwbacks to the Soviet era, ex-apparatchiki with Communist credentials who rouse fierce opposition from many of the original indigenous peoples.

As a longer-term solution, allowing Afghanistan to break up might make more sense than trying to cobble together an Afghan state out of such volatile and contentious elements. A compromise solution might be to create a federal Afghanistan with regional options to secede after, say, ten years if that were the wish of the majority of the region's population and that of the proposed recipient. The individual regions of Afghanistan might not be viable as separate entities, but if a unitary state is to survive they will need a great deal more autonomy in a very loose federal structure.

The fissiparous tendencies in Afghanistan became dramatically evident during the student riots of October 1965. A very shrewd American observer told me that the students naïvely believed that the armed police, mostly Uzbegs and Hazaras, would not be brutal to them or fire on demonstrating fellow countrymen, albeit Pathans. In fact, my informant told me, the police – simple country lads for the most part – revelled in the chance to "have a go" at the city-slickers from the Pathan capital of Kabul. The problem facing Afghan governments is an intractable one, for it is precisely those Pathan characteristics making for the efficient exercise of authority that also make unity among the different races difficult to attain. There can be little amity and sense of common purpose when one race feels itself innately superior to the others, whom it considers as irremediably second-class citizens.

5

BEFORE THE CIVIL WAR

Great contrasts between wealth and poverty were not so dramatically evident in Afghanistan prior to the Communist coup as in most Third World countries, though even before 1979 it was one of the half-dozen or so poorest countries in the world. This was because even the middle and upper classes, or the majority of individuals among them, were relatively poor and there were few outlets for conspicuous consumption.

Buildings, carpets, flocks and land and, in the north, the superb buzkashi horses on which a man would gladly spend a small fortune, have been almost the only investments for accumulated wealth. Moreover, the commodities on which in a consumer economy the rich spend their wealth have never been easy to obtain outside Kabul and one or two other urban centres, due to lack of foreign exchange. Access to them is largely dependent on smuggling, now, with transport, Afghanistan's second largest business. The nomad families with the largest herds were then probably among the richest people in Afghanistan, although their wealth could not readily be converted to measurable terms. However, the drug barons and the transport mafia have usurped their place at the top of the greasy pole.

Yet if evidence of the heights of wealth was scarce before 1979, it was also fairly rare to come across any stark display of the depths of poverty which are so harrowing in more densely populated, if richer, underdeveloped countries. The children, boys and girls, were generally well cared for and fed, and often almost extravagantly well clothed. While it is true that the signs of disease were plentiful and infant mortality was among the highest in the world, the emaciated limbs and swollen stomachs of severe malnutrition were seldom seen. There was some begging, but not the persistent buzzing swarm of importunate human flies common to other Eastern countries.

It was not easy, either, to tell rich from poor, or at least from relatively poor, by outward appearances. Their style of dress and diet was much the same, and their houses, although different in scale, were usually similar in external appearance and design. In Kabul, it is true, distinctions were beginning to emerge, but only because the capital was ceasing in many ways to be typically Afghan and was acquiring some of the features that seem, depressingly, to be common to all modern cities.

More objective assessment of poverty levels was hard to make in a land where fiction was preferred to figures. In 1977 a World Bank team estimated that between 20 and 40 per cent of the population fell below their poverty line. The number today is probably between 60 and 80 per cent. The average Afghan's income was only one-and-a-half times the poverty level. He spent two-thirds of it on food and, owing to the severity of the climate, 10 per cent on fuel and a further 10 per cent on clothing. In the rural areas, however, his house, made of mud and straw brick, accounted for only just over one per cent of his income. There has been no means of making such statistical analysis for 20 years, but visual evidence and extensive hearsay among Afghan refugees, make it clear that for all but the favoured few – mostly the combatants and criminals on either side – the poverty of 1979 would be the riches of 2001. Severe drought since 1998 has created famine conditions at the time of writing. According to the aid agencies, hundreds of thousands, perhaps millions, of Afghans, particularly children and the old, have nothing but charitable handouts from abroad between them and death from starvation and cold.

When every Pathan is a prince in his own eyes, and men of other races are strong in personal pride, it was not easy for the casual observer to detect local equivalents of those class differences that abound, with all their social minutiae, in Western societies. Evidence of a racial hierarchy we have already noted; the hierarchies within each community are much harder to detect. Where these existed, they tended only to be evident in the form of official positions in the military, administrative and government structure, for government activity embraced a far wider spectrum of activity than it does in Britain, for example. These positions in turn frequently depend on nepotism (it was thus pleasantly surprising in the 1960s to meet the Finance Minister's nephew working as a doctor in one of the remotest provinces) and on the extremely complex patterns of family relationships and rivalries, of which the blood feud has only been the most dramatic expression.

The art of family power politics depends largely upon the ability to marry off the women of the family in such a judicious way as to keep its wealth intact, and for the men to marry in such a way as to increase the family fortunes. The ramifications to which these marriages have led over the generations are almost impossible for the stranger to follow. In effect, however, for the "class" distinctions of Western society one can substitute the word "family". The privileged members of pre-Taliban Afghan society came from no more than a dozen or so families, but "family" has to be interpreted very widely to include degrees of kinship which would scarcely be traceable in Western society. Even so, it can fairly be said that Afghanistan does not suffer from those two divisive plagues of Western society: class antagonism and wealth snobbery.

The most strikingly obvious divisions in Afghanistan, even prior to the Taliban, were between the sexes. "Eve span and

Adam dozed" might be the proverb here, for while the men sat around chatting in the *chai khanas*, the women did much of the day-to-day work, not only in the house, but also in the field. This inequality is enshrined in the system of purdah: a conception which, incidentally, is quite alien to the pristine tenets of Islam. Purdah is not merely the wearing of the *chadhuri*;* this sartorial isolation only symbolizes the whole position of women in Afghan society as inferior beings set apart, animate chattels – valuable, but still chattels. The setting apart of women extends to every aspect of life: their rooms, their meals, their upbringing, their education and their medical treatment. Even in their love life their status as amatory partner is usually regarded as inferior to that of the male, whose universal jealousy can often be so extreme as to make Othello seem like a complacent cuckold. In pre-Taliban days, a man's love affair was as likely to involve another man or boy as a woman. Many of the poems of the great Pushtu poet, Khushal Khan, are unequivocally and unashamedly written to youths. It has to be said that the Taliban claim to be as severe on acts of homosexuality as they are on adultery. One punishment consists of partial burial alive before a wall is toppled on the condemned man.

Purdah is basically an urban phenomenon, less stringently practised and enforced in the villages, and by the nomads

---

* For a technical description, I am grateful to be able to quote that of the wife of a former Afghan Minister of the Interior. "It is a garment that has a cap which is usually very intricately embroidered, and from this falls yards and yards of material minutely pleated, like umbrella pleating in a skirt. Then in front of the face there is an embroidered section like a net, the embroidery so worked that the holes are large enough for the wearer to see through. Then there is a heavily embroidered piece falling down to the waist. The whole garment has such a wide skirt that it can be pulled around the wearer so that no part of her can be seen except her feet as she walks." One might think the garment, though cumbrous, is apt to keep out dust and heat: I am told this is not so. (The garment is also called burqa.)

scarcely at all. Its extension and retention were at least partly the fault of the women themselves, in the view of one shrewd lady (a foreigner married for many years to a very prominent Afghan). The chadhuri was seen as a social status symbol and the poorer women, particularly peasants moving into towns, would obtain one as soon as they possibly could in order to imitate their city sisters whom they regarded as their social superiors. Certainly, the chadhuri is a great leveller among women, cloaking all in equal obscurity. But differences in the material and workmanship, and the air of wearing it by one passing purdahed woman as against another, are nevertheless apparent.

Afghan women became officially quite free to dispense with the chadhuri after Daoud's 1959 pronouncement to this effect began the tactfully gradual introduction of female emancipation. Soon the brave among the more prominent women were showing the way and others followed suit. Yet, even pre-Taliban, in towns other than Kabul you could see the majority of the women still wearing the chadhuri. In the bigger provincial towns women, even foreign visitors, would sometimes attract contemptuous comments from the male bystanders if they were unveiled. Remonstrance that the unveiled one was only following royal precept left them unmoved, for the Afghan man is no fool and saw the immediate implications of the disappearance of purdah for his own easy way of life. Its strict re-imposition by the Taliban has met with little protest from Afghan men and is enforced with relish by the religious police. Unfortunately, few Afghan males seem yet to have recognized that, in the long run, purdah can only hamper the growth of their prosperity.

Whatever spurious arguments may be advanced by the mullahs, purdah, then and now, is based on the concept of a woman as a man's property. In the supposedly more liberal

1960s the governor of one district (Chahardarra in the province of Kunduz) explained to me with some pride the way in which the region's beautiful hand-woven carpets were made; how five or six women might work together for four or five months to make a patterned carpet, nine feet by six feet, for which they would get 4,600 afghanis (equivalent to about $90 in 1979), and how a man would pay a very good bride-price for a girl who was an accomplished carpet weaver. When I asked him who got the money for the carpets, he looked at me in astonishment and replied: "Why the man of course, the woman belongs to the man." Some of the nomads even tattoo their women with the same mark they put on their sheep! It is this attitude which is the chief obstacle facing the champions of women's emancipation in Afghanistan, many of whom continue to put their lives at risk in organizations such as the Revolutionary Association of the Women of Afghanistan. The denial of women's rights by theocratic and neo-theocratic regimes alike was a major reason for the enthusiastic support of "reform" and Communist regimes by many urban Afghan women.

Those Afghans who dislike the idea of feminine equality, but do not wish to oppose it outright, adopt many subtle arguments. They ask why there is any need for emancipation when Afghan women already wield so much power within the family. An analogy can be drawn with the Victorian ideal of the woman as moral guide and domestic guardian. After all, it is the women who arrange the all-important marriages on which the family fortunes may depend, and it is often the oldest woman in the family who manages its financial affairs. But these are subtle sophistries, for such power is exercised only on sufferance or by strength of will, and not as a recognized right. In fact, it is this very family structure which helps to perpetuate the inferior role of women. The value of a marriage arrangement often depends on the fact that a woman has no property rights in marriage, and that property, therefore, reverts to the male side of the family when a woman dies – contrary as this is to the Shari'at.

Under the old customs, it was virtually impossible for a girl to refuse to marry the man of her parents' choice, for the marriage was seen as an important property transaction, one not to be thwarted by mere personal whim. Moreover, the parents could invoke the law to support them in any conflict with an erring daughter who decided she was not attracted to her betrothed. However, although most marriages were still arranged even before the Taliban – and were not necessarily the less happy for that – in the thirty years prior to their advent a girl's wishes were normally consulted and no penalty was exacted for refusing to comply with the parental will. Among the newly educated more "love" matches were made on the initiative of the man and woman themselves. The shy pride of a doctor or a teacher who told you he married for love was something new on the Afghan scene.

There were two major weapons in the Afghan emancipator's armoury: education and economic opportunity. Through the first they could encourage women to rebel against their inferior status, through the second to rebel successfully. It is significant that practically all of the leading women in Afghan public life in the democratic period had been teachers of one kind or another, and were concentrating their efforts on creating wider educational opportunities for girls, though these remained very limited. By the mid-1960s women had begun to break into the professions in noticeable numbers. There were a few women doctors, and women engineers; as well as nurses, health visitors and malaria control officers who were coming forward in increasing numbers – in 1977 there were about 200 of these. But here the problem was always the same: to get them to go out into the provinces and the villages, where their influence was most desperately needed. Husbands and brothers still generally refused to let a woman involved in medical work stay away from home overnight. Treatment was at second hand when the doctor was a man and the patient a woman, and is still practised by this means in many areas. The husband or father relays questions from the doctor, symptoms from the patient and treatment back from the doctor, without doctor and patient ever meeting face to face. Under the Taliban a male doctor could treat a female patient in some circumstances, but when examining he was "only allowed to touch the affected part".

Life was not easy for the woman who went to the provinces and the counter-attractions of Kabul were very strong: not only the amenities and services, and the prospect of better health for her children, but the fact that in Kabul she was one of many women tasting freedom. In the provinces she would often be a lonely and conspicuous pioneer. If she wanted to further her education, her chances of doing so in the provinces were very small. The provision of such opportunity was thus a critical point in changing women's traditional role in Afghanistan. By Western standards the provision for women might have seemed pretty meagre – though by the time Kabul University was closed down over half the students were female – but for Afghan women it was an astonishing breakthrough which they bitterly resent being deprived of by the Taliban.

Yet education without economic opportunity can lead to frustration. If a woman is to have the courage to assert her right to live her own life, she must be able to feel confident that she can defy her family and social pressures and taboos, and yet still make her own living independently. She will also want to appear attractive out of purdah, to have good clothes, shoes and make-up when her form and features no longer have to hide behind the chadhuri – and this costs money.

By law, an Afghan woman was entitled to equal pay for equal work; in practice (as is not unknown in more progressive societies), she did not get it. In the first place, there was very little work for women outside the "ministering" activities of medicine and education. Under the Taliban, such opportunities have been reduced almost to zero. The most important and rapidly expanding new field used to be secretarial work, for which, with the gradual modernization of Afghan industry and commerce, there was an increasing and unsatisfied demand. Otherwise most women were employed in cottage industry rather than industrial manufacturing. There were exceptions as in the Spinzar Company's pottery works in Kunduz, and in some textile processes, but here, also, the inequalities were evident. When I visited Spinzar in the late 1960s women pottery workers with four years' experience of doing the delicate trimming operations on the unfired teapots and jugs, for which most men's hands are too clumsy, earned only about two-thirds of the pay of men doing similar and, if anything, slightly less delicate work further down the production line. Criticism of this disparity has to be tempered by the recognition that such companies were real pioneers in employing women at all. In the country, where the sudden and sweeping reforms introduced by Amanullah came to such a disastrous end, it seemed for a time as if a gradual pragmatic approach might be more successful.

The full rigours of purdah were normally imposed at the onset of puberty, a little before the age of 12. For those lucky enough to attend primary school the provision of further education and training institutions to bridge the gap between leaving and taking up relatively independent employment at 15 or 16 was of critical importance in enabling them to evade the imposition of purdah. Once this had been accomplished, it was much easier for them to maintain their emancipated condition.

A number of remarkable individual women, some of them foreigners, have campaigned for women's rights in Afghanistan since the 1950s. Its most prominent leaders in the mid-1960s were the four women deputies elected to the Wolesi Jirgah, the lower house of the Shura (parliament), in the elections of October 1965. In these, women were both allowed to vote and to stand, although few took advantage of their rights to do either. One of the women deputies for an area just outside Kandahar was certain that, in fact, not a single woman had supported her. (Her election was due to the last-minute withdrawal in her favour of two male opponents.) The others were opposed by men but, remarkable as it must seem, they were elected by a predominantly male electorate. These four women deputies – Mrs Mahsuma Wardaki, Mrs Rokyan Abu Bakr, Dr Anahita Ratebzad and Mrs Adija – made a considerable impact in parliament, showing themselves to be superior to the majority of male deputies. Their influence was principally exerted in the areas of special interest to them, such as education and women's welfare, but it was not confined to these.

Putting their views on the role of women in Afghanistan to me at that time, Mrs Wardaki and Mrs Abu Bakr argued most cogently that the inferior position of women in Afghan society offended against both the constitution of the state and the religion of Islam. The constitution demanded that laws and government should conform to the laws of Islam. The laws of Islam, the emancipators argued, protected the rights and status of women; hence, to the extent that the exploitation and domination of women was permitted, Afghanistan was an "ungodly" state in which the tenets of Islam and their constitutional embodiment were being ignored – not an argument that would be calculated to appeal to the Taliban in 2001.

It would need an expert in Islamic law to appraise this "liberal Muslim" argument properly. It is certainly arguable that there is less scriptural justification for the inferior status of women in the Koran than in the New Testament, where Saint Paul makes it very plain that wives should be in subjection to their husbands. Particularly striking is the way in which the Koran specifically mentions "men" and "women" separately rather than collectively in setting out such matters as rights to property and access to Paradise (e.g. *Surat al Tauba*, v. 71 *et seq*). On the other hand, there is the positive statement (*Surat al-Nisa*, v. 23) that "the men are set over the women" – although theologians have expended much energy in arguing just what "set over" means in this context. The argument of the emancipators may have been sound, but it did not carry much weight with the mullahs, the religious leaders, for these have come to epitomize in the name of Islam, the conservative opposition to female emancipation, and played no small role in seeing that no female deputies were elected to the 1969 Wolesi Jirgah.

The angry mullah mentioned earlier who declared, "When these reforms come in, Islam will go out", was promptly clapped in prison by Amir Amanullah, whose rash attempts to turn Afghanistan into a modern state overnight, with equality between the sexes, secularized education and democratic institutions, had provoked this declaration. The rising inspired by his fellow mullahs succeeded in putting the clock back again, and in due course Amanullah lost his throne.

From the initial progress under Zahir Shah in the 1960s until the overthrow of Daoud in 1978 these reforms were being reintroduced, more subtly, more effectively, and in a more welcoming climate of public opinion. The more overt commitment to emancipation of subsequent despised Marxist regimes may well have set back, rather than advanced, the cause of women by offending not only the mullahs, but also a deeply conservative people over whom their influence was paramount.

With the coming to power of the Taliban we have to ask ourselves again is it still right to assume with the mullah that Islam and the progressive social development of a modern state are incompatible? If it is, what will the outcome of the conflict be? Now, as in the past, the role of the ulema – the body of Islamic scholars who interpret Islamic law – in interpreting the Koran and of the mullahs in implementing that interpretation is critical. They are the only conduit of faith and law in most cases to a poorly educated but deeply religious people. If they claim that the woman's role is properly an inferior one, it will not make any difference for militant females and liberal scholars – especially foreign ones – to declare that such a conception is contrary to the true doctrines of Islam.

One element, albeit a minor one, in the extreme attitude of the Taliban to any form of emancipation for women is a reaction to the Daoud and PDPA reforms. Much more important, I believe, is the concept of the celibate army, the virgin mujahid dedicated to his cause and emotionally bonded with his fellow male warriors. To ensure that bond remains inviolate it is necessary to remove all temptation by making it virtually impossible for the young mujahid even to see, let alone meet, a woman not of his immediate family. The only way to guarantee this total separation of the sexes is to immure all women, whether it be behind the walls of their own homes or the cotton walls of the chadhuri; to deprive them of education and employment that might teach and enable them to defy such quarantine; and to break the spirit of any women who try to defy or ignore these restrictions by publicly humiliating or even terrorizing them. The restrictions imposed on women – from allowing them out only in the company of a close relative to forbidding them to "wear shoes that make a noise when they walk" – have so incensed feminist and liberal opinion worldwide that any positive explanation advanced by the Taliban is dismissed out of hand. Personally, I believe they are partly telling the truth when they say that one of their reasons for imposing full purdah is to protect women's virtue from the importunate attentions of young men. After all, a "virtuous woman" – a virgin or a faithful wife – is a much more valuable commodity domestically and in the marriage market than one whose reputation has been impugned by the least hint of sexual suspicion! When the priestly leadership of the Taliban says it will provide for female education and other needs when the time is ripe they should not be believed – in their eyes it never will be. That the Taliban are creating a potent fifth column that may play a crucial role in their eventual downfall does not seem to have occurred to them.

Islam has no ordained priesthood but rather a pastorate of knowledge – though it is sometimes permissible to refrain from adding "and of wisdom". The original thinker, particularly among the Taliban, is usually looked on as a dangerous man, for the whole pattern of religious learning is based on a process of repetitive ingestion and regurgitation, generation after generation, of the same arguments and doctrines with no attempt to adapt them to changing circumstances. Such a dogmatic process of instruction, exercised on those generally drawn from the lower and peasant class, tends to lead to bigotry and narrow-mindedness, in things temporal as well as spiritual. Anything which falls outside the compass of recorded knowledge and has no precise precedent is, for the mullahs, either insignificant or inimical. It would be wrong to suggest that there are no good and wise men among the mullahs, but the significant point is that training and circumstances reinforce the limitations and narrow-mindedness of the mediocre who make up the great majority.

Most are illiterate farmers and only part-time pastors, indeed, they sometimes seem rather to be Shamans, dealing in white magic, than religious leaders. The traffic in bogus and magical relics at many local shrines is quite as extensive as was that in Chaucer's "Pigges bones" and provides one of the many sources of material comforts and secular power which the mullahs fight to protect. Among other privileges in this category they are particularly jealous of the system by which, like the mediaeval monasteries in Britain, they are able to own land under the guise of religious, tax-exempt endowments (*wafqs*).

There are a multitude of detailed rules for the conduct of private and civil life which have to be learned by the mullah, and such is the number and complexity of these rules that the ordinary citizen who wishes to conduct his life in accordance with Koran and Sunna has no option but to seek the mullah's guidance. Indeed, the Muslim's word for the senior theologians, in the Sunni persuasion at least, is ulema, the learned, or those who know. In many villages and small towns, the mullah has often been the only focus of law and learning. Since the law is based on the Koran, the mullah lays claim not only to the authority which comes with the power of moral and spiritual judgement and leadership, but also to the authority derived from his role as an interpreter, however indirect, of the law governing the daily lives of the villagers. Moreover, the *madrasah* system of education has for long given the mullah a position of authority vis-à-vis the local people from their childhood onward. In this system, the mosque and the school are virtually synonymous, and the method of learning applied is a miniature reflection of the pattern of the mullah's own education. Until the 1960s this sterile form of rote learning was the only one available to all but a privileged few. We shall see its significance and that of the madrasah in the emergence and conditioning of the Taliban in Chapter 13. In fairness it must be admitted that, an oral tradition of learning is inevitable in a country where very few can read and write.

Illiteracy has largely resisted various attempts by central government to reduce it. Bureaucracy as a main weapon of control in the twentieth-century corporate state requires the citizen to be able to read his orders and fill in his forms; oral traditions confine obedience to ear-shot and the village mullah has, radio apart, the loudest voice. It is difficult to be precise about such figures, but probably only around one-eighth to one-fifth of the population could read and write by the late 1970s. Of those then over 40 living outside the four main cities of Afghanistan, almost none were literate. Four-fifths of the population had never been to school and that figure for women was over 90 per cent. Of course, things were better the further down the age scale you went, and half the Afghan population was under 15. Something like half the ten-year-old boys had attended school and although only 5 per cent to 10 per cent of the girls in the same age group had done so, this was a vast improvement on the education of girls as little as 15 years earlier. In 1975, for example, there were some 700,000 children in the 3,300 primary and village schools. This represents about one-third of the age group. 170,000 were receiving secondary education and 11,000 higher education, though it must be recognized that this latter category ranged in standard from about fifth-form level at a British secondary school to genuine university work. Even in the democratic period the Ministry of Education chose who should have higher education places, and what courses of study they should pursue and exacted in payment almost a lifetime of compulsory government service from most graduates who were often not free to strike out on their own until their fifties. Twenty years of unrelenting warfare have undone almost all the progress made in the previous twenty years. In 1989 it was estimated by the Afghan Foreign Minister, in an address to the UN, that 2,000 schools had been destroyed in Afghanistan. This may have been an exaggeration, but with the destruction of a further 12 years added since then, it is likely that fewer than one-quarter of those schools which were open in 1979 are still teaching pupils today. Moreover, the lack of secular educational facilities among the refugees is what has drawn many youngsters into the madrasahs there to be indoctrinated as well as taught.

Social and geographical mobility also plays its part in the power of local influences when set against central government wishes. More than 80 per cent of the population lives in the countryside and the same proportion lives, and has only lived, within a few miles of where they were born. Three-quarters of all Afghans live in the very village or town in which they were born. Influences established in youth thus remain paramount throughout adulthood and the whole pattern of family life – 99 per cent of all Afghans marry – is designed to maintain traditional patterns. The centre of that local authority is the village mullah and in most rural areas the local khan or tribal chief as well.

Religion was very much an ingredient in the perennial border clashes with British India, the Afghan War of Independence of 1919 and the revolutionary overthrow of the would-be reforming Amanullah in 1929. The mullahs would rouse their congregations to rebel with the cry of "Islam in danger!" Even in the more secular pre-invasion period the authority of the mullah and respect for him were virtually unquestioned in Afghanistan. He could jab a clear space for himself with his umbrella in the back of a dangerously overcrowded lorry without protest, and the foreigner who forcefully objected was in danger of being thrown off by the other passengers as an impudent feringi. Throughout the 1960s and 1970s the mullahs remained the mainstay of the conservative opposition to reform, indeed to change of any kind. They were shrewd enough to realize that reform could only mean the end of their almost exclusive authority and a decline in their status. The sequence of increasingly secular, socialist and foreign-dominated governments that followed Daoud's coup in 1973, gave them great opportunities to recover lost ground in the name of Islam, culminating once more in the cry of "Islam in danger" and the call to jihad against the invading Russians. Whether they could hold the ground regained under a reformist, *independent* Afghan government is another matter.

A decline in the influence of the mullahs had been taking place throughout the 1960s and 1970s to the extent that they were no longer in a position to veto all progress, provided changes were made gradually and tactfully. The main reason for this decline in influence was the growth of alternative sources for the authority and educational opportunity of which the mullahs once had a monopoly. Education, albeit still in short supply, was available through state schools. In those I visited the tenets of Islam were certainly still taught, but learning them by heart was no longer the only mode of instruction. As the economic and political structure of the country became more complex, so the tentacles of administrative, secular authority reached out further and further into the rural areas. The law was becoming more a matter of police and lawyers, legislation, courts and judges; although still based on the Koran, it had an increasingly secular flavour, in which nice legal arguments about evidence replaced inflexible interpretations of the Divine Will.

As subsequent events have clearly shown, the gradual decline in the influence of the mullahs did not necessarily imply any decline in the importance of the Islamic faith in Afghanistan – nor was it irreversible. Belief in Islam and the practice of its rituals was then, as it is now, the almost invariable rule throughout the country. Admittedly during the democratic period and Daoud's second term, I noticed a slight secularization – if that is the right word – of attitudes among some members of the upper and middle class. A bottle of Scotch would appear on the table and be drunk as willingly by the influential Muslim host as by his guest. A scientist would admit to scepticism. A government official regretted that he felt Islam might be an anachronism in the context of social reform, though usually adding that a return to the original purity of Islamic doctrine would be conducive to progress. But these few, sceptics and reformers alike, were the exceptions.

The great mass of the people accept and believe in Islam in exactly the form that their fathers have done for many generations, ever since their conversion at sword-point in the tenth century AD. There is no mistaking the way in which Islam has become a deep-rooted part of Afghan life. "Please excuse me while I say my prayers", says your host, gesturing for you to continue drinking your tea while he turns away into a corner, thus fitting his religion naturally into his daily life. Or perhaps it is the touching simplicity of the nomad who walks a little apart from his flock and kneels on his prayer mat, his brown clothes and black pugri standing out starkly against the evening skyline, to say the prescribed prayers; or that same mullah who so uncharitably wielded his umbrella on you who now climbs down from the lorry in some isolated clump of huts and under the single tree leads the villagers in prayer by lantern light.

For the Afghans, the observances of Islam have always been an integral part of life's daily routine. But sometimes I couldn't help feeling that the gesture of the hands spread behind the ears was indicative of nothing so much as the worshipper's own deafness to the strident cries of a new world. The mosques, of which there were some 15,000 in Afghanistan before the wars, are coolly beautiful. The pale blue and dark green glazed tiles, the simple curved architecture, the pleasantly laid out gardens, had all the dark unhurried calm which befits a place of worship. Yet how far was it the quiet of decay rather than of tranquillity? I could not help feeling in Afghanistan, even as I watched it strive to modernize, that the centuries-old faith had lost the capacity for change and would be left behind in the Middle Ages when every other aspect of national life had finally made its painful way into the modern era. The tragedy of Taliban rule is that it has precluded the bridging of that 700-year gap.

Of that trio of tolerances so frequently invoked in human rights' charters – "without discrimination in regard to race, sex or creed" – the first two, in Afghanistan, may be divisive factors; but the third, the religion of Islam, is very definitely a unifying factor. It is the major cultural and spiritual common denominator of ethnic groups that otherwise have little in common. Thus it enables governments to relate laws and administration to an acceptable premise, understood, however dimly, by all the people. While Islam, like Communism, is in some respects a materialistic and dogmatic faith, there was in Afghanistan a contrary factor which hampered the spread of Marx's creed in Afghanistan. Although Islam demands no less obedience and conformity, it is practised there by fiercely independent people. It is this individualism that provided the main antithesis to Communism rather than pure religious faith.

There are two other elements it is necessary to consider in order to appreciate the social background to current events in Afghanistan. The Pushtunwali, or code of honour, which dictates the conduct of life quite as much as religion or government in the Pathan areas of Afghanistan, and the process by which attempts were made to centralize administration, particularly of the law, during the twentieth century. The Pathan code of honour has its minor variations from tribe to tribe, but its central core revolves round the twin concepts of honour and what I term aptness in the aesthetic sense. The Ideal Man is the warrior-poet, the man bold in battle, eloquent in counsel and moving in love. Woman scarcely features in this code, except in so far as she is either the recipient of the benefits of the Pushtunwali, or bound, through her men-folk, by its obligations. But she is also, to some extent, the guardian of its standards, usually in her role as mother, paying "blood money" or denouncing the cowardice of a son.

The element of the code that the traveller in Afghanistan most often encounters is that of hospitality, an element which in my experience has rubbed off equally on the non-Pathans. The code obliges a man to be hospitable whenever the occasion offers and I have often been lodged and entertained by a villager who would not think twice before killing his last chicken for your supper and who it is very hard to recompense in any way without offending. The most important extension of this part of the code is the obligation to protect, with your life if necessary, the person and property of your guest and, if he specifically takes refuge with you, to take up his cause as well. Understanding Pushtunwali is crucial to understanding the vehemence of the Taliban intransigence about handing over or expelling bin Laden.

The second major element of the code is the obligation to avenge the spilling of blood. This is not just a matter of a death for a death, but in lesser degree of an eye for an eye, a tooth for a tooth. Such revenge quarrels can continue for many generations and to some extent serve as both a safety valve and a proving ground for manhood in a society where a boy has a gun put into his hand almost as soon as he can walk. Surprisingly few are actually killed in the fairly frequent inter-village or inter-tribal conflicts, which, if not triggered by a feud, usually centre on the right to water or land. In the context of the blood feud the Americans, like the combatants in the Afghan civil war and now the Soviets before them, are building up a debt which will not easily be redeemed.

A third element is, strange as it may seem, the concept of mercy. One does not kill women (adulteresses excepted) or small children, a poet or a Hindu, a priest or a man who has taken sanctuary in a mosque. Except where a blood feud is involved – and here only blood money will clear the debt – mercy is granted at the intercession of a woman or a priest and in battle even of the opponent himself when he begs for it. This last point may seem to contrast oddly with the bloodthirsty "no prisoners" talk of guerrilla leaders (fervently believed by the ordinary Russian soldier) and the sadistic tortures and inhumane killings for which the Afghan was, and still is, infamous. Perhaps the hardest thing about the Pushtunwali is to know to whom it extends, for that so often seems to depend on the whim of the man with the dagger or the gun in his hand. The rules are still fairly clear but the terrible exigencies of war have made their application more expedient.

No central government can clearly tolerate for long the quasi-anarchical state implicit in the Pushtunwali, so the struggle for control between the central authority and the tribes is a very old one. In this century the centre has gradually, albeit with many setbacks, begun to assert its supremacy. This process began in the late nineteenth century with the remarkable Abdur Rahman. Early in his reign Rahman declared that his unifying aim "was to impose law and order on all those hundreds of petty chiefs, plunderers, robbers and cut-throats. This necessitates breaking down the feudal and tribal systems and substituting one grand entity under one law and one rule."

To this end he created a regular national army, police and civil service who were in a way the embryo of the first Afghan nationalists. Their first major test came in 1891, when the ever-recalcitrant Hazara continued to ignore central legal and fiscal authority and resisted those sent to enforce it. Abdur Rahman sent in his troops and at first the Hazara did not resist them. However, when the Pathan troops got out of hand and seized property and women, a fierce and bloody rebellion broke out which was not finally put down until 1893. The victors turned over much Hazara pasture to the Kuchi nomads and sold many of them into slavery. More significantly, in the long term they imposed the rule of law on the basis of their own particular Sunni interpretation, which was anathema to the Shi'a Hazara, and broke the influence of the local leaders. That pattern has continued ever since. Throughout Afghanistan, the local Khans still provide some protection for their villagers against the not infrequent depredations of oppressive or corrupt government or central officials, though they are not themselves immune from these vices.

The counterpoint of local custom and central fiat, variety and consistency, wove its varied balance at least up until the closing stages of Daoud's second period of rule.

A good illustration of the practical realities of this system was the story told me in 1966 by Muhammad Hussein Massa, Governor of Balkh, about "the tooth that did not fit". Sitting on his verandah in Mazar-i-Sharif one day, he was suddenly confronted by an agitated citizen who claimed that he had been grievously assaulted and that the Governor must compel his assailant to recompense him financially. The Governor calmed him and bade him sit down and tell his story. This the complainant did with a wealth of graphic detail, his tale reaching its climax with the dramatic production of the tooth which the assailant was supposed to have struck from the victim's mouth.

"Indeed a monstrous blow," said the Governor, examining the tooth with great solicitude. "Tell me, from which part of your mouth was it struck? Please show me the wound."

Taken aback, the complainant thought hastily and then pointed to a gap in his teeth.

"But see," said the Governor, putting the tooth in the gap, "it does not fit. Now stop wasting my time and yours and go and devote your energy and ingenuity to more useful ends."

In a simple society of isolated communities, much depended on the ability, percipience and sympathy of the local representative of central government. Afghanistan was blessed during the 1960s with a number of capable administrators throughout the provinces, but there were far too few for the ever-growing range of tasks imposed by increasingly dirigiste governments in the 1970s.

The provincial governor, almost invariably short-staffed, had a two-pronged administrative machine. The first prong was that of his direct decision-making. The majority of decisions in the practical fields such as agriculture, industry, irrigation and mining were reached in conjunction with the local representatives of the appropriate ministries and were only rarely referred back to Kabul. In this relationship, the governor usually took the initiative. Both governors and Ministry representatives were working within the limits of the share of the departmental budget allocated to their province. There was – officially and legally – no local revenue, although the provincial officers were responsible for collecting national taxes. The various ministries were given their share of the national budget and then allocated this to different projects in the provinces. The provinces themselves were latterly encouraged to propose schemes of development, though with the revenue of the provincial municipalities accounting for no more than one per cent of total state revenues, their scope for independent initiative was negligible. The other prong of the provincial governor's administrative machine was provided through a series of district governors in charge of various sections of his province. They worked to his orders and had their own small staff.

The system demanded that both the greater and the lesser governor be accessible to the people of the province or district. It was a common sight, in the Pathan areas in particular, to find the local district governor being buttonholed in the street (literally, for he was probably the only one wearing European dress) by some loquacious citizen and urged to do or prevent something. Not that the Pathans are spineless beseechers of authority when some grievance exercises their concern; far from it. As one district governor pointed out to me, such is the initiative of the Pathan and his extraordinary capacity for voluntary corporate activity that, as often as not, the job has been done by the time the governor has even heard that it needs to be done.

The dialogue between governor and governed was formalized through elected Provincial Shuras or Councils. But in most provinces the real power and initiative still lay mainly in the hands of the governor. When I first went to Afghanistan in 1957 governors were quite willing to be guided in many things by public opinion in the various forms in which it was expressed to them. By the late 1970s they found themselves increasingly at odds with local leaders and more responsible for the maintenance of law and order than for the promotion of prosperity.

During the "democratic" period power was further centralized by diminishing local autonomy on matters of policing and local administration of the law, though these remained primarily the provincial governor's responsibility. He could also call in the military if he thought its help necessary to maintain public order, but he had no direct authority over the military in his province. The picture in this respect was a little ambiguous in those Pathan tribal areas where the administration was military and the governor a senior military officer, although at district level the military administrator acted, to all intents and purposes, as a civilian. Further confusion arose with the creation of a police investigation department directly responsible to the Attorney-General's office and not the provincial governor's. A certain amount of antagonism developed as a result of this division. The local police, at that time generally unarmed, felt that, despite their particular knowledge of the area, they were being relegated to an inferior peace-keeping position. The Attorney-General's department, by contrast, viewed its activities as an independent assurance of the objective investigation of a charge or a crime. The representative of the Attorney-General acted rather in the capacity of the French "Juge d'instruction", as both prosecutor and judge in examinations of first instance, but it was always open to the accused to appeal his decision to a higher court. Similarly, a tribesman could technically appeal to his district governor against a fine enforced by the local Jirgah, but he got short shrift from governor and fellow citizens alike in most cases. A determined man could take the matter still further by appeal to the provincial governor or to the courts.

The major legal problem in pre-invasion Afghanistan was to ensure the application of a "common" law to all parts of the country: a problem arising, not so much from abuse – although in the past the Afghan judiciary has certainly been open to corruption – as from tribal customs. In Pathan districts, the law has been a combination of custom and personal justice assessed by the local Jirgah, or Council. It worked very often on the basis of "everybody knows that so-and-so did such-and-such" rather than on careful accumulations of evidence. It contained a highly compensatory rather than a purely punitive element, and was much concerned with personal honour.

The story told to me of the old woman who, when her great-nephew could not produce the blood money to absolve him from the murder of a member of another family, threw on the ground the exact sum, untouched, which that family had once paid to her grandfather as blood money, illustrates the persistence of the "customary law".

In all of these frontier districts, the Afghan government had been trying gradually to replace a patchwork of different customs with a common law which did not sacrifice the element of true justice in the Jirgah system or so antagonize the local tribesmen that they ignored the courts and reverted to personal revenge. For a while the authorities had considerable success in this. One district governor told me in 1966 that in his area in the previous five years, which included the villages of the fierce and hitherto unruly Mangals, there had been no murders and only one case of manslaughter (in which the accused was a child). This view was confirmed by the fact that in 1966, for example, I was permitted to travel in these tribal areas without any escort, although my party included two women. This would not have been the case a decade before, and under Daoud, until 1977 at least, the rule of law was still further tightened.

A number of factors contributed to this acceptance of central and common control. In the first place, it was administered by the Afghan army, who the tribesmen could understand as fellow fighting men. Then again, central authority clearly brought with it a number of material improvements – in agricultural techniques, communication, medicine and education – so that the new ways as a whole were gradually identified as beneficial. Finally, the tribal Jirgah was not suddenly deprived of power and influence, but rather had its function changed to that of a local government council concerning itself with local construction and irrigation projects, and with disputes over property, the use of irrigation water, and so on. Only if such attitudes are taken into account in mounting a post-Taliban reconstruction programme will it bring peace as well as prosperity. Improvements in living standards would be unacceptable to most Afghans if they were achieved at the price of freedom. The increasing arbitrariness of Daoud's regime in the 1970s exacerbated the suspicion and hostility of the mullahs whose privileges were primarily at risk. By the time Taraki's PDP seized power, much of the ground won in the 1960s and early 1970s had been lost. Local people acquiesced sullenly in the military imposition of central authority when it could not be escaped or resisted, and reverted to local traditional codes and authorities as soon as the military back was turned.

Although so much has changed drastically since the Soviet invasion, I have written at some length in this chapter and the next about the state of Afghan society in the previous quarter-century for three reasons. The first is to try and dispel the common belief that Afghanistan was irredeemably backward and locked into the Middle Ages until the Soviet Union and the United States took so destructive a hand in its affairs. The second is to record a picture of the society that was largely destroyed by that intervention and the third is to outline the kind of pattern of progress which might be applicable – and I emphasize might – if peace and stability could be restored.

6

EARNING A LIVING – PRE-1979

If the British could once be described as a nation of shopkeepers, then the Afghans must be classified as a nation of peasants. In Afghanistan, a country three times the size of England and Wales, four-fifths of the land is desert, yet four-fifths of the population earns its living from agriculture or the cottage industries and crafts associated with it. The deserts or semi-deserts are not all immutable, and many of them in the west and south-west of the country were once highly fertile irrigated areas. Although not as easily as was once hoped, they can be rendered fertile again by the waters of those deserts of snow and ice high in the Afghan mountain ranges.

In total, about two-thirds of the land yields some kind of grazing, however sparse and seasonal. In parts of Afghanistan there is good soil but no water, while often where there is water the soil is poor or non-existent. The basic problem for Afghanistan is to mate soil and water to fertility. This is a problem which has been recognized by successive Afghan governments since the 1950s and some progress in the development of irrigation and hydroelectric power had been made. In 1979 there were some 3.5 million to 4 million hectares under irrigation, around one-third of the cultivatable land. The greater part of those irrigation systems has now been destroyed. Similarly, in 1979 cultivated land amounted to only 14 per cent of the total – in 2001 the figure is probably less than 10 per cent.

The problem of bringing water to the land has always been a major preoccupation at every level, from those who seek to dam the Oxus, the Helmand and the Hari Rud and use their waters for large-scale irrigation, to the peasant who is trying to

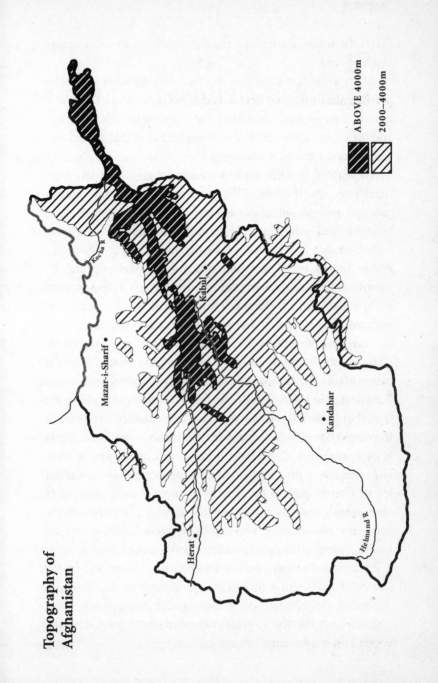

Topography of
Afghanistan

ABOVE 4000m

2000-4000m

Mazar-i-Sharif

Kabul

Kandahar

Herat

Kocha R

Helmand R

divert the water of a passing mountain stream to a few square yards of land.

Many years ago an elderly Pathan, steel-rimmed spectacles perched authoritatively on the end of his nose, accosted me one morning as we made breakfast camp in Paktya. His problem and his solution were typical – as was his belief that, since I was a European, I must be an engineer.

He wanted to raise water some six or eight feet from the small river which flowed 20 yards from his land to irrigate a patch of arid ground about the size of a tennis court. He had brought with him a couple of dozen neighbours (typically willing to join in a voluntary cooperative effort of this kind), and he hoped, by piling boulders across the river opposite the top end of his field, to divert sufficient water to it. However, even he had slight doubts about the feasibility of this. The river was swift but shallow, and at that point the water would have had to be raised considerably; yet in bursting out of a gorge higher up it made a shallower dam further upstream impossible. It was at this juncture that he consulted one highly unqualified British "engineer". No hydrodynamicist, it nevertheless occurred to me that, if only something as simple as a heavy concrete beam with the open ends of half-a-dozen plastic pipes embedded in it had been available, it might have been lodged in the fast moving river well above the point at which it was wanted and the water led by flexible pipe to the field as required. Such gadgets were not available and one could only talk about the best spot for the primitive boulder dam. We left our bespectacled friend noisily issuing orders to his neighbours to begin the work. I never knew if it achieved its object, but on its success or failure and on the success or failure of a thousand little enterprises like it, much depended. Despite attempts to industrialize in the past 50 years, Afghanistan's economic prosperity must, for a long time yet, depend on improvement in agriculture.

In normal times, with sensible reserve purchasing policies, Afghanistan was self-sufficient in food. The Soviet invasion and the civil war have had a catastrophic impact and widespread starvation, particularly in the more remote regions, can be expected in the winter of 2001/02. The fighting has destroyed most of the irrigation systems and more than five million mines and anti-personnel devices imperil the life and limb of those agricultural workers and their families still left in Afghanistan. Hundreds of thousands of farmers have vanished into the ranks of the combatants and, although many break off the fighting to return in time for sowing and harvest, agriculture has been left desperately short of labour.

An important factor in a land of such fiercely independent people is that the peasant has always been in charge of his own affairs. However, because the high cost of good land meant that the ordinary landless villager had no hope of saving enough to buy a viable plot, many Afghan peasants operated some form of sharecropping rather than direct ownership. About half of the agricultural land was owned by the cultivator, although part, if sometimes a large part, of his produce would usually be mortgaged to the local moneylender. The average holding was three hectares, the vast majority of holdings falling in the range of 0.5 to 6 hectares. The Taraki regime's promise to limit holdings to 15 acres and distribute the rest to the peasantry must at first have seemed attractive. But there were in fact very few large land-owners, other than the Wafqs, in Afghanistan, although absentee landlords were common. One estimate in 1960 identified only 30 landlords with over 200 hectares.

The aspiring landowner might once have tried to make his money from freelancing in the timber trade. The hills in Paktya are an impressive sight, stretching for miles and miles with trees dotted over their entire surface, but rather sparsely, each standing three or four yards from its neighbour, the whole looking like a hesitantly gathering crowd. The timber in the past was haphazardly felled and cultivated scarcely at all, but in 1965 a group of West German forestry experts set up a major forestry project near Ali Khel to increase timber exports to Pakistan and try to halt the depletion of Afghanistan's 3 per cent of forested land. A steady, if unofficial, trade in camel-borne cedar baulks developed. These fetched in Peshawar or Kohat three or four times what they could be sold for to the Kabul merchants. Now much of this standing timber has been destroyed.

Paktya was not, of course, the only prosperous agricultural area in Afghanistan. There was a relatively successful development in the Helmand Valley; and a much older flourishing agriculture in the main areas for cotton cultivation – *once* Afghanistan's chief cash crop – in Kataghan, round Mazar-i-Sharif, in the province of Kunduz, and in the Herat and Jalalabad regions. Khanabad in Kunduz claims to be "the seed gourd of Afghanistan".

However, yields were not high for most crops and most Afghan farmers thought in terms of subsistence, with only perhaps a small surplus for sale locally. Until the wars the motivation to produce surpluses or to plant cash crops was not strong enough because most were bought compulsorily by the government at less than their true market value.

Afghanistan's industrial expansion relied chiefly on cotton processing in the 1960s and 1970s. Gins, presses and oil-extraction and oil-processing plants were established in several areas. A major agent of this expansion was the Spinzar Company ("spinzar" means white gold), a combination of private and state enterprise in which the controlling power lay with the state. It was astonishing to see the transformation that a single enterprise such as this could bring to the remote towns and villages strung out along the Oxus. Most hospitals and many schools and housing projects were built or organized by Spinzar. On the other hand, on one occasion in Khwaja-i-Gar I was told that because a generator had broken down the factory gates had been locked, and the workers would not be paid for the days of enforced idleness. Afghan workers simply did not have trades unions – a difficult concept for a community-orientated society – although they would have been perfectly legal under the constitution.

In 1967 there were scarcely a dozen factories (in the Western sense) in the whole of Afghanistan and probably less than 10,000 industrial workers. By 1978 there were some 130 medium-sized firms in Afghanistan. A recent aid agency report suggested that, as a result of 20 years of war, this had been reduced to as few as six by 2001. As a result of Daoud's policies from 1973 onwards, the manufacturing sector became dominated, and the mining sector monopolized, by the state. In all, the industrial and mining sector employed only 41,000 people, about one in eight of them women, which represented less than 1 per cent of the workforce compared to the 85 per cent employed in agriculture and associated trades.

The Afghan industrial worker had no mass-production traditions behind him. He was just a retrained agricultural worker. He did not take easily to the disciplined regularity of modern industrial work, to the clocking in and out, and the necessity of keeping pace with a continuous production process. When harvest time came round, as often as not he would down tools and dash back to the fields where he could earn for a few weeks as much as double his normal wage. Harvest over, he was outside the factory gate again asking for his job back. The peasant recruited into the Afghan army or a mujehadin band wanted to behave in the same way so that in the midst of all the modern weaponry the medieval practice of a tacit suspension of hostilities at sowing and harvest time often survived.

It will take time for Afghanistan to embrace large-scale industrial activity. Until then, it will need to depend on the small factory or local workshop, and on producing wheat, cotton and rice, karakul skins, wool and dried fruit which can be used to feed its people and for export.

Afghan carpets are famous throughout the developed world, but before the wools can be woven, they must go through an elaborate process of vegetable dyeing; and little is known of the current state of the host of wild herbs and flowers needed to produce the acid and alkaline dyes in all the many shades that go into an Afghan carpet. Before the invasion more than half a million square metres of carpet were produced annually, and of this four-fifths were exported – principally to England and West Germany, often via Russia.

Equally beautiful and almost as lucrative are the thousands of karakul skins, known as Persian Lambs, which find their way to Afghan heads and the shoulders of the rich all over the world. The skins – black, brown, grey, gold, and, rarest of all, white – are of fine quality. The gold skins, with their infinite changes of shade and light, must surely be the inspiration for the Jason legend. Some ten million karakul skins were sold abroad annually in the late 1970s, fetching around $10 million in export earnings. Golden fleeces indeed – although the karakul farmer seldom gained his fair share of these rich rewards.

The major agricultural exports, however, were cotton ($35 million a year, mainly to the Soviet Union) and, largest contributor of all at $75 million, the fruit one saw drying in the sun on the flat mud roofs of the Afghan villages and the fresh fruit and nuts that made summer and autumn travel in Afghanistan such a delight. The remaining cottage industries – leatherworking, sheepskin jackets, and the delightfully intricate pieces of hand-beaten copper – were important mainly for saving scarce foreign currency by supplying the domestic market.

At the best of times these agricultural products are not easy to nurture in the harsh climate of Afghanistan. If the winter is too severe and late, it affects the karakul lambs; if it is too mild and ends too early with little rain, then it fails to keep down the grubs that destroy the grass roots. If the herds and flocks are too small, there is not enough wool for the carpets; if they are too large and graze indiscriminately, then the earth is stripped bare and erosion sets in. If there are too few donkeys, then there is too little transport for what is grown; if there are too many donkeys, they destroy the vegetation. The need is for better husbandry, improved strains of seed and livestock and the development of the appropriate small-scale machinery, such as motorized hand tractors. In the past there have been too many generously given and totally useless ordinary farm tractors rusting in old forts, and even by the roadside, because they were far too large to use on the small plots characteristic of Afghan agriculture. All of these agricultural improvements have required the sort of capital investment which the Afghan small farmer could not afford. Apart from the poppy grower, he will have even less now unless he receives assistance from outside the country.

Two major discoveries made in Afghanistan in the 1960s offer rich promise for the future: natural gas at Shiberghan in the Balkh provinces and iron ore at Hajigak in Bamiyan. The gas reserves are estimated at 130 billion cubic metres and even throughout the fighting, production has varied between two and three billion cubic metres a year. Of this, 95 per cent was exported to the Soviet Union. The balance was used at a fertilizer plant at Mazar. I do not know if this plant is operational at present, but if not its restoration should be one of the first aid projects undertaken, particularly as the discovery of huge oil and gas reserves in the South Asian Republics of the former Soviet Union make Afghan gas superfluous to their and Russia's needs.

The iron-ore deposit at Hajigak is of the order of 1,760 million tons of a very high grade (62 per cent iron content was the official estimate). Only a few miles away there is a substantial deposit of the limestone needed for iron-ore smelting. The cost of mining, processing and transport in so remote a region would be high, but the eventual return would be substantial and the economic benefit to one of Afghanistan's poorest regions enormous.

Extensive traces of other mineral deposits have been found throughout Afghanistan. There is a large sulphur deposit near Nangarhar. Coal has been mined in small quantities in a dozen places for many years, but now recent surveys have revealed proven deposits of 100 million tons and an estimated further 400 million tons. Copper has also been discovered in substantial quantities at Ainak, where deposits are estimated at 4.7 million tons metal equivalent. Lead, manganese, marble, gypsum, barite, gold, beryl and uranium have all been found.

One of the oldest mining operations in Afghanistan is for the semi-precious and very beautiful lapis lazuli found only in the remote mountain regions of Badakshan, where some of the mines are so high that they can only be worked in summer. Between 30 and 40 tons of this ultramarine stone, shot through with threads of gold, was mined each year.

A quicker return would probably come from the building of the much-mooted oil pipeline from the huge fields of Turkmenistan to the Pakistan coast in Baluchistan. The lobbying of the US/Saudi combine UNOCAL/Delta played no little part in determining US policy towards the Taliban until 1997. Now that Iran is no longer quite the pariah that it once was this project has to compete with the shorter and cheaper

route into an existing pipeline system through northern Iran to the Caspian. However, as a reward to Pakistan for its cooperation over bin Laden and a means of helping to stabilize Afghanistan, America might think the subsidy necessary to make the project economically feasible was worth paying.*
The development of all of these mineral resources will require a very sophisticated level of planning in a country where there are too few trained administrators and where both private and state capital are in short supply.

Because of the Cold War game, Afghanistan seldom experienced much difficulty in obtaining large sums of foreign civil aid until the Soviet invasion. This not only distorted the Afghan economy in practical terms, as Dupree has pointed out, but also, in my view, much more seriously conditioned the attitude of Afghan governments to their economic problems. Many leading Afghans acquired the belief that little or no effort was required of them and that they did not have to modify, either individually or collectively, their conduct or customs in any way to achieve economic development. The failure of many enterprises undertaken in this spirit was almost inevitable. Foreign aid-funded projects seldom yielded even sufficient return to service the debts incurred in launching them. For this the donors must share the blame. Since the aim in the Soviet case was to create dependence, Russia did not presumably regard this as blameworthy. The conventional free market economists' remedy would be that Afghanistan should pull itself up by its own bootstraps. The trouble is that in Afghanistan there are now no bootstraps left. Only massive external investment can unlock Afghanistan's potential wealth and restore a modest level of prosperity, and perhaps the Afghans will prove unwilling to pay the price in

For a fascinating and exhaustive account of the "oil wars" see Ahmed Rashid's Taliban *referred to in the reading list.*

loss of economic freedom and customary practice that accepting it could entail.

The acid test of any economic policy must be whether or not the majority of the citizens are – or, perhaps more importantly, feel – better off as a result of it. In the 40 years from 1932 to 1972 real wages in Afghanistan doubled or trebled against an overall average inflation rate of about 5 per cent. These inflation figures, however, were based on urban prices and it is difficult to tell how accurately they reflected the domestic financial vicissitudes of the majority of Afghans. It is difficult in the absence of reliable statistics to give a definitive answer to the crucial question of whether the ordinary Afghan was better off shortly before the invasion than he was when I first went to Afghanistan 20 years earlier. One has to rely to some extent on impressions.

During the 1960s and 1970s a doctor would speak of extensive malnutrition in the Afghan population while the evidence of one's eyes suggests that food was both good and relatively cheap and plentiful throughout the country. Kebabs and kormas with plenty of meat, flat discs of coarse, tasty bread and bowls of rice, salt and spices, fruit from apricots to melons, high-quality tomatoes and cucumbers. On the other hand, the visual evidence of disease was also plentiful. Half of the children born did not live to their fifth birthday and life expectancy for the rest was still only 50 years. Rarely did one see an Afghan in rags, or the rows of sleeping beggars, which are a common sight in other Asian cities such as Calcutta. On the other hand the drainage and water supply were almost invariably unhygienic and inadequate, and your drink of water was more than likely to be brought to you in a fine copper cup filled from the jui (open ditch) which also served as laundry and latrine.

Afghanistan in 1979 was an incongruous blend of the old and the new, albeit one in which the old still predominated. It was a country suspended in a limbo between the Middle Ages and the twentieth century: purdah and green plastic sandals; Cadillacs and karakul skins; the rural host who would beggar himself in the name of hospitality, and the servant in the modern hotel who would drive you mad with his constant demands of *baksheesh*; the sophistication of supersonic jet fighters and the ancient creaking of a Cretan-style windmill pump; the imposing bulk of a massive hydroelectric scheme and the lines of *karez* or *qanat* holes dug down the hillside to irrigate a small patch of tired crops in some remote corner of the country. In all these antitheses the spectacular modern part had but little effect on most Afghans. Afghanistan remained a country which was poor, though poor without that desperation which characterizes so many other underdeveloped countries. The benefits of development had not been widespread. As an independent report put it in 1972, "Most Afghans can rightfully say that they are paying for the exclusive benefit of a privileged minority in privileged areas of the country." It was on those sentiments that the revolutionaries of the People's Democratic Party of Afghanistan (PDPA) tried to capitalize.

7
RED TO MOVE

The commercial and industrial development of Afghanistan, in modern terms, did not begin until the 1930s. In 1933 Abdul Majid Zabuli, surely one of the most remarkable entrepreneurs of this century, founded the Bank Melli and used it to establish a whole range of new industrial enterprises. His greatest stroke of genius lay in circumventing the Koranic prohibition against the charging of interest by inventing the "money ticket". By means of this the bank took a fixed "profit" on its money and thus casuistically avoided the prohibition. Zabuli thus released the capital needed for development and the bank itself provided the funds for more than 30 enterprises, from vehicle imports to hire purchase, electricity generation to cotton processing. In each of these the bank held a major and usually controlling interest, so that from the very outset the Afghan economy was based on the concept of centralized control of growth and development. No matter what the political complexion of the government, royalist, as at this time, or proto-democratic or neo-socialist, as it was to be in the 1950s, 1960s and 1970s, this principle remained paramount. In fact, it was the arch-capitalist Zabuli who introduced the concept of long-term economic planning to Afghanistan in the early 1930s.

Another characteristic of the Zabuli pre-war boom was the volume of trade with Russia; by the late 1930s this accounted for one third of Afghanistan's exports. The Second World War cut short both economic growth and, as a result of Russia's preoccupation with internal supply, the Soviet connection for neutral Afghanistan.

Once the war was over, Zabuli, who had spent most of it comfortably installed in Switzerland, returned at the King's request to try and restore the country's fortunes. However, a new and much more significant factor had now entered the equation. From now on economic growth and economic and other ties with Russia were largely determined by the state of relations between Afghanistan and the new state of Pakistan over the Pushtunistan issue.

Although the United States dominated Afghanistan's external trade, aid and cultural contacts until 1953, the level of activity was at less than $1 million a year. The turning point, almost unnoticed by a Britain trying to divest itself of an empire, a Europe rebuilding its shattered economy, and a United States concentrating on keeping Europe out of Communist hands, came in 1950.

In that year, as we saw in Chapter 3, following fierce exchanges on the border, Pakistan, through whose territory virtually all goods for Afghanistan had to pass, cut off its neighbour's petrol supplies. Russia immediately made a barter trade agreement with Afghanistan, exchanging oil and textiles for wool and cotton.

During the 1950s the Americans were handicapped by their commitment to the ill-fated Helmand Valley project, begun as a contract between Morrison-Knudsen (M-K), a private American company, and the Afghan government. In the early 1950s the high walls of the M-K compound symbolized the shuttered attitude of its employees. The Helmand Valley project was certainly imaginative in conception, aiming as it did to restore fertility to a vast desert area south-west of Kandahar and to revive something of Afghanistan's claim to its ancient title of "the granary of Central Asia". But a number of snags, in particular the salinity of the irrigated area and the unforeseen social consequences of the new pattern of agricultural settlement which was required, meant that more and more capital had to be sent chasing the initial investment. The Americans did not feel that Afghanistan was ready for industrialization, so they confined their aid to the Helmand and other agricultural projects and to education and, because of wholly understandable preoccupations elsewhere, paid only scant and spasmodic attention to Afghanistan.

While the Russian commentator, R.T. Akhramovich, writing in 1966 about the immediate post-war stage of Afghanistan's economic development, was exaggerating when he claimed that "developing Afghanistan, of course, did not find among her partners in the world capitalist market the slightest desire to co-operate in overcoming her economic difficulties", the West in general was certainly paying less attention than it should have to this strategically significant country. But America's dominant position in a neighbouring state was a cause of anxiety to the Soviet Union, at a time when the Cold War was at its chilliest and US Secretary of State Dulles was pursuing an aggressive foreign policy. That Russia feared that the "wicked imperialists" might pre-empt its own intentions in this part of the world is clear from Akhramovich's repeated accusations.

> By linking up its national development programme with the imperialist monopolies, Afghanistan very soon found herself in the position of a debtor, and the prospects of realizing her plan proved to be completely dependent on foreign monopolies.
>
> The US monopolists pressed these agreements on Afghanistan, regarding them as a means of penetrating that country's economy.
>
> US capital, by controlling roughly half of Afghanistan's exports, forced on her the contract thus making sure of getting a good part of Afghanistan's foreign currency receipts.

Fortunately for Russian ambitions, Prince Daoud became Prime Minister in 1953 and immediately embarked on those policies which were, unintentionally, to put Afghanistan under the paw of the bear. A fanatical Pathan, he stirred up the Pushtunistan dispute and, partly at least from resentment at the fact that Bank Melli had made the bulk of its investment in the non-Pathan North, stripped the main driving force of the free enterprise Afghan economy of much of its power and investment control. He also played with zeal and some skill the Cold War game of setting the two great powers to compete in giving aid. By 1955 US aid was running at some $2 million a year, and Russian post-war aid had by then reached about half the level of the US contribution. But Russia was already deploying its investment with great propaganda, skill and perhaps less regard for Afghanistan's real interests – though, to be fair, its emphasis on smaller-scale agricultural investment was valid in economic terms. Early projects, such as paving the roads of Kabul, building grain silos in which US gift wheat was stored as if it came from Russia, and the construction of huge public bakeries, all made a good impact in the capital where the decisions on future commitments would be taken. That these projects had no effect on the needier provinces, that in due course the asphalt cracked and the bread lacked flavour, mattered little at the time.

In 1955 trouble broke out again over Pushtunistan, Pakistan closed the border and the Soviet Union launched a major drive to gain the dominant position in the Afghan economy. It entered into a trade agreement which enabled Afghan goods, and particularly the then crucial export of Karakul skins to New York and London, to escape Pakistan's blockade. By the end of the year Russia was buying some 20 per cent of Afghan exports and, more importantly, had made its largest ever loan ($100 million) outside the socialist bloc at

2 per cent over 40 to 50 years – but it was a loan, not a grant. The Afghans got the full "complimentary treatment" when Bulganin and Khruschev descended on a state visit in that year, designed to show that Russia was anti-colonial, peace-loving and sympathetic. Khrushchev was at his table-banging best as he castigated "the criminal policy of the colonialists whose long years of rule in those countries cause the people tremendous damage and greatly hinder their economic development". He was particularly forthright in his support of Afghanistan over the issue of Pushtunistan.

At the same time the two countries entered into a new friendship treaty which, while being basically an extension of earlier treaties, edged a little nearer to the kind of arrangement which the Russians were to make in December 1978 and to exploit in December 1979. It did seem at the time to offer security from direct invasion for anyone willing to believe Soviet promises and Bulganin made all the right noises: "In its relations with Afghanistan the Soviet Union will continue to be guided by the principles of respect for territorial integrity and sovereignty, non-aggression, [and] non-interference in internal affairs." (It is an amusing sidelight on the ephemeral hagiography of Communist Russia that Akhramovich, writing after the disgrace of Bulganin and Khruschev, describes this and their subsequent state visit in 1960 as "by a Soviet delegation"!)

Even then the situation could still have been retrieved by the Western powers. In my view, Daoud was only ever pro-Soviet in so far as that stance promoted Afghan interests. Soviet influence at that time was still purely economic and Daoud was seeking economic aid from all sources to avoid a situation where Russian influence would also become political and military. As he said at the time, "If development is slow, poverty itself is a hotbed where communism or socialism might grow and prosper." Indeed, in 1956 it was to America that he first turned for military help and, it is rumoured, for a secret guarantee of his borders as well. However, America, as a member of SEATO and the Baghdad Pact, opted to support fellow member Pakistan in the Pushtunistan dispute and refused the Afghan request. Daoud was now genuinely concerned about the balance of power in the region, for not only was he in a state little short of war with the well-equipped Pakistan army on his south-eastern frontier, but he was also at odds with Iran over boundaries and water in the south-west. The anti-imperialist conditioned reflex by which America automatically repudiated former British assessments in areas where the US was called on to fill the vacuum left by the withdrawal of British imperial power, thus drove Afghanistan further into the Russian sphere of influence.

Military influence was usually the main goal of Russian economic penetration in the Third World in order to protect friendly regimes from military coups or to provide military backing for Communist-inspired ones. In 1956 Russia made a $25 million arms deal with Afghanistan to supply relatively modern tanks, aircraft and other technical aid. More significantly, it began that arrangement for the training of Afghan officers, technicians and specialists which, by the time of the 1979 invasion, had processed some 10,000 men, or about 10 per cent of Afghanistan's servicemen.

A few hundred Afghans, mainly pilots, had received their military training in the United States and towards the end of his presidency Daoud tried to loosen the Soviet grip by sending more officers to India. He also tried to broaden the base of military allegiance by introducing non-Pathans into the officer corps (not something he would have considered during his premiership) and to create a second power base by building a large quasi-security police force. This he did by setting up a special police college to take on the best of the many thousands of Kabul University graduates who left each year without jobs to go to. But these were the very students among whom the PDP, Afghanistan's Marxist organization (Communist parties were banned), had been recruiting so assiduously.

From the outset Russia kept a tight logistic grip on all the Afghan forces, deliberately restricting the supply of spares, fuel and ammunition, so that they would swiftly be rendered impotent if they chose to act against Soviet interest. The Afghan air force, for example, never had more than enough fuel in hand for ten to fourteen days' operations and diesel for tanks was doled out in similar penny packets. My own peacetime conversations with Afghan officers and the view of shrewd observers of the military scene, suggested that while Afghan aircraft could quickly be grounded, the Afghan spirit of independence was less easily earthbound. As so often happens, the great majority of Afghans exposed to the culture shock of life in Russia (or America for that matter) became more deeply attached to their own national prejudices rather than being won over to the official philosophy of their hosts. Nevertheless, a few were seduced and a number of the young lieutenants and captains of the 1960s became the impatient middle-aged revolutionaries who held key staff and regimental positions when the time came for the Afghan Marxists to strike in 1978.

In 1957 the Soviet Union entered into an agreement with Afghanistan in which they funded an oil exploration team which found some quite substantial deposits (for example, one field of approximately 500 million barrels) and gas deposits of more than 22 billion cubic metres. However, these resources took a considerable time to exploit and their output was committed in advance at a fixed price to the Soviet Union – the only market available.

Nevertheless, economically, Afghanistan was still in a position of relative independence. In 1956 Afghan/Soviet trade balanced out at some $17 million in each direction. But by the end of Daoud's first period of rule in 1963 the Soviet Union was exporting $72.5 million worth of goods to Afghanistan, but importing only $23 million. The heavy, unfavourable balance of trade into which Afghanistan had largely been tempted by the credit terms offered (and of which the Russians had been so critical when such a position was enjoyed by the Americans) became an additional means of controlling the Afghan economy, though once natural gas came on stream this imbalance was partially re-dressed.

As early as January 1960 a Mangal tribal leader fleeing from retribution in Afghanistan to Pakistan could say "the crux of the matter is that the Afghan government has taken strong exception to our objection to the growing Russian influence in Afghanistan, to giving the country into the iron grip of communists who are preaching their atheistic creed under one garb or another". This may well have been an excuse for "a little local difficulty", but it is interesting that it could be considered even then as an excuse for the difficulty.

It is doubtful if the Soviet Union would have achieved this position of dominance so swiftly but for the renewal of the dispute over Pushtunistan from 1961 to 1963, which erupted into open conflict and brought legitimate transit trade, including the materials required for American aid projects, to a standstill for two years. In 1962 the two great powers tried to help Afghanistan by airlifts of its important fruit harvest. America provided, free of charge, ten cargo flights a week to India for 40 weeks. In the same period Russia mounted 15 flights a day, almost all to the Soviet Union, and for which the Afghans ultimately had to pay. It was this third Pushtunistan dispute and its economic consequences which would bring about Daoud's fall from power and the advent of a more democratic style of government, led by prime ministers such as Yusuf and Maiwandwal who were sympathetic to the West. But, although America continued to step up its aid considerably and other Western countries such as West Germany came substantially into the picture (even China gave aid of $2 million), the battle was virtually over, although the Russians were careful to blow no premature trumpet blast of victory.

Writing in 1968 about the peaceful competition between the two powers in his country, an Afghan economist living in the United States could describe with equanimity a situation in which the, "Russians built the terminal building of Kabul Airport while the Americans supplied and supervised the communications system in the control tower. The majority of the trucks, automobiles and buses in Kabul are American-made and yet all of them are run on Russian gasoline. It is in Afghanistan that one finds American automobiles driven on Russian paved streets, American wheat used in Russian-made flour mills, Russian MiGs flown by American-trained Afghan pilots and American cigarettes lit by Russian matches."

My own favourite example was at Dilaram – Heart's Ease – where the Russians had just finished building a road over a bridge I had watched an American construct ten years earlier.

By 1968 Afghanistan had received more than twice as much Soviet aid as American: $550 million to $250 million. Eighty per cent of the US aid had been in the form of outright grant, whereas two-thirds of the Soviet contribution was in the form of loans. These admittedly were long term at low rates of interest and could be repaid in either commodities or Afghan currency, but the commodities were always valued by the Russians (and usually at lower rates than originally agreed on grounds of their poor quality) and the artificially high exchange rate with the rouble, which helped Afghanistan buy Soviet products, made repayment in local currency burdensome.

American efforts were concentrated on transport, which accounted for 40 per cent of US aid. This was spent mainly on road-building in the south, but also involved such "white elephants" as the largely unused Kandahar Airport. The second highest expenditure (22 per cent) was on the wretched Helmand Valley project, where yields were, for a long time, even lower than they had been before the project. With glee, Akhramovich could write "a telling blow was dealt to the prestige of the American 'friends' for from behind the cloak of 'assistance' the public saw the hated visage of colonialism which was threatening Afghanistan's independence". America's generous supply of wheat (17 per cent) went largely unnoticed by the general public in Afghanistan, though without it many people might have starved. Perhaps the most effective element of the American effort, though it comprised only 9 per cent of the total, was in education, particularly teacher training, so much so that it drew Akhramovich's special condemnation: "The US monopolists, like their partners in Western Europe, have considerably stepped up their penetration into Afghanistan under the guise of cultural assistance. Special attention has been given to education."

Soviet policy was to take advantage of every Afghan dispute with Pakistan to get the country more deeply into debt using techniques not unlike those of the rural moneylenders they had so strongly condemned. Fixed price contracts for purchase of commodities would be entered into at above world prices, but on such terms that long after the world price had risen above the agreed level Russia enjoyed the advantage. The Soviet Union would, it was true, take goods, such as poor quality Afghan wool, which no one else wanted, and supply commodities such as petrol, green tea, sugar, books and vehicles at below world prices. But it was noticeable that after 1963 Soviet trade agreements involved the sale to Afghanistan of such luxuries as cars, watches and cameras, the pursuit of which superfluities further strained the economy. They also included many more long-term infrastructure projects which Afghanistan's state of economic development scarcely justified, but which often had strategic and political advantages for the Soviet Union. The classic example was the road-building programme which was not designed to the advantage of the Afghan economy, but for military access.

Nineteenth-century British strategists, concerned to keep Afghanistan an impenetrable buffer state, often gave stern warnings against the construction of a road south from Herat to Kandahar, since this would outflank the Hindu Kush. By the mid-1960s, you could drive in five or six hours between these two cities on a Russian-built concrete highway, striking boldly across the brick-red desert. Babur, the great Mogul, once struggled to stay alive in the deadly cold of a pass in the Hindu Kush by crouching in the corpse of an eviscerated camel. Four hundred and sixty years later you could drive through the heart of these formidable mountains at any time of year along the Russian-built pass and tunnel at Salang, or fly over them in the aircraft of Aeroflot, Ariana and Bakhtar – and at prices considerably below those of the international commercial airlines.

A glance at the map on page 8 will show that the only good roads in Afghanistan were those which were part of the system completed, mainly by the Russians, in 1966. This system is shaped like the Russian letter Ц. Its lines of communication run from the Soviet border north of Herat, through the major towns of Afghanistan (with the base of the Ц thoughtfully provided by the Americans) and back to the

Russian border at the Oxus port of Qizil Qala. The tail of the Ц runs down to the Khyber, where there is access – via Peshawar and Karachi – to the sea. Transit trade agreements between Afghanistan and Pakistan allowed Russian goods, if not Russian guns, to roll unimpeded down to the Indian Ocean "in fulfilment of historic destiny".

This triumph for Soviet diplomacy tends to be overlooked in the West when discussing the Russian invasion little more than a decade later. In terms of that economic competition which was the corollary – often ignored in the West but never by the Russians – of peaceful coexistence, access to a warm-water port within easy reach of the seaboards of Africa and South Asia, and through which its goods could strategically be despatched, was as important to the Soviet Union as it was to tsarist Russia. Once the route was opened, the Russians had an even greater interest than had the government of British India in the stability of Afghanistan and in friendly relations across the Durand Line.

In the 1960s the Russian presence, if inescapable, was discreet and sometimes exhibited an almost psychotic sensitivity to the presence of curious Western visitors in Afghanistan. At this time the visitor to Qizil Qala, for example, however eminent the authority for his visit, would have found at his elbow, as I did, within moments of entering the dock area, a large blond Russian who claimed to be – and possibly was – a maintenance engineer, but whose only discernible function seemed to be the maintenance of a close watch on the visitor until safely out of the gate. All along the far bank of the Oxus there were squat gantry-legged observation posts even in peacetime. The visitor with a camera who stood for more than a moment on the Afghan bank might find himself the centre of a diplomatic protest sparked off by a telephone call before his return to Kabul. Although no one seemed to object in 1966 to my taking photographs at Ay Khanum* on the junction of the Oxus and Kochak rivers, this area – site of one of the great archaeological discoveries of modern times – was very difficult to visit, even under the monarchy.

Russia often markedly underbid when tendering for major construction work in order to secure the contract, only to charge two or three times the estimate at the end of the day. This was particularly true in hydroelectric work, where the Russians were anxious to elbow out the very successful West Germans. Soviet technical performance was sometimes not up to scratch either, but by the time disillusioned Afghans realized that their Marxist neighbours could deal as sharply as any Western capitalists they were too deeply committed to the deal to do much about it.

By the time Daoud seized power for the second time in 1973, Soviet aid – at $1,500 million between 1953 and 1973 – was more than three times that of the United States ($450 million) and there were probably some 3,000–4,000 Russian technicians working at all levels in Afghanistan. As Louis Dupree, a leading American authority on Afghanistan, wrote at the time of the coup:

The Hellenic site of Ay Khanum is remarkable almost as much for the way it was discovered as for what it contains. One day in 1963, the King of Afghanistan, an ardent huntsman and a keen student of his country's history, was out hunting along the Kochak river where it joins the Oxus. He came upon two unusual stones protruding from the ground: a Corinthian capital and an altar. He made no delay in getting these to the museum at Kunduz and in drawing them to the attention of the head of the French archaeological expedition, Dr Schlumberger. The early excavations conducted by the new head of the mission, M. Paul Bernard, revealed at Ay Khanum the first complete Hellenic city east of Mesopotamia. Ay Khanum was probably built in the second or third centuries BC in the wake of Alexander the Great's conquest. The city and its hilltop fortress occupy a commanding strategic position with strong natural defences. There is evidence both in situ and in documentary sources to suggest that it was probably sacked and burned to the ground towards the end of the second century BC by a tribe of nomads, the Urchi, from higher up the Oxus. Excited interest in the site, however, had to contend with "difficulties" in reaching it. The author went there without asking; this, luckily, avoided the "difficulties".

Afghanistan's economic problems are nothing new, but have been growing since the advent of overkill in foreign aid, which reached its peak during the 1953–63 decade of Daoud Khan's previous tenure. No matter how one viewed Afghanistan's economic problems, the outlook at first glance certainly appeared bleak. With most major infrastructure projects completed, with few real resources capable of earning vast sums of hard currency, with smuggling and corruption steadily eroding income from customs (a major source of government revenue), with little statistical data for intelligent planning, with minimal overall increases in agricultural production (and two years of drought, disastrous to men, livestock, and crops), with small success in attempted fiscal reforms, with debt repayment on foreign loans coming due, with annual budget deficits of about 500 million afghanis, with few of the country's limited industrial and power plants operating above 50% capacity, with a bureaucracy oriented toward perpetuation rather than innovation, Afghanistan offered any economist – free enterprise, socialist, or mixed – extreme challenges.

As was to be expected, the return to Kabul of an apparently sympathetic regime led to still further Soviet involvement in the Afghan economy. By the end of 1975 more than seventy new projects had been signed up, including major extensions of hydroelectric and irrigation schemes, particularly in the tribally important (and untamed) Jalalabad region, development of fertilizer production and the expansion of natural gas production so that 2.5 billion cubic feet per annum could be exported to the USSR from 1976.

There were the inevitable catches by which the Russians fixed the prices, measured the quantities and pronounced arbitrarily on the quality of the goods exported. Although between 1973 and 1976 Russia increased the price per thousand cubic metres of gas from $6.08 to $16.1 – in 1977 equivalent to $0.61 per btu – this has to be seen against a world price range of $0.60 to $1.45 per btu. By 1978, although aid at $400 million for the year made Afghanistan the fourth biggest recipient of Soviet bounty in total and the largest per head of population, more than 40 per cent of Afghanistan's exports, including all of its gas, were going to pay off its debts to the Soviet Union.

In imitation of the Soviet model, Daoud had nationalized existing industries and directed a disproportionate amount of Afghanistan's scarce capital to further industrialization. He was, however, both an able man and a patriot. By 1975/6 he had begun to reassess his economic strategy and the implications of excessively close ties with Russia (as he did in other spheres).

Detecting a change in attitude, Moscow became both less enthusiastic and less generous in its support. Counter-measures by the West were few and the United States diminished its economic and military commitments in the area, and particularly to Pakistan, when that country, in response to India's 1974 detonation of a nuclear device, began to pursue its own independent development of nuclear weapons with the aid of France. The completion of the Karakoram Highway linking Pakistan to China marked the end of a process which had begun with the collapse of SEATO, the Baghdad Pact and the Bhutto regime and which divorced Pakistan from Western interests. Minor and belated moves such as the Iranian/Afghan transit trade agreement of 1974 could have little influence on the great game which Russia appeared to have won.

The Soviet Union had seen Afghanistan as an exemplary opportunity to prove that a society could be changed in a

Marxist direction by economic penetration and the social impact of new technology. It was an artificially created state whose people had bitter memories of Western imperialism. There was a largely poor, non-literate population and a great gulf between a small and wealthy elite ruling group and the masses. There were a rising and frustrated number of technocrats and students and a varied and mutually antipathetic racial mixture. There was a border with Pakistan in a continual state of dispute over the Pushtunistan issue and a strong central government and military organization largely dependent for its effectiveness on Soviet support. The Soviet Union, in other words, appeared to be running a highly successful experiment in economic penetration as a means of achieving political objectives and in the bountiful reward of neutrality as a means of encouraging other Third World countries not to be drawn into the Western camp.

Making due allowance for cant, the coincidental protestations of altruism by Russian commentators had a certain ring of conviction about them. As Akhramovich wrote, "regardless of the obvious facts, they, the apologists of British colonialism, kept propagating the idea that Afghanistan was threatened by 'a fatal danger' from the North. The selfless and friendly support of the socialist countries, by their very nature are far removed from any designs that might threaten the Afghan state".

Since in the 1960s and early 1970s Russia appeared to be content to ignore political principles and to help a neutral country ruled by a monarchy, where the Communist Party was actually illegal, in order to secure its long-term advantages, the optimistic speculation of an Afghan commentator of the time seemed not unreasonable: "Looking at the Soviet intentions in Afghanistan one could reasonably rule out a direct Soviet invasion of Afghanistan. In addition to the fact that the

Afghans would defend themselves directly and through guerrilla war, the Soviet Union would lose the confidence of other neutral nations. She would suffer from world popular pressures and about 300 million Moslems of Asia and the Middle East would turn against her."

That was certainly a view shared by most commentators, myself included, at the time and it was a view that appeared to hold good at least until very shortly before the coup which overthrew Daoud in April 1978. In order to understand what changed the picture so dramatically it is necessary to retrace the development of a number of political forces in Afghanistan.

Peasant, poet and warrior, a pattern of life unchanged for two thousand years.
© JOHN C. GRIFFITHS

Purdah at puberty was the rule for Afghan women until Daoud's decree of 1956,
however the rise of the Taliban has seen this re-instated with severe punishment for
those women who fail to comply. © JOHN C. GRIFFITHS

Two Soviet soldiers struggle to carry a heavy box full of ammunition past a Soviet military poster at a base in Kabul during preparations for the Soviet withdrawal from Afghanistan (29 January 1989). © ASSOCIATED PRESS

Soldiers of Afghan president Burhanuddin Rabbini look over the ruins of a tank captured from the president's rival, Prime Minister Gulbuddin Hekmatyar, in the Soviet-built Microrayon in Kabul, which saw some of the bloodiest battles along the frontline during this power struggle (1 July 1994). © POPPERFOTO/REUTER

Afghan Shi'ite Muslims use bicycles, cars and trucks in their flight from Kabul and the advancing government troops (11 March 1995). © POPPERFOTO/REUTER

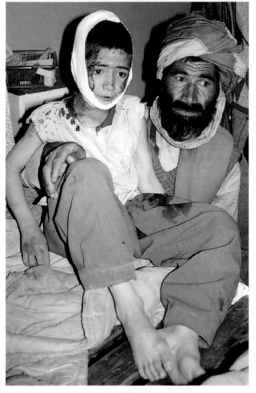

An Afghan boy helps his mother fill a sack with scrap salvaged from ruined houses in the battle-scarred city of Kabul (26 February 1995).
© POPPERFOTO/REUTER

An Afghan father, at the Red Cross hospital in Kabul, holds his son who was badly injured by a rocket fired by government forces
(17 February 1995).
© POPPERFOTO/REUTER

Afghans working in the poppy fields of Nangarhar province, a large opium growing area. Despite imposing a ban on the cultivation of the opium poppy, the Taliban has failed to completely stamp out production. © ASSOCIATED PRESS

The bodies of former Afghan President Najibullah (right) and his brother hang from a traffic kiosk after being captured and executed by the Taliban (27 September 1996). © ASSOCIATED PRESS

Taliban fighters fire a Soviet-made 122mm gun 30km north of Kabul (November 1996).
© POPPERFOTO/REUTER

Wakil Ahmed Muttawakil of the Taliban (left) and Fazl Hadi Shinwari (right) leader of the Northern Alliance are encouraged by Gohar Ayub, the Pakistani foreign minister, to embrace each other at the start of peace talks in Islamabad (26 April 1998).
© ASSOCIATED PRESS

Two Taliban militia hold US-made Stinger surface-to-air missiles as they pass by the hijacked Indian Airlines plane at Kandahar airport in Southern Afghanistan (30 December 1999). © POPPERFOTO/REUTER

A surface-to-air missile is driven past onlookers during Independence Day celebrations to mark the 72nd anniversary of Afghanistan's independence from Britain (19 August 2001). © POPPERFOTO/REUTER

A Taliban fighter sits on rubble in front of one of the demolished 1,500 year-old Buddha statues in the central Afghan province of Bamiyan (26 March 2001).

8

EXPERIMENTS IN DEMOCRACY

In the heady atmosphere after the Second World War, when so many underdeveloped nations either achieved or demanded their independence, in the much-abused name of democracy, Afghanistan indulged in its first mild and brief flirtation with that siren.

Louis Dupree aptly named the preceding two decades the "avuncular period" when government was almost entirely in the hands of members of the royal family. The pattern changed in 1950 with the law permitting some freedom in what had hitherto been a state press monopoly. Three main papers appeared which, while critical of the government and, in the context of 1950 Afghanistan, radical, were not revolutionary. Nor, of course, in an almost totally illiterate country did their circulation exceed a few hundred copies. Probably the most significant of them was *Afghan Mellat*, around which an informal national democratic socialist group coalesced. This group was in fact vehemently orthodox and irredentist over the issue of Pushtunistan. At the same time a student union was formed which naturally took an enthusiastic and iconoclastic interest in Afghan politics. The students' criticism, and that of the more left-wing papers, particularly of the corruption of members of the government and of the reactionary influence of Islam, became increasingly virulent.

After an abortive attempt to form its own political party in order to counter these critical organizations, the royal government reverted to type. In 1951 the students' union was closed and a few of its apprehensive leaders fled to Pakistan. By the end of 1952 all non-government papers had been closed and some 25 "liberal" leaders were sent to prison, where some of them died. The first taste of democracy had not been to the liking of the ruling establishment, but although in 1953 the strong man of Afghanistan, Prince Daoud, had become Prime Minister, the appetite of many intellectuals for the power denied to them by the nepotism of Afghan politics had been whetted.

The decade of Daoud's first period of rule will be considered elsewhere, but in examining the political development of Afghanistan it is significant in two respects.

In ten years Daoud enormously increased the grip of central government on Afghanistan at the expense of local rule and customs. Not since Abdur Rahman had an Afghan leader so effectively insisted that the writ of central government be paramount. Like his illustrious predecessor, he created a loyal, well-paid, well-trained army and used it, not only to govern the tribal districts, but also to enforce the law generally. It had been customary, for example, for the wealthier citizens of Kandahar to neglect to pay their taxes, proffering excuses in their stead year after year to governments which had no choice but to accept them. In 1959 they tried their usual ploy – sanctuary in the mosque for a few days until the tax collectors got bored and went home – only to find their road to the mosque barred by Daoud's troops. Immediately they instigated a riot, but Daoud's commander was not impressed and simply shot some of the rioters. Thereafter taxes were paid promptly.

This same willingness to exercise authority enabled Daoud to make reforms which would have been quite beyond the power of any progressive elements at that time. Again in 1959, on Daoud's initiative, a number of leading Afghan women abandoned purdah and its most public symbol – the chadhuri, or veil. The mullahs, ever quick to counter any threat to their absolute authority, sent a noisy deputation to protest to

Daoud. After fifty of them had spent a week in jail they acquiesced in the new reforms.

To carry out his economic and social programme Daoud needed resources beyond those Afghanistan could supply and so he began that process which was to put the Afghan economy in pawn to the Soviet Union and which, unfairly, earned him the sobriquet of "the Red Premier" from the Americans whose aid, though substantial, was no match for Russia's. By 1963 there was widespread, if relatively peaceful, unrest at Daoud's leftward tilt in the balance of Afghanistan's neutral stance and against his social and economic reforms. It is more than likely that his influence in the armed services could have enabled him to stage a coup even then, as it did a decade later. However, in a remarkable gesture of self-denial, he stepped down from office at the King's request and there slowly began Afghanistan's second experiment in democracy.

Within a decade the experiment had failed – largely from lack of courage by the man who launched it. In 1964, the King, Muhammad Zahir Shah, deliberately abandoned 200 years of autocratic rule and diminished his own personal power in order to give his country a system of government which could survive, as an absolute monarchy could not, the stress of the twentieth century.

The new constitution, which Zahir had a major hand in drafting, came into operation in 1965 following Afghanistan's first elections and imposed some surprising and shrewd restraints on the exercise of power. In particular, it barred the royal family from both politics and government, thus imposing on the recently ousted Prince Daoud perpetual exile from the legitimate exercise of power and closing the back door of quasi-constitutional usurpation to any possibly dissident relatives. It also set up a representative system of government formed by the Shura (parliament) consisting of the directly elected Wolesi Jirgah (House of the People) and the partly elected and partly appointed Meshrano Jirgah (House of the Elders). The older institution of the Loya Jirgah (Great Council) was composed of members of both houses of the Shura and the chairmen of elected provincial councils. The Loya Jirgah's functions were partly formal and partly to act as the sounding board of national opinion in times of great stress, such as a royal abdication or a state of emergency.

In promulgating this new constitution, the King seemed to be deliberately effacing himself and minimizing his power. An exquisitely well-mannered, highly civilized man, he was more interested in the culture and history of his country and in open-air sports than in the practice of government and the exercise of power. Yet he had a very real love of his country, and wisdom enough to know that the absolute authority of his family would ultimately be an obstacle to Afghanistan's progress.

As events were to prove, it was a mistake to look on the new constitution as a total abdication of the royal authority. Certainly, it imposed conditions and restraints: the King must be an Afghan national and, in effect, of the House of Nadir Shah; he must be a Muslim and a follower of the "Hanafi doctrine". But he also retained extensive reserve powers. Among royal prerogatives were the dissolution and summoning of the Shura, the appointment of the Prime Minister and other ministers, and of the Chief Justice and senior civil and military officials, and the proclamation of a state of emergency. It is true that the King was supposed to govern within the limits of the constitution, but that same constitution insisted that "the King is not accountable and shall be respected by all".

The restrictions on the political role of members of the royal family other than the King have to be seen in the context of Afghan history, in which the most likely suspects in any plot against the King's life were his nearest, though not necessarily his dearest. The constitution's caution was no more than realism demanded. The problem of the succession is always a delicate one in an autocratic system, whether the autocracy be regal or "proletarian". It is following the death of the ruler that the state is most prone to upheaval and to the chaos that accompanies any prolonged struggle for power among aspiring heirs. The new Afghan constitution went into considerable detail in setting out the line of succession in the royal house and the conduct of any necessary regency. Particularly significant was the provision by which no one who had acted as permanent regent could subsequently become King himself.

Two factors were critical if the experiment was to succeed: self-restraint on the part of the monarch and members of the royal house and the increasing derivation of government authority from the popular will, rather than from the whims of its appointed members. Whether such democracy is in fact the most beneficent form of government for a country such as Afghanistan is another matter. The issue was scarcely put to the test because both of the critical elements for success were missing.

The Wolesi Jirgah was to be directly elected every four years by the universal suffrage of all Afghans over the age of 20. (We shall see later how these elections were conducted.) It consisted of 216 members representing single-member constituencies and was elected by the single direct vote system as practised, for example, in Britain. The Wolesi Jirgah could, therefore, have become as truly representative as any parliament elected by this rather crude method can ever be. Of the 84 members of the Meshrano Jirgah, one-third were directly elected every four years from constituencies coextensive with the 28 provinces, one-third were representatives elected every three years by provincial councils to which they had previously been directly elected, and one-third were members appointed every five years by the King "from amongst well-informed and experienced persons". Thus, the composition of both houses of the Shura, and of the Loya Jirgah as well, was predominantly democratic, with members answerable to the voters at regular intervals.

At the first of these elections in the autumn of 1965 there were 1,358 candidates for the 216 seats in the Wolesi Jirgah (six of which were reserved for nomads), and 100 for the 28 directly elected seats in the Meshrano Jirgah. By no means all of these candidates were hand-picked nominees of the King and his administration. Many of the elections were quite heatedly contested, and one provincial governor at least (to judge from the interview I had shortly after the election with the governor of Kunduz) had considerable difficulty in keeping alive a warm interest without actually letting the contest come to the boil. On the other hand, the local election commissions did a considerable amount of preliminary screening to ensure that no "subversive" characters – that is to say, those who might too dramatically oppose the administration's programme – were allowed either to stand as candidates or to vote. They could also exercise a similar veto after a candidate had been elected, though I am not aware that they actually did so. The candidates themselves were largely local influential landowners – generally, but not always, of the predominant ethnic group in the locality. Six women candidates put themselves up for election and women were entitled to vote. Four of the women were elected, as we have seen, but the number of women voters was disappointingly small – mainly because husbands and fathers in many cases expressly forbade their womenfolk to participate in this open public activity.

The election campaign gave encouraging evidence of the government's desire for genuine debate between candidates, although in the absence of parties this had to be on a largely personal basis. Newspapers printed the name and picture of every candidate free of charge; candidates were able to purchase both advertising space and airtime on Kabul radio (at about £12 a minute for a maximum of five minutes); and the radio station itself ran an extensive series of explanatory programmes on how the elections were to work and what they were all about. (Television did not come to Kabul until 1978.)

Throughout the campaign, provincial governors and other prominent local officials spent much time explaining to voters what kind of people they ought to vote for, that is to say, they were soliciting support for candidates sympathetic to the administration. Yet there is no evidence of other direct pressures being brought to bear on the electorate to influence their voting. Clearly, a man had to be able to dip substantially into his own purse to finance a campaign, and, as in the United States, this naturally tended to limit candidature to the wealthier sections of the community; but, apart from this practical consideration, the field was open to all who could satisfy the provisions for qualification laid down in the constitution. Considerable pains were also taken with the conduct of the ballot itself, to ensure both its secrecy and its accuracy. Each candidate had a separate ballot box with his name, photograph and electoral symbol on it and into one of these, in the privacy of a screened booth, the voter dropped his ballot paper to indicate his choice.

Despite these efforts, however, the election remained largely confined to intellectuals and city dwellers, as one might expect for the first election among a generally illiterate population. Even in the cities the poll was not high – between 5 and 10 per cent of those eligible to vote – and in the rural areas it was often as little as 2 per cent. Thus the first elected deputies of the Shura could not reasonably be called representative of the people as a whole, though they certainly were representative of the politically aware and interested (or organizable), with the towns naturally returning the more radical and unusual members. Moreover, in assessing the poll in rural areas with a very low turnout of voters, one has to appraise with caution the merits of the multi-ballot box mode of voting. This reservation is reinforced by the fact that the concept of the secret ballot is quite alien to the long-established "open" democracy of the village or tribal jirgah where every man may be heard and in voting must be seen to have the courage of his convictions. Many Afghans – whose ideal is to have as little contact with officialdom as possible – were suspicious that the ballot was just a device to identify them for taxation or conscription.

Yet the 1965 election can be seen as a clear, if limited success for the democratizers. There was virtually no indication of corruption or coercion; there was a competitive campaign and a fair ballot. The next step was to try to extend the interest in the electoral process through the municipal elections of 1966. But the poll was again low, as it was in the following general election of 1969. So what went wrong?

The division between legislature and executive was absolute: and it is perhaps in the way that this separation was organized that there lay the principal weakness of the 1964 constitution. The Prime Minister was appointed directly by the King and then recommended a list of ministers to him. Neither the Premier nor other ministers could be members of either house of parliament. The Premier then submitted his government to the Wolesi Jirgah for approval, first outlining its general policies to the lower house. The Wolesi Jirgah had the power to grant or withhold its vote of confidence, and it was the lower house alone that had this power of veto. (The "all or nothing" powers of the Wolesi Jirgah were not dissimilar to those of the European Parliament of the time in its power to sack the whole European Commission but not an individual commissioner.) Only when the government received a vote of confidence could the King issue the necessary royal decree of appointment.

The Premier, however, had no machinery of party whips through which to exact that vote of confidence (the organized party as understood in the West being then still unknown in Afghanistan). The fall of the first government to hold power after the elections of October 1965, and its replacement by the next administration, demonstrated that the battle for ultimate power had yet to follow this preliminary skirmish between executive and legislature.

When Prince Daoud was forced to resign the premiership in 1963, Dr Yusuf, an able but not very determined man, was appointed and held office as Premier for more than two years until the 1965 elections. With a PhD from Gottingen University rather than influential family connections, Yusuf was the first meritocrat to reach the top in post-war Afghanistan. When the new Shura met, he was again appointed Prime Minister by the King and with much the same cabinet as before, almost as if there had been no elections. But, surprisingly and encouragingly, the Wolesi Jirgah, though unaccustomed to the business of parliamentary democracy, showed its teeth, accused some of the members of the Yusuf government of bribery and corruption, and was only with the greatest difficulty persuaded to give its vote of confidence. Certain left-wing members, led by Nur Mohammed Taraki, continued to protest and invited the students of Kabul University to come in a body to support their objection. The mass of the students were forcibly restrained from entering the parliamentary building; the inspirers of their demonstration urged them to force their way in on the following day on the grounds that it was their right to be present.* In the riots which ensued three people were killed, one a bystander, but the crackdown on legal outlets for student opinion that followed was to contribute significantly to the still more tragic demise of all party democracy. Many who were students then carried their resentment into the towns and villages where they were teachers and officials. This disturbance was largely instrumental in inducing Dr Yusuf to resign – in anguish of conscience, his supporters claimed, at the three deaths which occurred – and Muhammad Maiwandwal was invited to form a government. But the tension between government and Shura was by no means over, although it was to be much less severe than before.

Maiwandwal submitted his government and its policy for approval, and comfortably got his vote of confidence. He then interpreted the constitution as permitting him to make individual changes in the composition of his cabinet without submitting them for approval to the Wolesi Jirgah. This interpretation he acted on, and he insisted (as I found in conversation with him) that he was correct in so doing. Members of the parliament thereupon exercised their right to question ministers and used it to criticize the Prime Minister for making these new appointments without first seeking the approval of the Wolesi Jirgah. However, since debate was not permitted on ministerial replies, they could do nothing more, short of moving a "specific and direct" vote of no confidence in the government as a whole and this, in the country's unsettled state, they were reluctant to do for some time.

Maiwandwal, plagued with ill-health, resigned and Nur

---

*An unquestionable breach of Article 57, paragraph 3 of the constitution which stated that "Nobody may enter the meeting place of the Shura by force".

Ahmed Etemadi took office. In 1968, after much delay and fierce debate, the bill legalizing political parties – but not of course the non-Islamic, atheist, Communist Party – was passed by the Shura, but when the second election under the new constitution was called in 1969, the King had still not had the confidence to sign and so enact the bill. Fatally, therefore, the elections were contested only by independents. Though the 10 per cent plus poll was a slight improvement on the 1965 election, it could scarcely be described as a triumph for the democratic process. As independents, candidates were virtually all extremely conservative landowners or businessmen able to finance their own campaigns. Many more non-Pathans were elected, but not a single woman, and almost three-quarters of the members of the Wolesi Jirgah were taking a parliamentary seat for the first time. There was some rigging of these elections and much influence was used to ensure the defeat of such able opponents of the government as Farhang and Maiwandwal. Polling outside the urban areas was negligible and the crypto-Marxist faction in the Wolesi Jirgah was reduced from five to three. Among the Leftists was a new member, a certain Mr Hafizullah Amin.

Amin, an American-educated maths teacher, claimed that he had become a socialist as a result of his experiences in the United States. A man of ruthless ambition, brutality and administrative skills, but without any family connection with the essential power bloodlines of Afghanistan, Amin saw the extra-parliamentary activities of the recently formed (but unofficial) People's Democratic Party (PDP) as his best means of climbing from his lower middle-class origins to a position of power. He rapidly became a key member of the PDP and a staunch, though it later transpired expedient, supporter of Taraki. The PDP therefore continued to concentrate on extra-parliamentary activities amongst students and junior officers, both now going to Russia in increasing numbers for training. The arbitrary change of the entry conditions to Kabul University to favour applicants from the American school, and perhaps surreptitious pot-stirring by the Chinese, made the young a more fruitful, if still limited, source of recruitment for the Marxist groups.

The deadlock in parliament between the legislature and executive grew worse. In the 1969/70 session, for example, only one, very minor bill was passed.

A major reason for this situation was to be found in the composition of the Wolesi Jirgah. The standard of debate was poor, the quality of members in general, poorer. There was an enormous contrast between the handful of able members and the rest, most of whom merely fulfilled the minimum requirements of sanity, literacy and attainment of their twenty-fifth birthday. For the most part they were small landowners, chosen for their local influence rather than for any wider ability or knowledge. Ultra-conservative in outlook, they yet lacked any coherent philosophy of conservatism. They concentrated simply on resisting any proposal for taxing land or animals which might diminish their own wealth. It was not simply that the Shura's debates, if those I saw were anything to go by, were considerably more disorderly than those of the House of Commons, and its members inexperienced in the art of parliamentary discussion. More serious was the lack of any imaginative approach to the country's problems. Although legislators in many a Western state can be just as unimaginative, in Afghanistan this deficiency was not compensated for by a strong outside body of political thinking or an informed public opinion capable of perceiving national needs and the policies necessary to meet them. The initiative lay almost exclusively with the government, apart from a handful of deputies with the ability to devise and present legislative proposals. The members of the Maiwandwal administration and the subsequent Etemadi, Zahir and Shafiq cabinets were, generally speaking, able men whose ideas were tempered with realism. The political weakness of the system lay in the absence of any real collective alternative other than that of the former Yusuf cabinet, which contained a number of able ministers relegated to impotent obscurity in the provinces. However unjustly to individuals, this alternative group carried a collective label of venality.

Corruption has always presented a major problem in Afghan government, whether under an absolute monarchy, a democratic monarchy, or a Marxist autocracy. In 1966, for example, the imprisonment of a judge for taking bribes was a courageous initial step against the acceptance of corruption as a normal and inevitable ingredient in the Afghan way of life. The problem was to draw a dividing line between corruption and the customarily permissible nepotism – indeed, to know just how far it is practicable to go in the tightly-knit society of the Afghan governing classes in breaking down that nepotism in favour of a meritocracy. A former Minister of the Interior once pointed out to me with tolerant cynicism that, within hours of a great set-to at question time in the Wolesi Jirgah, the very deputies who had denounced his supposed corruption would be round at his office to beg posts for their sons, cousins and nephews.

Such practices were bound to continue as long as the government remained the only considerable source of patronage and as long as parliamentary, ministerial and civil service salaries were so low that they made some form of supplementary income – by private enterprise in some instances, by taking bribes in many others – almost a matter of survival. Moreover, it was unreasonable to expect wholly "clean" democratic government so long as there was no united opposition ready to replace the government at the first sign of failure. But with that perverse yet encouragingly characteristic Afghan independence of mind, the members of the Wolesi Jirgah were perfectly capable of banding together for the purpose of harassing the government. The weapon they chiefly used was the repeated demand that individual ministers answer questions on demand, not just on the rare occasions when the premier of the day put them up before the Wolesi Jirgah. In 1971 they brought down Etemadi's government by a threat of a vote of no confidence on this issue. His successor, Dr Zahir, lasted a bare year to December 1972. Famine had afflicted much of the north part of the country and Zahir, too, fell to a no confidence vote. Dr Shafiq's ensuing six months in office ended rather differently. It is against such a background of confusion and frustration in the official machinery of democracy that the development of the underground Marxist parties in Afghanistan has to be seen.

The People's Democratic Party of Afghanistan was founded – unofficially, of course – in 1965. Its structure was strongly influenced by that of the Soviet Communist Party. Its two leading lights were Nur Mohammed Taraki and Babrak Karmal, a lawyer with a flair for the dramatic. (Dupree recounts how, when injured in hospital after a Wolesi Jirgah fight in 1966, Karmal hastily bound a few extra bandages round his head before coming the window to wave to his supporters.) Karmal was elected to the Wolesi Jirgah in 1965 and my discussions with him shortly afterwards indicated that while he was a conventional Marxist ideologue – where Taraki was a very impractical romantic revolutionary – he then envisaged an advance to socialism through the electoral process under cover of the traditional United Democratic Front. This was an optimistic, or perhaps expedient view, considering that his parliamentary support was no more than two or three members including the woman member, Dr Anahita Ratebzad. Taraki, however, an intellectual and competent man of letters, was generally regarded as the leader of the Afghan Left and though his weekly magazine *Khalq* (the masses) only appeared for half-a-dozen editions before it was closed down, it gave its name to the predominant group in the PDP and indicated the staunchly nationalist and independent line adopted by the majority of the Party. Karmal was much more an orthodox international Marxist toeing the Moscow line as required.

The differences between the two leaders were eventually to lead to a split in the Party and just prior to the 1969 elections it was Karmal's Parcham (the flag) faction of the Party which was to produce the Party weekly of that name – as short-lived as its predecessor and closed before the polls opened. After the 1969 election, Amin, from his new position of influence in the Wolesi Jirgah, began to take over much of the role as Taraki's first lieutenant. The split between the two factions became open in 1973. Taraki refused to obey the Moscow directive to support the coup in which Daoud overthrew the monarchy and declared himself President, but Karmal moved himself and his Parchamis into the mainstream of power by doing so. Not until most of the Parchamis had been banished to the wilderness and it was clear that the orthodox Left would get nowhere as long as President Daoud ruled, did the two factions, under considerable pressure from Moscow, reunite to plot the Prince's overthrow.

Both factions had tried hard to recruit in the 1960s and 1970s, not just among the intellectuals, but also in the army, air force, and police, into whose ranks they also infiltrated their own men. Amin played a key role in this strategy, though Parcham perhaps did a little better among those actually influenced while training abroad. It should be emphasized, however, that very few of the 10,000 or so military personnel who had been trained abroad to that date were sympathetic, let alone recruited to the PDP. At the very height of its strength, just before the Daoud overthrow in 1978, it is doubtful whether the PDP ever had more than five or six thousand members in total.

But the Khalq and Parcham groups did not occupy the most leftward position in Afghan politics in the late 1960s; that position was reserved for the group involved with another short-lived journal *Shu'la-yi-Jawed*, published by the brothers Mahmudi. This mounted verbal attacks indiscriminately against the Russians, the Americans, the irredentist nationalists, the mullahs and the royal family, though reserving its sharpest abuse and the vilest epithet – revisionist – for its political neighbours in the PDP.

Largely because political parties were illegal at this time, a profusion of publications and associated unofficial groupings sprang up at the time of the 1965 elections. Many of the ablest deputies belonged to a group which centred round the shrewd, able and pleasant personality of Mohammed Siddiq Farhang, one of the deputies for Kabul, who gave up a ministerial appointment in order to take part in the genesis of politics in Afghanistan. When I questioned him about the formation of a political party, he laughingly told me that he was a very legalistically minded man and that, since parties were not yet legal, he had taken no steps to form one. Then, watching me with a twinkle, he added after a pause that, of course, he had sounded out his fellow deputies' opinions on political subjects and discovered those who were like-minded. There seemed to be only about a dozen or 15 of these "like-minded" deputies (although, in contesting the office of Secretary of the Wolesi Jirgah, Farhang obtained a quarter of the total votes). The "like-minded" might be encompassed by the term he used to indicate his own affiliation with international political elements: "liberal democratic parties with social tendencies". Certainly, he and his colleagues drew inspiration from the European social democrats, but more particularly from the progressive parties from such other underdeveloped countries as Burma, India and Egypt.

The basis of his economic policy was that the state must play a major role, almost an exclusive one, in the development of the backward economy of such an underdeveloped nation as Afghanistan, and that the consequence of the need for capital resources to achieve this development must be a policy of neutrality – a line not so far removed from that of Karmal.

The constitution certainly made provision for this type of policy to be exercised subject to certain limitations, and, paradoxically, it was at least partially carried out by a government most of whose individual members looked on Farhang himself as a dangerous radical. Farhang also appreciated what the fundamental nature of Afghan politics would be for the next decade – the politics of the intellectuals and not of the masses. He realized, as clearly as his leftist rivals, that whoever secured the allegiance of the increasing numbers of technocrats who could not be fitted into the old nepotistic family patterns, would gradually establish political ascendancy.

Any political approach to the masses, (I wrote in 1980) *other than perhaps one based on a simple and fanatical dressing up of Islam*, could have little hope of success when the national literacy level was below 10 per cent, communications were physically so difficult, and the radio, and to a considerable extent the press, was under government control. The other informal groups in the Wolesi Jirgah were perhaps less aware of this crucial fact. The largest was a traditional religious party led by Sibghatulla Mojadidi and his family who later headed one of the more religiously moderate groups of freedom fighters. There was, in addition, a small economically conservative group committed to laissez-faire and private enterprise, a group whose principal objective was to create the wider Pathan empire envisaged in Pushtunistan and a national party headed by Khalilullah Khalili, a poet and very much a King's man committed to seeing the constitution evolve along the lines envisaged by Zahir Shah. After he left office Maiwandwal also set up a highly personalized party (confusingly also known as the PDP), which pursued a line very similar to Khalili's.

Formal political debate on any large scale outside the Shura was made very difficult by a nervous administration. When Khalq appeared in April 1966, its editorial style was slightly hysterical and many of its articles (and the particular style of Tajiki Persian) seemed to reflect the influence of the banned Tudeh (Communist) Party in neighbouring Persia. This need not, however, have been a permanent defect and friends of free expression in the country were privately urging Taraki to make his journal more typically Afghan. The government did not give the paper the chance; after only five issues, it was closed down on the grounds that it violated the constitution, ostensibly in response to demands for its suppression by members of the Shura. No specific charges were made to justify this, but I was told by the head of the government news agency that its advocacy of public ownership and the abolition of private property was the specific aspect that was regarded as impugning the constitution. Also the government put a number of other small papers out of business by much more subtle methods, such as persuading the editor to resign (under the press laws, no newspaper could be published without an editor).

Of the 30 newspapers and journals listed by Louis Dupree in 1973, two-thirds were banned for at least a time in the democratic decade, most of them for good and many within weeks of their first publication. Some, of course, collapsed under financial pressures in a country where commercial advertising was virtually unknown and the support of either the government or a wealthy individual was essential. The majority, however, were closed like Khalq because they had in some way offended the authorities.

The development of a Western-style democratic political system in the 1960s was hampered by many factors, but to me three of them were clearly crucial. When barely a tenth of the adult population could read, there could be no mass circulation press and therefore no popular political movement involving the mass of the people. But freedom of speech is the natural birthright of the Afghan. The pungently expressed views that can be heard in the chai khanas are an indication that, when the majority of Afghans can read and write, successive administrations will find themselves appraised with equal vigour on paper. During the 1960s, however, party politics were confined to the few and those electors who could overcome their suspicion of the whole system were influenced more by the local power of candidates than by their doctrines.

The deputies who were elected in the main proved themselves to be both inflexible and intemperate and the total separation of the elected element from the executive resulted in the absence of that process of mutual accommodation necessary to effective democratic government.

Finally the reflexive panic of the King and his family associates whenever they or the system they had devised came under fire, meant that no coherent, legitimate opposition could develop. The only alternatives to the appointed government were, therefore, autocracy or anarchy.

9

COUPS SANS SURPRISE

"I have acted to abolish a corrupt and effete government, a pseudo-democracy based on personal and class interests which has taken Afghanistan to the edge of an abyss." The Afghan citizen tuning in to Kabul radio on July 17 1973 would have learned with those words that the experiment in democracy was over and his country had returned to its more usual method of changing government. There would have been little else to tell him that Prince Daoud, the "Red Premier" of the 1950s, had finally grown tired of political emasculation. Daoud's coup, involving only a few hundred key members of the army and air force and masterminded by the man who was to become Afghanistan's coup specialist, Colonel Abdul Qadir, Deputy Commander-in-Chief of the Air Force, had been virtually bloodless. Fewer than half-a-dozen people had died in the process. The King was "conveniently" out of the country. In view of the speed with which members of his family and entourage were released from captivity and sent to join him in Italy, it is hard to escape the conclusion that Zahir Shah, always more interested in sport and archaeology than government, had done a deal with his ambitious uncle.

It is hard, too, not to share Daoud's frustration and his strictures on the proto-democracy he swept aside. Deprived of the legitimate development of political parties and of a free press, it never had a chance. It was more surprising, perhaps, that an aristocrat of the old ruling clan and not one of the Marxist parties had staged the coup. The fact is, however, that the latter were still far too weak to act and were wisely biding their time. They were, too, in some disarray among themselves, and had already divided into the Khalq and Parcham factions whose relationship we shall examine in greater detail later. Moscow had decreed that the PDP should support Daoud, but Taraki's majority Khalq group had declined to do so. Karmal's Parchami, however, toed the party line both from conviction and expediency. Daoud soon received further Soviet endorsement in the shape of a state visit from President Podgorny.

Following the classic pattern, within two months Daoud had "discovered" a counter-plot and imprisoned its leaders – that is to say, his critics. One of them, former Premier Maiwandwal, was supposed to have hanged himself in his cell.

Inevitably, Pakistan was accused of involvement in the counter-revolution, as indeed it was again in the following summer of 1974 when a further unsuccessful attempt was made to overthrow Daoud. Pakistan firmly rejected all such accusations, Zulfikar Ali Bhutto's government trying to keep a delicate balance between the needs of stability on its north-western border and the loyalty of the Pathan tribes on its side of the same frontier.

At the outset of the five years of his second rule, Daoud firmly suppressed any dissident Islamic groups such as the Muslim League, which objected to the degree of his involvement with the Soviet Union. With Russian economic backing, he was able, in the early years at least, to improve the Afghan economy and even to achieve a small balance of payments surplus. But like virtually every other Afghan ruler in similar circumstances, he found it increasingly necessary, psychologically and politically, to assert his independence of his patrons. In 1975 he began to purge the Marxists from the army and subtly diminish their political influence by despatching the enthusiastic young apparatchiki, the

Parchamis,* to spread the socialist word in remote tribal wildernesses, where he well knew it would fall on stony ground. He is reputed to have engineered the assassination of half-a-dozen prominent Leftists and was certainly exiling even his moderate critics. He also began to repair his relations with religious leaders. By 1977 he had not only begun to modify his hard line on the "Pushtunistan question" and to arrange an exchange of state visits to Pakistan, but had also promised new legislative elections in 1979 which would inevitably have brought substantial conservative elements back into the political arena. This antagonized the members of the People's Democratic Party (PDP) whom he had used as the political basis of his own team at the time of the coup.

In 1978 Daoud began purging again, still more drastically, and when he openly expressed the view that Cuba, Russia's proxy in Africa, should be expelled from the non-aligned nations group for its interference in that continent, his days were numbered. Daoud's Marxism was expedient rather than ideological. He used it, and the Soviet and PDP support that were its corollary, as a means to obtain and hold power in pursuit of purely Afghan objectives, an approach which neither Moscow nor its loyal Afghan disciples could allow to prevail for long.

His opponents initiated their counter-measures in November 1977 when they assassinated his close associate Ali Ahmed Khoram, the Minister of Planning. The inevitable "trial" followed against a background of food shortages and student unrest. The accused did not yet include the key political and military figures who were Daoud's real enemies, amongst and against whom he did not yet feel secure enough to move openly. Nevertheless, no suitable pretext for his overthrow immediately

---

*Again we must remember that we are thinking in terms of very small numbers only – in this case some 150 men.

offered itself to this opposition group. However, on April 17 1978 Mir Akbar Khaiber, a former leader of Parcham, was assassinated – by whom it was not clear, although the KGB, with a "team" now in Afghanistan, came under some suspicion and was undeniably involved in helping to engineer the subsequent coup. The funeral on April 19 turned into a large-scale anti-American demonstration which gave Daoud the excuse he needed to arrest the PDP ruling triumvirate of Taraki, Amin and Karmal a week later. However, he made the mistake of leaving a number of his other former 1973 fellow conspirators at large, including Mr Coup himself, Colonel Abdul Qadir. On April 28 the Colonel struck again, using carefully selected units of the army and air force headed by Soviet-trained officers who were either members of PDP or sympathetic to it.

This time the coup was far from bloodless. Tanks and MiG 21s attacked the presidential palace, army head-quarters and other key points. In many of these places, the revolutionaries were resisted, because Daoud had strong support among the armed forces. Daoud himself was shot in cold blood, but not before he had seen more than a score of his family and close supporters butchered before his eyes. In the land of the blood feud it is always considered safer to kill possible avengers pre-emptively while you are at the business of murder.

By the end of the month, the PDP trio had been released and the new Democratic Republic of Afghanistan had been established under a Revolutionary Council whose chairman, Nur Muhammed Taraki, also became Premier. The two other PDP leaders, Amin and Karmal, both became Deputy Premiers. At this stage the Council still contained some influential former supporters of Daoud, such as Aslam Watanyar, who was, however, moved away from the key Portfolio of Defence to the relatively harmless one of Communications.

Taraki probably owed his emergence as leader of the new regime more to his reputation for being independent of the Soviet line than to his personality. I had found him likeable to talk to, but clearly a man of ideas rather than action. It was important to the newcomers to try to prevent tribal resistance to the first purely Marxist, non-dynastic government of Afghanistan both by paying lip service to the pre-eminence of Islam in the philosophy of government, and by denying that their coup was Communist or Soviet-inspired. Much evasive language was employed on Kabul radio. Qadir explained that while the revolution was Marxist in a popular sense, there was no Communist Party as such in Afghanistan and that the new leaders were all good Muslims.

Nevertheless, between May and July, some 25 trade agreements were signed with the Soviet Union and others with Eastern Bloc countries. Particularly important were those for the additional exploitation of oil and gas and for the building of a linking road and rail bridge and associated communication system across the Oxus at Hairatan. It soon became clear that the Afghan economy could function only by grace of Russian aid.

Taraki sought to popularize his government by cancelling all debts and mortgages to moneylenders and promising to limit landholdings to 15 acres and to distribute the surplus of the feudal landowners' agricultural land, to poor peasants. He also planned to abolish the traditional bride-price and launch a national literacy campaign aimed equally at both sexes – all of these measures would have seriously undermined the privileges of the exclusively male, conservative and primitively Muslim leaders of the rural communities. It was also his intention, in his own words, "to nationalize anything that is worth nationalizing".

At the outset of Taraki's regime all the provincial governors, even those in non-tribal areas, had been replaced by military commanders, but tribal unrest continued to increase throughout the summer of 1978 and was not even checked by Taraki's resumption of an irredentist line over Pushtunistan. It also soon emerged that several thousand people had been killed and some 5,000 imprisoned during the coup rather than the "not more than seventy-two or seventy-three" that Taraki had been claiming.

Strongman of the new triumvirate was undoubtedly Amin, who was soon drastically to step up the volume of execution and imprisonment. Although some thousand PDP prisoners were released, by the end of May, non-PDP politicians, including anyone who had been a minister during the previous 20 years, senior officers of the armed forces, civil servants and merchants, had been arrested and imprisoned in considerable numbers. It was Amin's influence too, which in July secured the dismissal of Parcham leaders Babrak Karmal and Nur Ahmed Nur (the Interior Minister), and their despatch to embassies abroad, while he had himself made Party Secretary of the PDP.

Early in August Karmal attempted to return from Moscow, but he was arrested after a gunfight at Kabul airport and again despatched abroad. It is hard to see why he was not executed, but the logic of Afghan acts of mercy is often as inexplicable as some of their wanton killings. A certain whimsical arbitrariness has pervaded Afghan power struggles throughout the country's history. A few days later yet another plot was discovered and several men who had been instrumental in the overthrow of Daoud, were themselves arrested, including Abdul Qadir.

Afghanistan's economic survival was by now firmly dependent on the patronage of the Soviet Union. Its Russian paymasters suggested to a more than willing Taraki that he insure his regime against counter-revolution by entering, in

December 1978, into the kind of defence treaty which had enabled the Soviet Union to secure unpopular regimes by military force elsewhere.

Early in February 1979 newly arrived American ambassador Dubs was kidnapped by a "bandit gang" in Kabul and shot, possibly by the Russians involved in the subsequent rescue. It was subsequently alleged that Dubs was a specialist in subversion and insurgency and although there is absolutely no proof of his involvement at this stage, the rest of the year was certainly to see a dramatic growth in the scale and scope of revolt against the Taraki regime and its open dependence on the Soviet Union.

On March 12, almost as soon as spring broke the paralysis of the Afghan winter, there was a major uprising in Herat in which several hundred PDP members and their families and sympathizers were killed. A number of those killed and reportedly flayed alive were Soviet advisers, and it was not long before a top-level military team under General Alexei Yepishev, First Deputy Minister of Defence and General Secretary of Political Affairs for the Russian Army and Navy, arrived on a "tour of inspection". General Yepishev had played a major role in the 1968 Russian invasion of Czechoslovakia.

There was, moreover, a considerable build-up in the influx of Soviet military hardware, though the equipment (MiG 21 fighters and Mi24 helicopter gunships and T62 tanks) was by no means the most modern available. Estimates of the numbers killed in the retaliatory action to restore government control in Herat varied from one thousand to five thousand, mostly students and religious leaders. Between May and September there were ever more frequent and substantial desertions from the Afghan army and increasingly successful and savage attacks by guerrillas on convoys and military and administrative posts. Again Soviet advisers were numbered amongst those killed. In March Amin had replaced Taraki as Prime Minister, but Taraki remained titular Head of State. There were only four new ministers in Amin's first cabinet and although Taraki relinquished the Defence Portfolio, it passed to his loyal supporter Colonel Watanyar, while the Interior Ministry was put into the hands of another Taraki man.

Amin was now progressively taking charge of the Afghan government and his response to the combination of growing insurgency and the diminishing reliability of the Afghan army was to try to establish a military arm of the PDP, to be known as khalqis, and introducing "people's courts" to mete out instant "justice" to "counter-revolutionaries", among whom members of the Parcham wing of PDP were to be numbered. In July, Amin took over executive responsibility for defence, although Taraki remained nominally responsible and Commander-in-Chief of the Armed Forces. At the same time Colonel Watanyar was demoted from Defence to the still important Interior Ministry, and the Interior Minister was moved to Border Affairs.

More disturbing was the ferocity of Amin's punitive raids on recalcitrant villages. It is clear not only from Karmal's subsequent denunciatory catalogue of his crimes, but also from numerous rebel sources that children were being tortured and butchered before their parents' eyes, villages were razed to the ground and their entire populations either massacred or forcibly moved to other parts of the country.

In an unconvincing attempt to explain the total inability of the government to control many areas in a country which it claimed to be "98 per cent behind the revolution" the state-controlled media put out a steady spate of accusations of "foreign intervention by Iranian and Pakistani imperialists sending troops disguised as civilians into Afghanistan". The United States and China were inevitably bracketed in these accusations, although publicly, at least, America had done no more than stress through one or two influential senators and at the UN that outside intervention in the troubled affairs of Afghanistan should at all costs be avoided! The governments of Iran and Pakistan repeatedly denied that they played any role in the insurgency within Afghanistan, other than as humanitarian hosts to refugees. International reaction was succinctly summed up by the Indian Prime Minister, Morarji Desai – so very different from Mrs Gandhi's view that Pakistan was to blame for everything – when he told President Brezhnev that "the Kabul government should try to acquire credibility among the Afghan people instead of blaming Pakistani interference for its troubles".

It is not easy to trace clearly the events that led Amin to dispense with the umbrella of Taraki's reputation and replace him as Head of State. Taraki made a visit to Moscow in September 1979 during which his sponsors expressed their disquiet at the imminent prospect of a successful right-wing counter-revolution if Amin's brutalities were not halted. Such a view accorded with Taraki's own repugnance at the retributive policies of his powerful Prime Minister, but that same squeamishness led him to forego the usual Afghan argument of a bullet in the brain and try persuasion. Amin was quick to see what was in the wind. When Watanyar issued orders for the arrest of the Prime Minister and key supporters, Amin countermanded them and organized his own counter-stroke.

On the same day it appears that the Russian Ambassador later invited Amin and Taraki to a meeting, ostensibly to discuss the current situation but in practice, it seems, to neutralize Amin. In the ensuing shootout, however, it was Taraki who was fatally wounded, although Kabul radio kept up the pretence that he was alive for some two weeks and then suggested that he had died from natural causes. Taraki's pictures vanished from public places within days of the shooting incident, and as early as September 17 Moscow had cut its losses and endorsed the new incumbent in a congratulatory telegram. The following week Russian combat troops entered Afghanistan in strength for the first time. The three battalions involved were probably largely made up of the specialist troops used to make ready the way for more substantial forces – as they had in Czechoslovakia. It is difficult to believe that this was done without the consent of Amin, if not by his direct invitation.

During the same week Amin made sweeping cabinet changes to bring in his own men, including his brother as Chief of Intelligence, and dismissed the governors of a number of provinces. He was faced, however, with the virtually insoluble problem presented by the fact that even at the height of its success the PDP probably had no more than 5,000–6,000 members, a figure drastically reduced by the internecine quarrels of the previous 18 months. Outsiders would clearly have to be brought in and there would be few of these to be found in Afghanistan itself. The Afghan armed services were already threaded through with an extensive network of Soviet advisers, even down to company level. In order to ensure loyalty Amin had no option but to further extend this network.

Amin's regime was short-lived and expired in as thick a cloud of mystery as that in which it was born. Although rebel claims to control half the country's 26 provinces were certainly exaggerated, there were unarguably major "no-go" areas for the government. By tacit admission Badakshan in the north-east was virtually in Tajik and Pathan hands. The Hazarajat, Nuristan and large parts of the provinces of Paktya and Kunar had also broken free of government control. Incidents such as that in which an Afghan army unit, sent to attack Hazara rebels in Wardak, simply handed over its weapons to them, made certain control beyond the capital almost impossible.

Against this deteriorating background it seems to me perfectly plausible that Amin did ask for Soviet military help. How else can one explain the fact that he did not publicly object to the arrival of Soviet airborne troops on December 17* – at least a week before he fell from power? After all, such an objection, if they had been present against his will, would have been both politically expedient – in demonstrating to the tribesmen that he was independent of Russia – and diplomatically expedient – in enlisting world opinion to forestall the more massive Soviet intervention which followed. It seems more likely that following the invasion he was killed by accident when his bodyguard started fighting the "protective" encircling Russians, or that he was simply doublecrossed. In view of his response to Taraki's earlier suggestion that he step aside, Amin may well have reacted violently again to the proposal that he quietly make way for the very men he had banished and was killed by the Russian troops of General Viktor Paputin, the Soviet general in charge of the coup. The embarrassment caused by the elimination of the one man who could "legitimize" their invasion would have infuriated the Russian leadership, already frustrated at the major failure in their foreign policy implicit in the necessity to intervene militarily in Afghanistan.

The best was made of a bad job on December 27 by announcing that Amin had been "executed" in the hope that this would win Karmal some support among those who had been outraged by Amin's atrocities. The anticipated anger of the Politburo would certainly account for General Paputin's suicide soon afterwards. But speculation, though it may be

*My sources always insisted that small numbers of specialist airborne forces arrived in Afghanistan to secure airfields and other key points ten days before the officially acknowledged date of December 27. This fits in logically with a timetable of events initiated by Brezhnev and the Politburo inner cabinet on December 12.

fun, is quite irrelevant, since it had long been apparent that without the Soviet prop, any left-wing reformist government in Kabul must fall in the face of reaction. So thin were the remaining ranks of indigenous Marxists that there were scarcely any members of the PDP in Karmal's government.

The pattern of the Soviet invasion is interesting. Once the advance units had secured the key airfields of Bagram and Kabul in late autumn, the invasion was spearheaded by the elite of the Soviet armed forces – the Airborne Divisions. These seven divisions (a division is made up of three regiments of three battalions, each containing about 400 to 500 men) were the best trained, best paid and best equipped in the USSR. Indeed it was their equipment, the ASU 85 armoured infantry fighting vehicle and the new AKS 74 automatic rifle, which betrayed the identity of these early troops, although they were not displaying their normal insignia when they first invaded. The Airborne Divisions (the 4th and 105th were probably involved, although regiments from others may have been included to "blood" a good cross-section) do not come under any army command, answering directly to the Politburo. A large proportion of the other ranks are also regulars (in contrast to the rest of the army, in which they are virtually all conscripts) and members of the Communist Party or Komsomol, thus suiting them to politically sensitive tasks. They are also almost all Greater (i.e. European) Russians, unlike other units of the Russian army, where, right down to company level, the races are deliberately mixed. The back-up troops, numbering some 80,000 by the beginning of March 1980, were probably of this mixed nature, although such is the flexibility of the Soviet army that while there may have been an initial preponderance of troops from the Asiatic republics, many of them were reported to have been replaced by non-Asian troops in March.

The main army invaded almost entirely through the long-prepared Kushka/Herat highway and through the Oxus ports of Termez and Sher Khan Banda and down the Kunduz/Kabul road. The Russian advisers were able to neutralize many of the units to which they were attached and for the first time an Afghan coup was carried out entirely by Russian troops.

Unpopular as Amin was, no Afghan unit could be counted on to participate in what was virtually a foreign invasion. By the end of December, while the West still digested its turkey and Christmas pudding, the Russians had occupied all the key towns, airfields and highways before the winter snows had completely restricted movement and reduced guerrilla actions to bands of small number. The Soviet Invasion had begun. It was not to end for another nine years.

10

THE BEAR BURNS ITS PAWS

The nine-year invasion of Afghanistan by the Soviet Union may conveniently be considered in purely military terms in four overlapping phases.

Phase One was short-lived, as the extent of spontaneous opposition at local level to both the Kabul regime's forces and their Soviet allies increased and their large-scale sweeps proved largely ineffective because of the fragmented nature of the various mujehadin groups. From the outset units of the Kabul regime's forces were defecting with their weapons and equipment to the still rather primitively armed mujehadin. Russian troops kept a low profile and were seldom engaged in direct combat with Afghans, except in dealing with rebellious units of the Afghan army or when Afghan troops faced certain defeat, as they did at Faizabad in January. Soviet-piloted helicopter gunships and MiG 21s had, on the other hand, carried out many strikes, although the majority of air attacks had been flown by Soviet-trained Afghan pilots. Until the summer of 1980 Russian forces could have disengaged relatively easily and quickly. Thereafter, without some accommodation with the freedom fighters, such a withdrawal would have been fraught with military hazard. The ferocity and fanaticism of Afghan reaction were underestimated by the Russians, many of whom were quite genuinely shocked to find that they were not welcomed as liberators but execrated as invaders.

During Phase Two, from late 1980 onwards, although Soviet involvement was now more direct and substantial, there was still some hope that the timescale for a major withdrawal and handover to Kabul's forces would be relatively short, being measured in months rather than years. Throughout 1981 there was intensified aerial bombardment of such mujehadin targets as could be located. Then, as in 2001, bombing the Afghans was no more effective than tossing a rock into a pond to empty it: it makes plenty of noise and a big splash and all but a few drops of water flow back to where they were before. Numerous smaller-scale offensives, rather than the major sweeps of the initial phase, backed up the bombing. The aim was to secure major bases and cities and, although this was largely achieved, little else was accomplished in the way of field victories over the mujehadin, despite their relatively low level of outside help. Soviet troops, mostly conscripts now, seemed reluctant to follow up heavy bombardment of enemy positions with the necessary infantry support which would have entailed leaving the relative protection of their armoured columns.

Phase Three began in 1982, as it became increasingly apparent that Afghan forces were often unreliable and the trickle of defections to the mujehadin became a flood. The Soviets resigned themselves to a long haul, although even then there were advocates of withdrawal in the Politburo. In 1983 Andropov told the UN Secretary-General that he had a plan for an eight-month programme for withdrawal. So icy was the Cold War at this time that the US turned the tentative offer down, although Pakistan was willing to ignore American advice and consider it. The tactic of the large-scale sweep by mainly Soviet troops was resumed but now in coordination with helicopter-mobile deployment to surround mujehadin strongholds and resistance points. By now the Soviet air force was implementing a sustained aerial bombardment intended both to depopulate combat areas and to destroy the means of sustenance for the mujehadin – by 1989 agricultural production was less than half what it had been in 1979.

Particularly effective in this regard was the systematic blowing up of the centuries-old Qanat irrigation systems.

Air raids were followed up by ground forces and high-quality troops deployed by helicopter behind a mujehadin band, but still within range of an artillery umbrella thus catching the enemy between the "hammer and anvil" of these two forces. Among the operations of this phase were a number of fruitless assaults on Ahmed Shah Masood's stronghold in the Panshir Valley in which government forces suffered heavy losses while Masood's casualties were probably less than 10 per cent.

In 1983 the Masood problem was temporarily solved by making a one-year truce with him which Kabul would come to regret. During this lull in fighting, Masood used his undoubted military genius* to begin the organization of mujehadin in other parts of Dari-speaking northern Afghanistan on a more professional basis – a move that would prove very effective in the later stages of the war. No doubt recognizing its mistake, KhAD, Karmal's secret police, headed by Najibullah, tried to assassinate him in 1984. However, the agent they employed was a double and handed over his 24-man hit squad to the Panshiris as soon as they reached the valley. Masood was not to be so lucky in September 2001 when he was killed in a suicide bomb attack. His death was seen by some as a preliminary to the September 11 World Trade Center massacre and a severe blow to the anti-Taliban forces. While his military gifts will undoubtedly be missed by the Northern Alliance, his demise may turn out to be a blessing in disguise because it removes the one man willing and capable of imposing an unforgiving minority Tajik government on the

---

*Rogers, Tom, The Soviet Withdrawal from Afghanistan (see reading list at the end of the book) takes a slightly more cynical view of Masood's reputation, but whatever the exact balance between reality and perception, the psychological impact of the image was highly significant both within and outside Afghanistan.

whole of Afghanistan and restarting the whole sorry cycle that began in 1992.

Phase Four of the war crept up on the Soviet invaders by stages. In the winter of 1985\6 they seemed to have achieved a number of significant victories as a result of Gorbachev's last push for a military solution. But these were victories Pyrrhus would have been glad to acknowledge. Soviet and government losses were high and the military objectives were seldom held for long before being relinquished to the ever-present and persistent mujehadin. I suspect it was these "victories" rather than the numerous minor defeats that finally confirmed Gorbachev in his view that withdrawal at the earliest opportunity was the only sensible option.

The scale of the Soviet campaign had been colossal. Soviet troop strength varied from 94,000 to 104,000 – half the US numbers in Vietnam in a land five times as big. A total of 642,000 Soviet troops passed through Afghanistan as part of a deliberate policy of rotation. Such a large number of witnesses to how badly the war was going made the censorship that presented a rosy patriotic success look highly cynical. Moreover, this was an army which had been trained to fight an enemy supposed obligingly to take up defensive positions across a wide front rather than scatter like mice when confronted by superior force.

When the war was over senior analysts of the Soviet Frunze Military Academy made a remarkably candid assessment of the reasons for their failure, albeit in the stilted soldierspeak that seems common the world over. Their description of mujehadin tactics is worth quoting in full:

> Several combat principles lay at the heart of mujehadeen tactics. First, they avoided direct contact with the superior might of regular forces which could have wiped them out.

Second the mujehadeen practically never conducted positional warfare and, when threatened with encirclement, would abandon their positions. Third in all forms of combat the mujehadeen always strove to achieve surprise. Fourth the mujehadeen employed terror and ideological conditioning on a peaceful populace as well as on local government representatives.

The mujehadeen knew the terrain intimately, were natural scouts, and were capable of transmitting the necessary information about secret Soviet unit and subunit movements over great distances using rudimentary communications gear and signaling devices. [Echoes of the nineteenth-century heliographs that tracked the British army's retreat from Kabul].

Among the guerrilla forces tactical strong suits were all types of night actions, the ability to rapidly and clandestinely move in the mountains, and the fielding of a very broad agent reconnaissance network.

A copy of the Frunze report should lie on Colin Powell's desk permanently open at this page!

In the course of the conflict 14,263 Soviet combatants were killed or reported missing presumed killed, 49,985 were wounded (i.e. permanently or long-term unfit for combat duties) and almost three-quarters of the entire Soviet forces employed were either minor casualties or were incapacitated by disease. However, heavy as the casualties may seem, they were incurred at only half the annual rate of fatalities in the peacetime Soviet forces. It was the manner and concentration of the losses in Afghanistan that had such adverse repercussions at home. Death in combat in an unpopular war is a very different thing from a peacetime accident. Astonishingly to anyone who was unfamiliar with the history and topography of Afghanistan, this considerable force was unable to provide security much beyond the major cities and selected supply routes. Soviet material losses, often through capture by the mujehadin, were substantial; 118 jets, 333 helicopters, 147 tanks, 1,314 APCs, 433 artillery pieces and mortars and 11,369 trucks.

Afghan casualties are harder to estimate. Well over a million Afghans died, many more were wounded and more than six million were driven into exile. The worst military casualties came when the mujehadin's foreign military advisers mistakenly talked them into fighting the fixed battles to which their style of warfare was quite unsuited. The main killers of Afghan civilians were the millions (as many as ten million) of land and anti-personnel mines, sewn by the contending forces, the majority unmapped, It is estimated that more than five million unexploded mines still lie in the ground. It is astonishing that some American feminists should have called for the suspension of the UN mine-clearing programme because of Taliban policy towards women – who along with children are the principal peacetime victims of landmines.

The financial cost of the Soviet–Mujehadin war is dwarfed by the social, military and economic costs we have already considered, but, in so far as it is measurable, it does give some indication of the colossal scale of the conflict. We have to distinguish between governmental contributions and private ones although the complex and clandestine nature of all these transactions makes any attempt to quantify them except in orders of magnitude highly suspect. The United States admits to approximately $10 billion during the course of the war and the Saudi government contributed a similar sum. Other Mujehadin backers, Pakistan in particular, also made smaller cash payments but enormous contributions in kind – especially weapons, munitions, fuel and training. My guess is that these probably amounted to as much as the state's cash contributions.

Then there were the large private donations, mostly from Muslims, all around the world but particularly in Saudi Arabia and the Gulf. Osama bin Laden, at this time a highly esteemed conduit for CIA and Saudi intelligence funds, used his construction companies to build bunkers, arms depots, roads and many other facilities for the mujehadin groups he favoured. He also acted as a major collecting and distribution agent for other large-scale donors, particularly Saudi businessmen and religious charities. These private contributions may have amounted to between $10 billion and $12 billion and continued to flow to the mujehadin groups and foreign mujehadin when official sources dried up. We are looking, I believe, at a figure of $75 billion to $100 billion over the ten-year course of the war.

On the Soviet side the cost was that firstly of sustaining a nine-year war and then of upholding a Marxist government for a further two years at some $2 billion to $3 billion a year. The cost alone of paying 100,000 officers and men, even at the Red Army's meagre rates, was probably of the order of $1 billion. The materiel costs must have been between 30 and 40 times that if you consider that in one year (admittedly the worst) the value of aircraft lost alone was $2.5 billion.

In February 1986, at the 27th Congress of the Communist Party of the Soviet Union, Gorbachev went public with what seems to have been in his mind since shortly after he came to power. He indicated that he wished to withdraw Soviet forces and he described Afghanistan as "a bleeding wound". Afghanistan was a problem he wanted speedily resolved because it was a distraction from far more important matters nearer to home. His initial policy, however, was to intensify the military action. This was a hedged bet. Either victory would be achieved – or something sufficiently like it to guarantee keeping the PDPA government in power for some years – or conditions would be created for a safe Soviet withdrawal that would also satisfy the military hawks.

If Pakistan, Saudi Arabia and the United States had had the foresight to restrain rather than encourage their protégés it might not have taken a further three years to evict the Soviet forces. However, President Reagan wanted to see the bear get its paws burnt, so he actually stepped up the supply of military equipment at this point. In August 1984 Reagan had authorized military supplies for the mujehadin at the rate of $280 million a month. In April 1985 he announced that the effort to drive out the Russians was to be conducted "by all means available" – some of them, as it transpired, highly dubious. The US President also announced that America would supply the mujehadin with Stinger ground-to-air missiles and the training to use them. They first came into Afghan hands in September 1986 and immediately altered the course of the war from stalemate to a Soviet resignation of the Great Game as its aircraft losses began to run at the rate of almost one a day. Consequently, it lost the ability to offer air cover to its troops on the ground. Nearly half of all Soviet aircraft losses were sustained in 1987. Thereafter the rate fell as Soviet strategy switched to the use of the pandemonic but less effective BM22 long-range Multiple Rocket Launcher. The critical question in the winter of 2001/2 is how many Stingers remain in Taliban hands.

The US delivered approximately 900. A small number of other Stingers, including copies, were given by supportive regimes, although the United States kept a pretty tight control on who got their hands on them. Even its European allies were barred from selling them on. The total supplied was probably between 1,000 and 1,100. In addition there were smaller numbers of British Blowpipe and Russian SAM 7 ground-to-air missiles. If the reported 75 per cent mujehadin hit rate is accurate and allowing for aircraft brought down by other means, then no more than 400 or 500 were used against Soviet aircraft. A few Stingers were captured by Soviet troops and a few more were sold after the war by mujehadin leaders – for example, 16 for $1 million by Hekmatyar to the Iranian Revolutionary Guards. At a conservative estimate, despite the secret (and unsuccessful) CIA attempt to buy them back, there are some 300 to 400 still in Afghanistan, the great majority in Taliban hands.

Although these Stingers are officially obsolete they do have a much longer shelf life if properly cared for. The ancillary equipment needed to fire them accurately may be harder to maintain effectively. Counter-measures have also been developed by the Americans, but are by no means foolproof. If even a quarter of the remaining Stingers were to find their targets it would cause serious, and perhaps unacceptable, losses to US Alliance helicopters and ground support aircraft. The Taliban will not have been so foolish as to waste them on the high-altitude bombers with which the US October 2001 bombardment began. But I am getting ahead of the story.

In addition to Gorbachev's political change of heart, 1986 saw two critical military developments. The one most often referred to was the introduction of Stinger ground-to-air missiles in September 1986 discussed above. The other, no less significant in its way but seldom mentioned, was Masood's development of both his strategy and his tactics. The "Tajik Napoleon" created a number of 120-man special units whose members were drawn from all parts of the north, not just the Panshir, and were paid salaries, thus freeing them from sumptuary dependence on a local home base. These units could be deployed for action in any part of northern Afghanistan – from Mazar to the outskirts of Kabul itself.

Supported by a well-integrated political and logistic organization they quickly achieved spectacular success. They staged a devastating attack on the Bagram airbase, frequently disrupted the all-important Salang highway with well-targeted ambushes, and even captured the garrison town of Farkhar. Prior to this, attacks on garrisons were almost invariably launched only by those mujehadin whose home bases were nearest. Thus in 1986, the impact of the Stingers, the greater cohesion and mobility of mujehadin forces and Gorbachev's change of strategy decisively altered the outcome of the Soviet invasion as it entered its final phase – Soviet withdrawal.

The Soviet forces managed their retreat by handing over outlying garrisons they had previously manned themselves to Afghan government troops and concentrating their own men in and around half-a-dozen more defensible cities and air bases. As a consequence many of the abandoned outposts either went over to the mujehadin or were easily overrun. On June 18 Kalat became the first provincial capital to fall to the mujehadin since the war had begun. The "anvil" was thus removed from the Soviet military equation and Red Army strategy transformed into a defensive one.

The larger mujehadin groups eventually decided not to harass the retreating enemy for fear of delaying the withdrawal, but, excited by their minor triumphs, many of the smaller independent mujehadin commands continued to do so relentlessly. So piqued was the Soviet command by the constant attacks that on November 5 it protested to America, halted the retreat and threatened to return. The US said and did nothing, knowing full well, as indeed did the Russians, that the withdrawal process was by this stage irreversible without a far greater involvement than the Soviet Union, with its commitment to perestroika, was prepared to make. Nor were the desperate tricks and blandishments of Najibullah able to delay the inevitable. The retreat resumed.

Not only did the arrival of Gorbachev in the Kremlin signal a change in the Soviet approach to Afghanistan, but as a consequence it altered the power structure in the Kabul government itself. Three months after his "bleeding wound" speech, Gorbachev decided that Karmal was the wrong doctor to staunch the flow of blood and would have to go. Atypically for Afghanistan he was quietly flown out to Moscow and replaced by Najibullah, his loyal right-hand man and head of the dreaded secret police, the KhAD. Despite the change at the top of the Afghan government, there was no improvement in the military situation. On December 12 1986, seven years to the day since the Politburo inner cabinet had decided to send Soviet troops into Afghanistan, Najibullah was summoned to Moscow to be told that they would definitely be leaving. He pleaded in vain for a stay of what he must have sensed would be his own execution, but earned only the partial reprieve of promised financial and munitions support. Some of the weaponry the Soviets left him turned out to be too sophisticated to be much use to the technically unskilled officers and men of the Afghan military. Even more debilitating than technical ignorance was the long-standing rivalry within the armed forces between the Khalq and Parchami factions which even the prospect of losing Soviet military support could not abate.

Alarmed by the apparent imminence of Soviet withdrawal, Najibullah went on the diplomatic offensive. In January 1987 Najibullah's declaration of a unilateral ceasefire and call for a government of national unity and reconciliation stimulated the moribund diplomatic process presided over by the UN and what was by now Geneva VII resumed.

The prospects for a settlement only really improved with Gorbachev's visit to Washington in December 1987 when he privately told the Americans he was willing to pull out. In January 1980 Brezhnev had gone on television to tell the Russian public why Soviet forces were "going to the aid of a friendly regime". On February 8 1988 Gorbachev told the television audience that he proposed to pull out starting on May 15 and that they would see the last Soviet uniformed soldier cross the Oxus on his way home by February 15 1989.

The Geneva talks that had begun as far back as June 1982 were handicapped from the outset by the fact that both the mujehadin and Moscow had been represented only at second hand. On April 14 1988 the Geneva Accord that eventually emerged from Geneva VII was signed by America, Russia, Pakistan and Najibullah's Kabul government. The mujehadin were not even party to the discussions, let alone signatories of the Accord.

Apart from the timetable for the withdrawal of Soviet forces, none of the terms were observed in either spirit or practice by any of the parties. I shall not, therefore, pursue the intricate and protracted detail of the numerous Geneva conferences, from I to VI, that led up to it. Suffice it to say that in theory the US, the USSR, and Pakistan conditionally agreed to cease military support for their respective protégés, to withdraw from the arena and to endorse a neutral government for Afghanistan. Pakistan and Afghanistan agreed not to interfere in each other's affairs. Having had no say in the matter, most of the mujehadin had either never heard of the Geneva Accord or ignored it completely. Gulbadin Hekmatyar went so far as to denounce it as a conspiracy entered into by his bete noire, America, with the Russians. While that was probably true only in the tacit sense, the sheer lunacy of the proviso that the Accord was not a peace treaty so that the US and the USSR were entitled to go on arming their respective Afghan allies shows that it was entered into with fairly cynical intent on both sides.

Surprisingly, perhaps, the timetable for withdrawal was scrupulously adhered to. Intensified mujehadin harassment of the withdrawing Soviet army at the behest of the US provoked angry responses from Moscow, but by then it would have been impossible to reverse the retreat. In a symbolic gesture, General Boris Gromov, the last uniformed Soviet soldier to leave Afghanistan, walked across the bridge over the Oxus at Termez on St Valentine's Day 1989 exactly as promised. As the general told reporters, "This is the day millions of Soviet people have been waiting for. The nine year war is over." Of course, it was not, but the means of waging it had changed.

In 1993 the Russian military analysts Sarin and Dvoretsky could openly confess that the Soviet leadership had been "responsible for millions of killed and wounded Afghans, not only the mujehadin, but civilians as well. The thousands of killed and crippled Soviet soldiers were the result of Soviet military interference in the home affairs of another country." As they said, "The Soviet Union we have known and served faithfully has ceased to exist." The very fact that such a statement could be made showed just how much the situation had changed. Their conclusions about the effect of the war on Russia itself are worth repeating. "Probably none of the Soviet leaders who made the decision to give military support to the PDPA could have seen the economic and social damage their act was to inflict on the Soviet Union itself… What the Afghan war did to the Soviet people was to make them become more aware of their own problems."

Thus ended the first failure of Soviet arms since the Second World War and so closed a disastrous episode in Soviet history. On February 16 President George Bush announced that America would continue to support the rebels.

The role of the war in contributing to the collapse of Communism in the Soviet Union is not part of this study, but four main effects can briefly be summarized.

1. Belief in Soviet ability always to impose cohesion by military means had been destroyed.
2. This changed the perception of the ability of the Red Army to hold the empire together with such eventual consequences as the rebellion and declaration of independence in Chechnya.
3. The Red Army itself was discredited, which encouraged the non-Russian republics to push for greater autonomy.
4. The effect of reporting in the media, which censorship was unable completely to curb, and the hearsay evidence of returning veterans weakened the grip of the Communist Party and legitimized challenges by non-Russians to Russian rule.

Apart from staunching the "bleeding wound", Gorbachev had achieved none of his long-term objectives in withdrawing from Afghanistan. There was no US undertaking to cease supplying the mujehadin with arms and there was no guarantee of a neutral Afghanistan, let alone one acknowledged as being within the Soviet sphere of influence. In fact the then US Secretary of State George Schultz made it clear that America would continue to equip the mujehadin until the Soviet Union stopped supplying Najibullah's Kabul regime. By this policy America hoped a broad-based mujehadin government would quickly oust Najibullah and take power. Wrong again, as we shall see in the next chapter. However, one thing that Gorbachev did gain, which he needed as much as an Afghan victory, was the lifting of the West's crippling trade embargo on the high-technology products Russia urgently needed to reconstruct its faltering economy.

Only after the failed coup in Moscow in August 1991 did Russia stop underwriting the Najibullah regime and thereby signal its rapid demise. In April 1992, after the usual defections and betrayals, it duly fell and Najibullah, cut off from the airport, sought refuge in the UN compound in Kabul.

But, tragically, a new and even bloodier phase of the Afghan civil war was about to begin. Those "glorious mujehadin" who had inflicted a "signal catastrophe"* on the fabled Red Army and the Soviet air force as their forbears had done on the British retreating from Kabul in 1842 conspicuously failed to unite to pluck the fruits of victory and bring peace to a united and victorious country.

So who were these men who, from being heroes in the eyes of the world, were soon deemed to be little more than self-serving bandits?

---

*A highly entertaining account of this British military disaster is given in Patrick Macrory's book Signal Catastrophe: The Retreat from Kabul.

11
FIGHTERS FOR GOD?

The roots of the mujehadin can be traced back to the perennial recalcitrance of all Afghans. No one tells a Pathan – or a Tajik, an Uzbeg, or a Hazara – what to do except his father, his khan or his mullah. Long before the Soviet invasion, the founders of the mujehadin had been protesting, more or less violently, against Daoud and then the PDP of Taraki and Amin. Of these mujehadin groups, ten play major roles in the story of the resistance. The story is greatly complicated by the patronage of the mujehadin by outside backers all with objectives only tenuously connected to the welfare of the Afghans. In Afghanistan there were more fingers than pie, so we shall try to establish whose were the stickiest!

In talking about the diverse and disparate movement loosely referred to as the mujehadin we must first define our terms. As all parties are devout Muslims, I shall follow the broad terminology suggested by the French Afghan specialist Olivier Roy. Rather than the pejorative "fundamentalist" and the usually misleading "moderate" I shall refer to them as the radical parties on the one hand, and the traditionalist on the other. Within most parties views could range from fairly traditionalist radicals to almost radical traditionalists! I shall sometimes refer to the parties and groups as Pathan, Uzbeg and so on, by which it should be understood that those are the ethnic groups predominating, but, with the exception of a few of the Pathan organizations, nearly all parties also embrace mujehadin of other races. It is also necessary occasionally to discriminate between the parties formed by the leading political figures and the combat groups in Afghanistan connected to them with varying degrees of loyalty and closeness. It will, I hope, be obvious from the context when I refer individually to a particular leader and when the reference also incorporates his supporters.

The seven Sunni parties of the mujehadin all eventually based themselves in Peshawar. Only one of these, the root stock Tajik Jamiat-i-Islami (Jamiat)* was not Pathan – as might be expected along the North-West Frontier of Pakistan. Intriguingly, none of the other six was led by Durrani Pathans from the tribe that had ruled Afghanistan for most of the previous two hundred years. Four of the seven were radical parties.

Jamiat was founded in 1972 by Burhannudin Rabbani. Rabbani was a Tajik and a multilingual, highly cultivated Islamic theologian at Kabul University. He believed that all aspects of society should be shaped by Islam but that the wider beliefs and traditions of Afghanistan, particularly the custom of collective decision-making down to the very lowest level, must also be accommodated in the civil structure. Fearful that Daoud might curb his opposition in the traditional Afghan way, Rabbani fled to Pakistan. He was later joined there by Ahmed Shah Masood, a young student from the resistance-fecund engineering faculty of Kabul University. Masood was to become the master tactician of the guerrilla campaign against the Russians. In his early days in Pakistan he and a fellow engineering student in Jamiat, Gulbedin Hekmatyar, quarrelled often and bitterly over the direction their party should take, generating a personal enmity which was to have serious repercussions for Afghan unity in the years ahead. As one of his spokesmen once announced, "Hekmatyar cannot agree to anything that includes Ahmed Shah Masood".

The abbreviations in brackets are how these organizations will be referred to hereafter.

So acute did their rivalry become that in 1979 Hekmatyar broke away from Jamiat to form Hizb-i-Islami (Hizb). The only secular leader of the seven Sunni parties, Hekmatyar was nevertheless the most radical in his pursuit of an absolutely Islamic state. This became evident from his brief tenure as Prime Minister in 1996 when he began to insist on the observance of purdah and other restrictive Muslim practices. He rejected the dominance of the ulema and what we might think of as an accumulated body of case law created by precedent established in the light of changing circumstances that modified basic doctrine. For Hekmatyar it was always "back to basics". Paradoxically, however, he modelled his party organization on the cellular structure of the Communist Party of the Soviet Union. A senior Pakistani army officer described him as, "not only the youngest but the toughest and most vigorous of all the mujehadin leaders in Pakistan. He was a staunch believer in an Islamic government for Afghanistan, an excellent administrator. Despite his comparative wealth he lives a frugal life. He is also ruthless, arrogant, inflexible, a stern disciplinarian, and he does not get on with Americans."

The Americans were to discover this for themselves when, having blindly picked Hekmatyar as their favourite recipient of aid and arms, he sank his teeth into the feeding hand. Not that his fellow countrymen fared much better – he is reputed to have killed more Afghans than Russians, 25,000 in Kabul alone.

To ensure both ideological control and attract as many recruits as possible, Hizb established its own educational institutions, orphanages and refugee camps. So exclusive was Hekmatyar's approach that not only did recruits have to undergo a probationary period, but he also vetoed all political cooperation with the traditionalist parties, especially the more liberal, such as Gailani's. But while he made no political deals, temporary military alliances were another matter, provided they suited his immediate aims. These were made and broken equally casually.

The next radical party, Hizb-i-Islami (Khalis), was to splinter from Hekmatyar's splinter almost immediately. This party was founded by Mohammed Yunus Khalis, a Deobandi-trained tribal leader from Paktia who, like so many others, had fled to Pakistan to escape the Daoud regime. From there he attracted a following of religious leaders and local commanders in south-east Afghanistan over whom he presided autocratically. Mullah Omar, the Taliban leader, is reputed to have joined and done his fighting with Khalis.

The final member of the radical group was Abdul Rasul Sayyaf, another theology academic from Kabul and once Rabbani's deputy. He is probably best known to the world at large as the man whose mujehadin, after the Soviet withdrawal, moved to the Philippines. There, under his name, they wreaked havoc, aiding their fellow Muslims in rebellion against the government. His party, Ittihad-i-Islami (Ittihad), had little indigenous support outside Kabul, but its Arabic-speaking leader secured a disproportionately large share of Saudi Arabian finance. Ittihad denies being Wahabi, but not very convincingly, and is particularly hostile to Shi'a Muslims. Sayyaf was briefly jailed by the PDP before fleeing to Pakistan.

The oldest, and in many ways the most revered, of the southern mujehadin leaders was Sibghatullah Mojadidi. In 1959 Daoud lost patience with this former radical with connections with the Muslim Brotherhood in Egypt and put him in prison for four-and-a-half years when he campaigned against a visit by the Soviet premier Khruschev. In 1980 Mojadidi founded the first of our three traditionalist parties, the Afghan National Liberation Front (ANLF). Coming from a prominent Pathan family, Mojadidi drew his support from the Afghan peasantry, but got little from the armouries of the West.

Harakat-i-Inqilab-i-Islami is usually also classed as a traditionalist party, but it drew its support from the ulema and the mullahs and students of the madrasahs. It was founded by Nabi Muhammadi, whose non-political insistence on strict adherence to the Shari'at was not dissimilar to that of the Taliban. Immensely popular during the immediate aftermath of the Soviet invasion it was too badly organized and unfocussed to sustain its momentum and adherents leaked away to Jamiat and Khalis.

Mahaz-i-Milli-i-Islami (Mahaz), the National Islamic Front for Afghanistan, was the party with which Western intellectuals felt it easiest to identify. Its leader Pir Sayed Gailani, a hereditary Sufi spiritual leader, is urbane and relatively liberal in outlook. Connected by marriage to both Zahir Shah and Daoud, he espouses the return of the monarchy as the means of restabilizing Afghanistan. Many Afghan intellectuals were drawn to his party which had its strongest popular support in what later became the Taliban core of Kandahar.

In 1980 these three traditionalist parties formed an alliance, the National Liberation Front of Afghanistan (NLFA), which outlasted the Soviet invasion and was, at one time, seen by the UN as the possible basis for a post-Soviet government. Not until May 1985 did all seven Sunni parties form a nominal coalition, the Ittihad-i-Islami Mujehadin Afghanistan (the Alliance of Islamic Warriors of Afghanistan), but Hekmatyar's support for this coalition was lukewarm at best and all seven kept a weather eye out for the best way to strengthen their own positions. At first the US did not seem to understand that they needed to supply seven different armies fighting seven different wars. It may have been America's belated recognition of the confusion that this could cause that led them to plump so heavily for the ISI favourite, Hekmatyar.

The Shi'a Muslim heartland in Afghanistan lies in the Hazarajat and there the eight* larger groups, under pressure from their Iranian Shi'a paymasters, also eventually agreed in June 1987 to coordinate their efforts in a single organization known as Hizb-i-Wahdat (Wahdat). This all-Hazara force was led by Abdul Ali Mazari, who recognized that only a unified Shi'a voice could hope to be heard in the haggle for power after the Russians withdrew. The infighting between Shi'a groups in the Hazarajat was unfettered by external threats from either government or Soviet troops. The internecine struggle between radical and traditionalist groups in this part of the country was a harbinger of what was to afflict all Afghanistan once the Soviet army had left. There was also a Hazara mujehadin group, Harakat-i-Islami, that retained its independence of action, by declining Iranian support. It was led by Sheikh Asef Mohsini, who often acted as an acceptably neutral intermediary in negotiations between mujehadin of all allegiances.

One of the most influential and volatile participants in the ebb and flow of both mujehadin and post-Soviet power politics was Abdul Rashid Dostam. Dostam commanded a large force of Uzbegs, at its peak numbering as many as 25,000, who were based on Mazar-i-Sharif. Interestingly, this group was usually referred to by its leader's name rather than as the National Islamic Movement. Dostam, who had once been a general in Najibullah's army, should properly be termed a warlord rather than a mujehadin leader, for, despite his involvement with the Northern Alliance, he showed almost as much skill in opportunist coat-changing as Hekmatyar. His

---

At one time I was told that there were as many as sixty of these based in Iran amongst the refugees who had fled west.

troops came to be known as the Jauzjani, or "carpet snatchers", for obvious reasons.

Finally, the Persian speakers of Herat and westwards to the Iranian border fought under the inspiring, if not always strategically inspired, Ismail Khan. Another former Afghan army senior officer, Ismail Khan also proved himself a capable civilian administrator who made post-Soviet Herat the envy of the many more turbulent parts of Afghanistan. His group of mujehadin was loosely connected to Jamiat, but in practice it operated quite independently.

The total number of mujehadin in the field at any one time is difficult to estimate accurately, but once the war was well under way it probably slightly exceeded that of the Russians. Like the Red Army the mujehadin rotated many of its combatants, but in a rather different way. Inside Afghanistan itself many would fight for a while, go home to attend to the harvest or for some family crisis, and then return to the "front". Of course, no conventional front existed and for the majority it meant their part of the country whenever Soviet or government forces were in it.

From outside the borders of Afghanistan recruits came from the numerous madrasahs in Pakistan (some 40,000 of them it is estimated) in particular, but also from the orphanages and the refugee camps. To get food and other necessities, the refugees in Pakistan had to join one of the seven recognized parties, thus greatly facilitating recruitment of mujehadin for training. Those condemning the mercenary nature of many recruits should not forget that joining one of the mujehadin groups in or out of Afghanistan was the only way for many Afghan men to provide for their uprooted families.

The other source of recruits for the jihad were the non-Afghans, mainly Saudis and Pakistanis, who joined the fight for a variety of motives, of which more later. This then is the main mujehadin cast list. There were also more than a hundred extras in the shape of highly localized mujehadin commanders who usually only played a part in fighting the Russians in their own areas or in the inter-factionary struggle when it was to their advantage in their own limited regions of influence. A few of these deserve a brief passing mention.

There were a substantial number of Pathans of the Diaspora fighting in the north of the country. The most spectacularly successful of these was Haji Meheidin,* a rough and ready man very different from the sophisticated intellectuals and religious leaders who headed the Pakistan-based groups. Together with the Tajik freedom fighters operating independently in the same province, he had virtually removed Badakshan from Russian and Afghan army control by the spring of 1980. Indeed the Russians had to mount one of their biggest operations to save the government forces in Faizabad from being totally destroyed. Yet the Tajiks and the Pathans in this region had only the most rudimentary liaison. In fact the Tajik group, the Setem-i-Melli, was founded as a political movement to resist Pathan domination. Other centres of non-Pathan resistance were, as might be expected, in the Hazarajat, where ex-MP Wali Beg led a force of some 5,000 Hazara fighting men, the Hedadia Mujaheddin Islam Afghani. These had links with Mohseni's Pathan group in Iran and arms from sympathetic Pathan units in the Afghan regular army.

In Nuristan, where rebellion against the Russian-backed Taraki regime and its successors began, resistance was both fierce and fiercely and brutally repressed. Here Khalilu Nuristani led a group of guerrillas, probably some three or four thousand strong, who received clothes, money and moral

---

See the author's thriller The Queen of Spades, *in which Haji Mehedin and the hero, Alexander Burnes, thwart a Soviet plan to deploy chemical weapons.*

support from Gailani's group. In Baluchistan Mir Chaus Bux Bizenjo, chief of one of the three main Baluch tribes, actively encouraged his clansmen on the Afghan side of the border.

Until a number of intrepid journalists entered Afghanistan itself it was virtually impossible to gauge the effectiveness of the Afghan freedom fighters. The Afghans must be strong contenders for the title of the world's greatest self-deceiving storytellers. If all mujehadin claims were added up, the Russian army would have been wiped out several times over. This is in their classic tradition. A typical example is a village tale of Bachha-i-Saqao, the brigand who seized the throne for a few weeks in 1929. "Shah Wali took a force to Kabul and found Bachha-i-Saqao in the Bala (fort) with only four hundred men. Forty thousand of the army of Shah Wali surrounded the Bacha who came forth alone with machine guns and drove off the entire force."

There is nothing new in the Afghan proclivity for exaggerating military success!

There was some spasmodic cooperation between various groups, but the general pattern was one of a large number of independent guerrilla leaders conducting their feudal, warlord-style campaigns. The Pathans were divided into two main factions and many lesser ones – all wary of each other. The attitude of the non-Pathan mujehadin to the Pathans was encapsulated in the old Tajik proverb "Trust a snake before a harlot and a harlot before a Pathan". There is no doubt of the widespread loathing of the Russians and the determination of the vast majority of the (male) population to resist the invaders at all costs, but this did little to diminish their mutual antipathies. Yes, they were all Muslims, but such an assertion is no more meaningful than lumping together all the numerous and widely differing churches of the United States or Britain as Christians.

While some mujehadin party leaders did take part in the fighting against the Russians, the majority remained outside the actual battle areas of Afghanistan. The battlefield commanders were of necessity younger and more adaptable and pragmatic than their nominal party leaders based in Peshawar. The commanders' links with the parties were inevitably somewhat tenuous and although those in the field usually expressed loyalty to their political leaders, the bonds were seldom strong and often grew weaker as the struggle for power progressed. For lengthy periods these field commanders also came to exercise political, administrative and judicial authority in areas cut off from communication with Peshawar. From mid-1987 onwards they acted ever more independently of their nominal headquarters. In July that year, on the initiative of Ismail Khan, some 1,200 of them met and formed the Allied Commanders' Council (AIC) which resolved that the destiny of Afghanistan should lie in their hands, on the grounds that those who risked their lives should decide the nation's fate. In October, the AIC meeting in Badakshan called on Najibullah to step down and independently offered amnesty to all who would cooperate with them. Najibullah, with substantial Soviet support still behind him, felt no necessity to consider the offer.

No doubt he knew how short lived opposition unity would be. By January the wheels, deals and betrayals were in full spate again as commanders tried to reinforce their personal positions by making their own private arrangements as the prospect of Soviet withdrawal grew stronger. While Masood seemed genuinely to seek "the national unity of all the jihad forces of Afghanistan", a number of his subordinates combined with some of Dostam's Uzbegs and with the Ismaili militia to unseat Najibullah by force when he started filling their posts in the administration with Pathans. They failed and, rather unfairly tarnished by these manoeuvres of his lieutenants, Masood was seen by many Pathans as just another Tajik on the make. Masood thus found himself eventually leading a predominantly non-Pathan* north irrevocably divided against a predominantly Pathan south. By March 1992 the AIC had more or less disintegrated.

Another problem in trying to unite the mujehadin parties was finding a leader of sufficient character and charisma to be acceptable to all them – or even all the Pathans. The Afghans can unite under the leadership of a truly great man, one who fulfils the image described and exemplified by Khushal Khan Khattaq, but these are once-in-a-century figures and there was no sign of one in 1979 (or now for that matter). Candidates, as far as the Pathan groups were concerned, ranged from the slightly absurd suggestion of a "restoration" of Amanullah's son Hassan Durrani, then a parfumier in New York, to a more plausible figurehead, ex-King Zahir Shah (now 86). However, the fact is that mutual suspicion comes much more naturally to the Pathans than mutual admiration and although family, village, clan and tribal loyalties are very important to them, so is their absolute, almost anarchic, love of personal independence. Not for nothing does the Pushtu word for enmity (*turburgalay*) derive from the word for cousin (*tur-bur*).

For all their courage and ferocity the mujehadin would have been fighting the Russians with "a ten rupee jezail"** if it had not been for the material support they received from abroad.

---

*Jamiat, with at least quantifiable numbers of Uzbegs and Pathans among its Tajiks, had the best racial balance of all the mujehadin parties.

**Rudyard Kipling, "Arithmetic on the Frontier"
A scrimmage in some border station
A canter down a dark defile
Two thousand pounds of education
Drops to a ten rupee jezail.

Although it did not seem at first to most outside observers that the resistance was getting much help, it transpired on later analysis that some military and financial support was provided quite quickly. Indeed, the Americans had begun surreptitious assistance in July 1979 before the Soviet Union had actually invaded the country. In their anxiety to defeat the Soviets and generally undermine the USSR none of the eager supporters of the mujehadin seem to have even paused to consider, let alone foresee, the possible consequences of their indiscriminate recruitment of such potentially fissile allies and their boomerang methods.

Let us first consider the second division players. The doubts of the usually cautious and well-informed Afghan desk at the British Foreign Office and its advisers were set aside by Margaret Thatcher's militaristic enthusiasm to seize any stick with which to beat Communism. However, the experts did prevail in so far as the fairly modest amount of British support was directed towards the traditionalists, such as Gailani. This may account for the Afghan and Soviet press, which seemed to be stuck in a time warp, accusing him and Mojadidi of being British agents. The UK also provided training by the SAS, and SAS veterans working through various, rather disreputable private mercenary companies, for a number of mujehadin field officers who were smuggled into Britain as tourists. SAS and ex-SAS also conducted covert operations in Afghanistan itself, usually connected with either supply and training for specialist weapons or missions to bring back specific items of Soviet equipment for analysis. Britain's difficulty was that although its historic involvement with Afghanistan meant that it probably had better intelligence and wiser policies, it was no longer influential enough to ensure that its views prevailed.

Two countries which relied heavily on American patronage, Egypt and Israel, responded quickly to the US diplomatic appeal for arms for the mujehadin. Because Israel's own forces being were equipped with US weapons, it could well afford to release the substantial quantities of Russian weapons that it had captured from Egypt. Some of these were to find their way back into the hands of Hezbollah in the Lebanon and Hamas and other Palestinian terrorist groups to Israel's cost.

At the time of the Soviet invasion of Afghanistan, Egypt had been the inspiration for radical Muslims for 53 years through the example of the Muslim Brotherhood. Although the Islamist Brotherhood had been a permanent itch under the skin of succeeding predominantly secular Egyptian governments, President Sadat was the first to respond to the US plea to supply arms to the mujehadin. At first this consisted of discarded equipment such as obsolete Lee Enfield .303 rifles with which, nevertheless, the superb Afghan marksmen sniped most effectively. Soon, however, they were followed by the latest Russian equipment, particularly the latest models of the peasant-proof Kalashnikov automatic rifles and machine guns. The Russians felt this to be a particularly unkind way for Egypt to repay the generosity of a former friend. Another irony for the Soviets was the purchase of SAM7s from Poland for use against them.

Egyptians were among the most numerous foreign recruits to the jihad and the price Egypt later paid was to range from the assassination of President Sadat on October 5 1981 to the massacre of 58 unsuspecting tourists at Luxor in November 1997, which crippled the country's tourist trade. Despite the obvious personal risks entailed, Sadat's successor as Egyptian president, Hosni Mubarak, nevertheless continued the policy of support for the Afghan resistance by supplying arms. In these circumstances it would not have been logical for Mubarak to prevent Egyptians joining the jihad, although he was all too well aware of the potential aggravation returning mujehadin would add to the threat from his own Muslim radicals.

China, with its short border with Afghanistan in the province of Xinjiang, where the peaks tower over 20,000 feet, stuck another of the smaller sticky fingers into the Afghan pie. China supported the jihad for both practical and political considerations. It desperately needed better trading relations with the United States if it was to obtain the many items of advanced technology crucial to its economic transformation. Politically, its struggle with the Soviet Union for dominance of the Communist world had become ingrained, and Afghanistan looked like a good chance to embarrass its rival. In the ten years of the war, China is estimated to have trained some 55,000 fighters, the great majority of whom where Muslim Uighar tribesmen from both sides of the common border. Other Chinese Uighar were sent to its ally Pakistan for training. China's arms shipments were on a much smaller scale than those coming in via Pakistan and consisted of small arms, field artillery and rocket launchers, including a specially designed single-barrel launcher. The significant point to make about the Chinese weapons contribution is that all the equipment actually reached the mujehadin (if so much as a single bullet was unaccounted for, they kicked up a fuss until it was traced). Moreover, with the exception of the Red Arrow anti-tank weapon, all of the weaponry was in good condition and worked. The unforeseen consequence for China was that it transpired that it was training and equipping the future Muslim revolt that was to seethe in Xinjiang from when the Russians withdrew from Afghanistan to the present day. In May 1980 China was duly rewarded for its support, and for allowing two US listening posts on its territory, by the lifting of the US trade embargo on a wide range of sophisticated technical goods.

The interference in Afghan affairs described so far was insignificant compared to that of the Soviet Union and the three other first division players – Pakistan, Saudi Arabia and the United States.

Saudi Arabia's motives are the simplest to describe. This was a genuine response to the cry of "Islam in danger", but one that also saw an opportunity to further its own particular Wahabi version of Islam. There was also the necessity to keep in with the most important Saudi ally, the United States, and financially supporting the mujehadin to the tune of almost $1bn a year was a good way of doing so without further unsettling its own restless population.

Pakistan's relatively new military dictator, General Zia ul Haq, must have breathed an enormous sigh of relief when the Soviet Union invaded Afghanistan. At the time his regime was in deep trouble, so the chance to join the "good guys" was a lifeline. Crippled by the burden of sustaining the proxy war with India in Kashmir, militarily and psychologically debilitated by the three defeats it had suffered at the hands of the despised Indian Army, still rife with the corruption that was the perennial excuse for military coups, the economy of Pakistan was in a desperate state. The situation was greatly worsened by the fact that America and the majority of the other Western nations had responded to Pakistan's "secret" nuclear weapons programme – not unreasonably undertaken in response to India's detonation of nuclear devices in 1974 – by cutting off the economic aid on which the country's economy depended so heavily. Only a modest amount of humanitarian help was unaffected.

Thus when America needed Pakistan's help in pursuit of its global anti-Soviet policy Zia was in a position not only to aid the mujehadin out of ethnic sympathy but also to restore his credit with America as the only friendly contiguous country.

In addition, Pakistan was able to insist that if its cooperation was required then all weapons supplies must pass through Pakistan military hands, or, more particularly, the far from spotless hands of the Inter Services Intelligence directorate (ISI). As a consequence only about half of all the equipment supplied by the various sympathetic governments reached the mujehadin in Afghanistan itself. The rest was siphoned off by the Pakistan military and the seven mujehadin parties who were the only officially permitted recipients of material support, either for their own use in any anticipated power struggle or to be sold abroad to fund their activities.

Pakistan had its advocates of a "forward policy" as keen as any Victorian Briton to advance its frontiers beyond the Hindu Kush, indeed as far as the River Oxus that formed Afghanistan's northern boundary with the USSR. This view was to be found most prominently among the military and the ISI, the majority of whose senior officers were themselves Pathans. This was not to be achieved by direct conquest, but by ensuring a regime in Kabul that would carry out policies that suited Pakistan. It was in pursuit of this objective that the ISI and Pakistan's Jamaat-i-Islami decided to back Hekmatyar to a much greater extent than any of the other mujehadin parties. This was a policy in which the United States fully concurred. Neither seem to have been able, or willing, to recognize that the ambitious but egocentric Ghilzai leader was happy to play along with them for his own ends. They seemed unable to look beyond their immediate goals of a stable border and access to the oil and trade of the southern Russian republics, but it seems strange that they ignored the implications that the history of Afghan Pathan irredentism should have taught them.

The situation was also confused by the rapid influx of refugees into Pakistan as soon as the Soviet Union invaded

Afghanistan. Zia allowed in large numbers of refugees on humanitarian grounds – an act for which Pakistan is seldom given sufficient credit. Estimates vary greatly, but by the summer of 1980 they seem to number between three-quarters of a million and a million in Pakistan alone. How many of these were nomads who would re-cross the border in their traditional seasonal migrations was hard for the Pakistani border authorities to tell. Nor could a figure easily be put on that proportion of the refugees who were, in fact, undercover guerrillas, training, recruiting or simply enjoying some R&R in a safe area. By 1989 there were three-and-a-quarter million in Pakistan and almost three million in Iran. By 1994, as relative stability returned, the parties in Pakistan were urging their adherents to go back home in order to strengthen their hands in the domestic power struggle. By this time the numbers of refugees had already fallen to just under one-and-a-half and under two million respectively. Many returnees were scornful of their leaders in exile and preferred to attach themselves to groups that had actually fought in Afghanistan itself. At the time of writing (October 2001), the UNHCR figures were already rising at an alarming rate in Pakistan and Iran as the bombs fell again in Afghanistan. They stood at a little under and a little over two million respectively, in addition to those in the CIS and much further afield.

Although General Zia gave asylum to Pathan rebel leaders in the 1970s and tacitly condoned their campaigning and coordinating in Peshawar, he repeatedly denied that he either encouraged or allowed training or armed attacks on Afghanistan to be based in Pakistan until that policy became internationally respectable. The Pakistan President was also wary initially because if his armed forces were tied down on the frontier they could not be employed to maintain order throughout the rest of the country, and his hold on power would weaken further. His possible successors, the Bhuttos, had already criticized the support that he had given to the Afghan rebels and scorned his fears of a Russian follow-up invasion as panic or self-preservation. They claimed that they would abandon his relatively hard line and try to preserve the security of their frontiers by appeasement – not a conspicuously successful policy in dealing with the Soviets. In fact, when Benazir Bhutto came to power in 1988 she continued Zia's policy – to have done anything else would probably have toppled her government.

In many respects the USSR had a more legitimate excuse for its intervention in Afghanistan than all of the other protagonists. In the first place it had a treaty with the de facto rulers of Afghanistan which provided for military assistance, including direct military intervention, in the event of being asked for such help. As I have said earlier, I believe the treaty was invoked by Hafizullah Amin some time early in December 1979. It may be objected that the government of Afghanistan had come to power by means of a coup and did not, therefore, have the democratic mandate to make such a request lawful. That is true. At the time it was also equally true of every one of Afghanistan's neighbours who, likewise, had no democratic credentials. Nor, of course, had one or two of the more distant participants, such as Saudi Arabia.

Legal niceties were not, in any case, of the essence in determining Soviet policy towards Afghanistan. Since the withdrawal of the British from India, Russia had regarded Afghanistan as indisputably part of its legitimate sphere of influence. It had amply demonstrated that relationship by being the largest, if most exacting, donor of economic aid. If the Soviet Union was to maintain its hegemony in Europe and its influence in the Third World from Cuba to Tanzania, it could not afford to let the friendly Marxist government of a client state be overthrown by a reactionary, and religiously driven, insurgency. A successful intervention would demonstrate that Russia could and would use military force to impose or uphold friendly left-wing governments. What happened in the event was that every day Soviet troops were on Afghan soil diminished, rather than enhanced, Russia's ability to influence Third World countries. With inexorable military and diplomatic logic, the world's second superpower was faced with a choice between genocide, which would have been politically disastrous, or retreat, which would be politically debilitating.

A second potent reason for intervention was the fact that rebellious Islamic elements in the Soviet Republics of Tajikistan, Uzbekistan, Turkmenistan, and Khyrgizia were looking hopefully across the Oxus at the efforts of their ethnic cousins and their attempt to overthrow a government imposed, to all intents and purposes, by Moscow.

To have allowed the PDPA to fall would have sent the wrong signal nearer home. Despite the few in the Politburo voicing doubts, the Soviet decision to invade was inevitable. Although it might seem that the United States had far fewer pragmatic reasons, the intensity of the Cold War and America's phobia about Communism made its intervention equally inevitable.

Sometimes the altruistic motives of the USA are rather unfairly discounted by Western liberals and there is no doubt these played their part in the American decision to support the mujehadin. There were also more selfish considerations to be weighed. The hawks in the CIA and the administration believed that the only thing that would check Russia's worldwide neo-colonial ambitions was burned fingers and that Afghanistan provided the best opportunity yet to light the fire. Out-manoeuvred in Africa and frustrated in Iran, the administration soon yielded to the temptation to try to score off Russia in Afghanistan. In doing so they repeated a mistake that had been made many times before in the history of Afghanistan.

When America first started clandestine aid in July 1979 to the groups forcibly opposing Babrak Karmal's Marxist regime in Kabul, it was to embarrass the Cold War devil-figure of the time by undermining its protégé. It also hoped to weaken Zia's ties with China by alleviating Pakistan's anxieties over the implications for the "Pushtunistan issue" of an unfriendly Marxist government in Kabul.

Once Soviet forces had entered Afghanistan, the emphasis immediately switched to open support for the mujehadin, as President Carter announced publicly within days of the event. When in January 1979 America's ally, the Shah of Persia, was ousted in a revolutionary coup and was replaced by the fervently Islamic regime of Ayatollah Khomeini a second devil-figure was conjured up who had to be quarantined at all costs. It was felt that such quarantine necessitated a stable, Sunni-dominated regime in Kabul that would not look kindly on Shi'a Tehran. However illogically, the United States became embroiled for the first time in Afghanistan. Once the US had achieved its main objectives, it turned its back on Afghanistan and it will no doubt do so again. Military aid ceased at the end of December 1991 and USAID stopped helping Afghanistan's displaced and hungry early in 1993. Cynics may wait to see if the pattern is repeated after America's third intrusion in less than a quarter of a century.

In 1980, some American commentators were tempted to draw warning parallels between Afghanistan and Vietnam, but the very different circumstances of the anti-government forces is only one of the many ways in which that analogy is false. The Afghans did not then have the significant military support of a contiguous major power, they did not have a single large base territory under their own control from which to operate, they did not have the support of a peace movement in their enemy's home country, and, above all, they did not have the unity of either purpose or belief enjoyed by the Viet Cong.

This last assertion may seem strange in view of the frequent claims made by rebel leaders that they were conducting a jihad against the Russian invaders. Certainly the fact that the Russians subscribed to an atheist view of life repugnant to Muslims was used as a means of inciting groups of rebels on a local and immediate basis to wage war on the invaders, but the Western assumption that the defence of Islam in the face of the ungodly was the prime motivating force for the ordinary mujehadin is wrong. As an Afghan commentator put it in 1951, in the context of the Pushtunistan dispute, "thus the real source of the uprising . . . lay in the passionate desire of the inhabitants for the independence of their fatherland. Since the British belonged to a different faith, they habitually interpreted any opposition as arising from the religious sentiment of the people and ignored their impatience for independence from all foreign influence."

Perhaps the support with the gravest long-term adverse consequences for the West was that provided privately, by individual Muslims and Muslim groups from around the world through such dubious organizations as the Tablighi Jamaat or through then respectable businessmen, such as bin Laden. These private sources originated mainly in Saudi Arabia, but, ironically in the light of subsequent events, financial support also came from other Gulf States, especially Kuwait. No accurate figure can be given for the number of foreigners who fought at some stage or other with the mujehadin in Afghanistan, but at one time a probably not unreasonable combined figure of 50,000 was estimated for the mercenaries and fugitives from their own regimes who were to be found in Pakistan and inside Afghanistan. Ahmed Rashid estimates that as many as 100,000 were involved in the jihad at some stage, directly or indirectly, in combatant, training and other support roles.

How then did these various mujehadin heroes, these glamorous freedom fighters, come to be regarded as fanatical Islamist terrorists as soon as the Red Army went home?

12

THE LAST MARXIST AND OTHERS

So long as they were fighting the arch-enemy the numerous quarrels amongst the mujehadin could be conveniently overlooked by their patrons. Only the UN, to its credit, tried hard to effect reconciliation before the fight against Najibullah's Marxist government ended in the hope that it would hold afterwards. Just how uphill the UN's task was is perhaps indicated by the fact that when they built a new sports stadium for the people of Kandahar the first event to be held there was a public execution with an audience of 10,000.

By the late 1980s, particularly around Kabul, the various mujehadin groups were already arming themselves, not just for fighting the Russians but for the coming power struggle as well. There are well-authenticated accounts of rival groups ambushing each other's weapons supply columns. A shared Islamic ideology was not compelling enough to sublimate ethnic suspicion and personal rivalry once the unifying foe had departed. Indeed, differing interpretations of that ideology served to exacerbate the struggle for secular power. When the Soviets were there to be fought, national pride and the perennial rallying cry "Islam in danger" resulted in a pattern of mujehadin relationships that was religious and local with an overriding national purpose. Once the external threat had gone, the pattern changed to an ethnic and regional one with little purpose other than the carving out of personal or group fiefdoms.

Not surprisingly in an atmosphere of so much mutual animosity and suspicion, the UN's attempts to put together a broad-based government acceptable to all Afghans failed. One has to ask, when the same animosities and suspicions are still clearly evident today, whether any post-Taliban UN power brokering will be any more successful.

The attitudes of all those involved in or with Afghanistan once Gorbachev had made it clear he would withdraw all Russian forces were mistakenly founded on the fallacy that control of Kabul meant control of Afghanistan and the expectation that the Marxist regime would fall in a matter of weeks. Najibullah was made of sterner stuff and even boasted that "nobody has taken Kabul in the past and nobody will take it in the future". As the disunited Opposition* assaulted the capital in vain it began to look as if he was right, or at least more right than Henry Kissinger, who categorically predicted Najibullah's fall "within three months".

Najibullah, as ex-head of KhAD, the Afghan KGB, a Parchami and a Pathan was in an ideal position to control the levers of power – precisely the reason he had been chosen by Moscow to replace the clever but unsuccessful Karmal. Najibullah's control of the government machinery was not, however, absolute. The Khalqi remained in the military key positions and refused to accept Parchami commanders. Attempts to reconcile the two factions led to greater antipathy and even greater rivalry with the result that in 1990 General Tanai, the senior Khalqi officer, attempted a coup that failed. He fled to join the ever-inconstant Hekmatyar who claimed credit for trying without taking the risk of actual involvement. Aware of the urgent need for more allies, Najibullah tried to distance his government party from its Marxist past by changing its name to the Watan (homeland) party and the PDPA ceased to exist in name only a quarter of a century after

As a naked struggle for power was involved I no longer use the honourable term "mujehadin", but describe whatever forces oppose the de facto government of the day as the Opposition.

its formation. The Afghans were not fooled and the Opposition rejected all deals proposed by Najibullah for a more broadly based government to include key figures from their ranks. In such circumstances it took $3–4 billion worth of aid a year that the Soviet Union could ill afford to prop up the Kabul regime. This support included air strikes on resistance bases from Afghan airfields, SCUD attacks and military, technical and support missions by Russian troops in mufti.

General Zia also adopted a more pragmatic approach when it looked as if Najibullah might hang on for some time without some incentive to depart. In January 1988, well before the Soviet withdrawal, Pakistan accepted that former members of the Najibullah regime (although not Najibullah himself) could participate in a successor government, much to the annoyance of the Americans still locked into their "anti-Communist" obsession. This was a magnanimous as well as pragmatic move by Zia knowing, as he must have done, who was behind the terrorist attacks carried out the previous year against his regime.

In 1987 KhAD (by then WAD, a full-blown Ministry of Security), with KGB assistance, launched a campaign of bombings and assassinations in Pakistan against both the mujehadin leadership and its Pakistani supporters. The campaign's aim was to pressurize Pakistan into ceasing to support the Opposition, but Zia played down such incidents and held fast to his line. When his C130 transport plane was brought down by sabotage on August 17 1988, killing the President, a number of senior Pakistan military officers and the American ambassador Arnold Raphel, suspicion immediately fell on KhAD. The CIA, factions in the ISI and Bhutto supporters were also variously blamed, but no proof has ever been produced as to who actually planned and carried out the sabotage, although much evidence appears to have been "lost" or suppressed. Whoever the assassins were they gained nothing, for Benazir Bhutto's successor government made no immediate major changes of policy towards Afghanistan. With her father's adviser on Frontier policy, the Pathan general Nasrullah Babur, appointed Minister of the Interior and thus overlord of the ISI, Pakistan's pro-Pathan stance if anything hardened. All that changed in due course was its chosen surrogate.

Hekmatyar's support had always been more or less confined to his own warlike Ghilzai, but even amongst his own people his was only one of three groups calling for their allegiance. In the end his bid for control of the whole of Afghanistan failed because of his narrow power base and his refusal to broaden it except by recruiting foreigners towards whom the attitude of the Afghans was ambivalent – their support was welcome, their foreign and very un-Afghan ways were not. Pakistan welcomed Hekmatyar's strength and effectiveness, which lay in his considerable material resources, financed by Saudi Arabia and by opium profits and processing, and in his personal energy and ability.

Once he proved incapable of delivering the pro-Pakistan Afghanistan he had promised, Hekmatyar's usefulness ceased. But that day was a little way off yet. At the same time the Peshawar-based party leaders – Gailani, Hekmatyar, Khalis, Mojadidi and Rabbani – all ventured back into Afghanistan to try to muster support, while those already based inside the country – Masood, Dostam and Ismail Khan – were off to a flying start in the race for power.

Najibullah's problems were compounded by the unreliable nature of the allies on whom he had to depend to keep open his vital road link with the Soviet Union. To protect the route he had to use Dostam's Uzbegs, the Jauzjanis, to hold the gasfields, so important to the Russians, round Mazar and the road north to the border while the Ismaili Hazaras of Sayyid

Mansur Nadiri guarded the next section of the route south to the Salang Tunnel. When Najibullah refused to pay salaries to the phantom soldiers on Dostam's payroll, Dostam took his real soldiers over to the other side.

We have seen how the failure of the Soviet invasion was a contributory factor, but by no means a decisive one, in the fall of the Communist regime in the Soviet Union. On the other hand, the disintegration of that Soviet regime was a decisive factor in the fall of Najibullah's Marxist government in Afghanistan. Once the Soviet transfusion was cut off following the collapse of Communism in the USSR, Najibullah was doomed and it was soon clear that he could not hold out on his own for much longer. As soon as he realized that he was to be abandoned, he appealed to the West for support in opposing "Islamic Fundamentalism" – his own words. Because he had been placed in power by the Soviets the appeal was ignored and no alternative support was offered. In vain he pointed to the emancipation of women and other liberal measures under his regime and the contrast he predicted, how rightly it transpired, if such radicals as Hekmatyar and Rabbani were to take power.

Against the background of Najibullah's weakening control even of Kabul, the foreign ministers of USSR, Russia and Tajikistan met in Moscow in November 1991, with Jamiat, the three traditionalist parties and Wahdat. However, Najibullah and the three other radical parties, still supported by the ISI and Arab Islamists, were not invited as they had refused to take part in earlier meetings organized by the foreign secretaries of Iran and Pakistan. Some thought that Russian selectivity demonstrated the success of the US policy of excluding both Najibullah (who had agreed not to insist on being part of any new government) and the then most extreme radical, Hekmatyar. It was, of course, folly to suppose that any agreement not endorsed by the Islamic radical parties could last longer than it took the ink to dry on its pages. Moreover, while Najibullah was prepared to relinquish power to an interim Loya Jirgah headed by King Zahir Shah or some other neutral body, he was not willing to do so to a divided group of mujehadin who had failed to defeat him. Hekmatyar immediately contacted Kabul via Colonel Qadhafi with offers to join forces, but by now his offers were being treated with the suspicion they had rightly earned.

The traditionalists and Wahdat kept faith by nominating their delegates to the proposed Loya Jirgah, but Zahir, who had sat out the war comfortably in Rome, refused to nominate a team to any body that gave so much representation to the mujehadin parties. For his part Najibullah was constantly pressured by Pakistan and America to agree to go unconditionally in return for his personal safety. Ever the realist, on March 18 1992 he announced on Afghan television that he would hand over power as soon as there was an interim government in place. Hardly had the programme credits gone up than all the contending parties, traditionalists as well as radicals, advanced their plans to take the place he was about to vacate. The very next day Dostam and his allies seized control of Mazar-i-Sharif while the Peshawar-based parties haggled over the composition of any new government.

Masood at least appreciated that stability would depend on a power sharing agreement among the various Opposition leaders that would cut across ethnic lines. Helped by Nawaz Sharif, the Pakistan Premier, the NLFA took the initiative in forming an Afghan Interim Government (AIG) that was supposed to take office after the departure of Najibullah. This gave way to a Leadership Council and a concordat was cobbled together and signed in Peshawar on April 24 1992. It provided for a two-month presidency by Mojadidi to be followed by a four-month term with Rabbani and then the convening of an Interim Shura to prepare the way for elections in a further 18 months. Like so many theoretically reasonable initiatives in Afghanistan, it was unsuccessful. It was boycotted by Hekmatyar and had only lukewarm support from the radical and non-Pathan groups. Hekmatyar took this as a signal to send his own men into Kabul to seize key positions from which Masood and Dostam only succeeded in driving him on April 28. However, Hizb managed to retain a foothold in the southern suburbs.

Dostam, together with some Parchami rebels, had already seized Kabul airport on April 16 1992. As a result a few days later Najibullah was unable to reach the UN plane to fly him to safety in India and had to take refuge in the UN mission. There he remained until he was dragged out with his brother by the Taliban in September 1996 tortured and then hanged from the traffic kiosk outside.

Masood, the Tajik, also tried to reassure the Pathans that he was not another Bacha-i-Saqao seeking power for himself, but all the same he rejected the UN peace plan on similar lines as he had not been consulted about it. Belatedly the interim government, with Mojadidi as its nominated President, finally arrived by road in the capital on April 28 and proclaimed the Islamic State of Afghanistan. It exemplifies the bitterness of the rivalry among Opposition parties that the Leadership Council had to abandon its original intention of flying in the previous day because Hekmatyar had threatened to shoot down the plane. In any case, due to its wrangling, the Leadership Council had left things rather late for by now local mujehadin commanders, even those who had fought each other, had ganged up to form local shuras and pocket the levies from the customs posts in their areas. Apart from foreign aid and such payments for natural gas as could be squeezed out of the Soviet

Union's successor states, these should have been the government's main source of revenue. Without them it was driven to even greater dependence on its foreign backers.

At the end of two months Mojadidi, an honourable man, duly stood down as President and Rabbani took office, but when it came to his turn to give way to the planned Shura he produced a string of excuses to stay put. Rabbani, on whom the US seemed to place so much reliance post-September 11, was as ruthless and autocratic as his opponents and under his aegis acts of brutality and barbarism as bad as those of the later Taliban were committed. By packing a speciously convened Loya Jirgah to extend his Presidency for what must have looked like an indefinite term, he destroyed any pretensions he and Masood might have to legitimacy and gave those excluded from government no option, as they saw it, but to try to topple him by force. His willingness, twice, to embrace his arch-enemy Hekmatyar by making him Premier could be seen as statesmanship, or, alternatively, as a well-developed instinct for survival at any cost. This intransigence simply rekindled the ever-glowing embers of civil war.

The Peshawar Agreement had looked like a non-runner from the outset. Hekmatyar, still hoping for sole power, refused to subscribe to it and Rabbani had no intention of relinquishing office once he had it, particularly when he had Masood at his right hand as his defence minister. Rabbani's forces occupied most of the city, but Hizb still held the southern outskirts and Wahdat the western. A frustrated Hekmatyar decided a sustained rocket bombardment of Kabul might set the various factions within the city violently against each other and so open the way for his takeover. Unsurprisingly, some of the capital's citizens looked enviously westwards to the stability and returning prosperity of Herat under Ismail Khan.

In June 1993, though accepting the post of prime minister in Rabbani's government, Hekmatyar declined to put his personal safety at risk by taking up residence in the city and exercised his office, in so far as he did so, from his stronghold in Sarobi. In January 1994, switching options yet again, he linked up with his former enemy, Rashid Dostam, to launch another massive bombardment on Kabul. All in all he managed to destroy half the city and kill some 25,000 of its citizens before turning coat once more and accepting the Premiership rather desperately offered by Rabbani in June 1996. He did not last long. Pakistan, recognizing that he was a broken reed as far as their policy of using him to control the future government of Afghanistan was concerned, switched their support to the nascent Taliban and began to consider other ways of removing Rabbani. Early in 1995 Bhutto declared the Rabbani government "illegitimate" – as if all governments of Afghanistan have not always been legitimate in the democratic sense. There is considerable irony in an Oxford-educated female premier endorsing the female-suppressing Taliban. With Pakistan's ever-greater involvement through its sponsorship of the Taliban, Afghanistan's other neighbours became increasingly nervous and felt the need once again to strengthen their own allies. Iran supplied both Wahdat and the Rabbani government.

Uzbekistan underwrote Dostam and the Tajikistan government backed Masood in the hope that he would help end the civil war that had rumbled on since 1992 between his fellow Tajik Islamists and an autocratic government inherited from the Soviet era. The conflict in Tajikistan did not end until 1997 and its potential recrudescence is a complicating factor in any post-Taliban restructuring of Afghanistan.

Let us return to the events of spring 1992. At this time, there were four main contenders for power:

- Dostam's Uzbegs, with a sprinkling of other northern ethnic groups and former key Parcham leaders such as Babrak Karmal. Dostam was financed by Uzbekistan and probably Russia.
- The mainly Tajik forces, together with a small Shi'a party not tied to Iran, were led by Rabbani and Masood. They had their regional base in the north-east. Once they were officially installed in Kabul, they were financed with a little in cash and kind from Saudi Arabia and by printing the official currency and collecting such official taxes as were collectable.
- Hekmatyar led the mainly Ghilzai Pathans – few of the other tribes got involved at this stage – and was reinforced by former Khalqis and Arab and Pakistani radicals. He was well funded by both Pakistan and Saudi Arabia. Hizb-i-Islami supplemented its income through drug trafficking (as, to a lesser extent, did the other groups at this time) and printing counterfeit money.
- Finally, with its base in the Hazarajat and support in Kabul, the Wahdat and the Parchamis of Najibullah's regime continued to draw both military and financial support from Iran.

In 1992 the initial alignment was into two opposing groups; a non-Pathan axis of Rabbani, Dostam and Wahdat opposed to Pathan Hekmatyar's Hizb-i-Islami while the rest hovered about waiting for the outcome. This set the Afghan allies of Pakistan and Saudi Arabia against those of Iran, but, as with most alignments in Afghanistan, it did not last for long. With the Tajiks holding most of the reins of power in the capital, the Uzbegs and Shi'a Hazara of Dostam and Wahdat were not long in joining forces with Hekmatyar.

The contest was now one between the "Ins" and the "Outs"

and the new divisions reflected the parallel struggle for power in the newly independent Asian Republics of the former Soviet Union between Tajiks and Uzbegs. The first military manifestation of these changes of allegiance was when Masood turned on the Wahdat in West Kabul. Wahdat responded by signing a pact with Hekmatyar, who had given up the premiership by the autumn of 1993 and was joined by Dostam in besieging the capital. Against this background it was scarcely surprising that UN efforts to establish a broadly acceptable legitimate government came to nothing. The UN made the best of a bad job and recognized the de facto government of Rabbani as the official government of Afghanistan.

At the beginning of 1994 there was a kind of uneasy stability in Afghanistan. Kabul and some other centres south of the Hindu Kush were held by the government forces of Rabbani and Masood. While they could not extend their grip further, nor could their opponents topple them. Hekmatyar, despite his brief tenure in absentia in 1993 of the Premiership under Rabbani, joined forces with Dostam and continued to rocket the capital right up to the end of 1994 in his attempt to oust the Rabbani government in Kabul. When that did not work, and finding himself defeated by the Taliban and out of favour with Pakistan, he once more became Rabbani's premier during the last few months before Kabul's fall to the Taliban in September 1996. In his second term as prime minister, Hekmatyar began to introduce much more strict conformity to an Islamic lifestyle, just as Najibullah had predicted. Unwisely, Rabbani sacked Masood from the Defence Ministry, though he remained in command of the government's forces.

In Herat the Jamiat leader Ismail Khan had taken control as soon as the Najibullah regime fell and this ancient city enjoyed three years during which peace and some prosperity gradually returned. For example before the city fell to the Taliban more than 20,000 girls, as well as a slightly greater number of boys, were in school. As most of the teachers were women, virtually all of the schools were closed again when the Taliban forbade women to work outside the home.

Mazar under Dostam was in a not dissimilar, although potentially less stable situation, with Dostam's number two, Abdul Malik, waiting for the chance to replace his boss. The Tajiks in the north-east had also established a rudimentary civil administration again.

However, in the south and west, apart from relatively well-ordered enclaves in Khost and Ghazni, anarchy prevailed, with the cities of Kandahar and Gardez particularly lawless as the contending warlords, like street gangs in New York or London, fought for territory at the expense of the local population. Rape, robbery and murder were the order of the day so it was unsurprising that it was here that the Taliban first and swiftly gained a foothold.

Amid such chaos the UN continued to try to broker a peace deal. It had become clear from the response to the UN peace commission tour of the main Afghan centres and neighbouring states that the people were eager for peace. However, they had not the means to secure it for themselves, the UN could not raise the essential international force to give it to them, and outside powers continued to encourage their clients to bid for power. Peace there was none. Towards the end of 1994 five main commanders controlled the greater part of Afghanistan. Ismail Khan from Herat, Rashid Dostam from Mazar, Abdul Qaderi in Nangahar, Jalalludin Haqqaniin in Paktia and Ahmed Masood, nominally under Rabbani, in the north-east and in Kabul itself. Then late in the year there joined this pretty gang of rogues one who would put them all in the shade.

13

THE TALIBAN PHENOMENON

If we are to take effective account of the Taliban phenomenon in such a way as not to inflict even greater harm on the long-suffering people of Afghanistan, we need to try at least to look more sympathetically on their antecedents and attitudes. It will not suffice to promise post-Taliban aid, or to make the kind of generalized statements of which Blair and Bush are so fond to the effect that they "are not at war with the Afghan people but only with the Taliban and the terrorists they harbour".

Substitute the word German for Afghan, Nazi for Taliban, and you have very much what some Western leaders were saying more than 60 years earlier, at the outbreak of the Second World War. The fact is that neither the Nazis nor the Taliban could have come to power without the cooperation, or at least the acquiescence, of the majority of the people over whom they ruled. The analogy between the two regimes is not exact because the Taliban, nominally in control of 85 per cent of the country, have only brought the principal cities and highways under their direct rule. Many towns, hundreds of villages, and large swathes of the countryside remain the fiefdoms of various warlords and local tribal khans, petty and grand alike.

Taliban is a plural of talib, a student or seeker in an Islamic madrasah, or religious school. Britain, too, has religious schools, where a particular religious doctrine is inculcated, albeit against the background of a state-prescribed secular syllabus. As we shall see later in this chapter, it is to the more than 40,000 madrasahs in Pakistan that we shall have to look for the origins of the eponymous movement that has usurped the meaning of the general term Taliban in the Western public mind. The Taliban movement soon came to embrace a much wider range of adherents than the original groups of "students". Even former Communists were welcomed, though watchful eyes were kept on them to ensure there was no backsliding.

The Taliban theocracy in Afghanistan promotes a set of values which would have been largely acceptable to the majority of our Victorian forbears and even to some traditionalists today, particularly in their emphasis on the family, the role of women as mothers and home-makers, and draconian punishment for crime. In Afghanistan, women are prohibited from working because it is felt that they should be at home bringing up their children and teaching them to be good Muslims. The imposition of strict purdah, literally a veil or curtain, is seen as shielding women from sexual harassment or, as the Taliban put it, "to protect their sisters from corrupt people". The difficulty, as Nancy Dupree* pointed out, is to secure certain human rights "without compromising the national cultural perspective".

The Taliban are quite open about their conduct, genuinely believing it to be in accordance with the beliefs of Islam and the Shari'at. They believe that imposing their rules strengthens society, but have no wish to export their beliefs or their doctrines. These rules are much more strictly enforced in the cities – in particular in Kandahar, Kabul and Herat – than in the rural areas over which the Taliban not only have less control but where they encourage the traditional role of the village jirgah. Their own structure is not so different from that of the Roman Catholic Church with its priests at ground level and College of Cardinals electing a Pope who thus acquires

---

Louis Dupree's widow and an expert on the lives of Afghan women.

absolute infallibility. Under the Taliban system, the ulema – that is the theologians, their College of Cardinals – is frequently consulted. The generality of mullahs, the parish priests, who are usually no more learned or literate than is necessary to lead prayers, are not. Then there are the Shuras, or governing councils, in Kabul, Kandahar and Herat, with the latter two having to refer their decisions for ratification to the inner cabinet in Kandahar. Over all of these bodies stands Mullah Muhammad Omar Akhunzade himself, the Amir al Mu'minim, the Commander of the Faithful – rather as the British Queen is described on British coins as *Fidei Defensor*, Defender of the Faith. Like the Pope, Omar is regarded as infallible and all decisions, theological and secular, ultimately rest with him.

Omar is reclusive, pious, and frugal, with little knowledge of the outside world and narrow intellectual horizons. Almost psychotically introspective, he rarely meets people from the outside world. Tall, thin and, according to one of the few Western journalists to have met him, elegant, his edicts are pronounced in an almost inaudible voice that detracts nothing from their binding power. This intelligent and charismatic man, himself a thrice-wounded hero of the resistance, commands deep respect among his followers even if to us he seems congenitally unfit to rule a nation in the twenty-first century.

The impact he and the billionaire businessman and terrorist Osama bin Laden made upon each other was thus both remarkable and catalytic. When bin Laden first used the Binoori mosque in Karachi as his base for coordinating assistance to the jihad, he was impressed by Mullah Omar, who was the young prayer leader there. Bin Laden, like Omar, also had the added heroic charisma of having been wounded fighting in the jihad. Both men subsequently exploited their "stigmata" to full effect.

Unlike other Islamist parties Taliban has no aim to create a *political* ideology, which may account for the slightly incoherent nature of its administration. This was made worse by the practice of frequently moving officials from one place to another. Intended to remove the opportunities for corruption, this simply destroyed continuity of interpretation and application of government policy and, for example, partly accounts for the conflicting statements made about bin Laden.

The Taliban regime could not make the concessions demanded by the West over bin Laden for fear not only of offending the Pathan sense of obligation, but also of being thought to have betrayed the jihad for which so many martyrs had already died. Jihad, incidentally, is another much abused term. While it can be interpreted as meaning military action against others, the emphasis, in the Koran at least, is on defence against aggression rather than aggression in order to proselytize, which is prohibited. It also means a personal struggle – a struggle to make oneself a better person, a struggle to follow the path of God. The fanatic hostility with which jihad has come to be associated in the West has much to do with the human vices of ambition, greed, hatred, revenge and lust for cruelty and very little with the divine precepts of the Islamic faith.

Saudi Arabia practices with almost the same degree of severity as the Taliban all those restrictions on what the West sees as human rights, particularly with regard to women, and punishments under the Shari'at, such as stoning, amputation and public execution. The only distinction is that the one is in a state of draconian and undemocratic peace and the other is in the throes of a civil war. The question has to be asked why one was warmly embraced as friend and ally when the other is anathematized as the Evil One that American politics seems always to need. Many other states, Islamic and non-Islamic alike, from Syria and Indonesia to China and Zimbabwe, practice many of the same "abuses" as the Taliban while subscribing with public hypocrisy to the UN Charter of Human Rights and thus gaining the international recognition denied the Afghan regime.

Why pick on Afghanistan? Is it sufficient to insist that it is solely because the Taliban harbours bin Laden and the al Qaida terrorists who so callously destroyed the World Trade Center and massacred around 5,000 people of many nationalities? After all, the biggest single racial component of the suicide teams was Saudi, the Wahabism that drove them is a Saudi phenomenon and bin Laden himself is a Saudi – although his citizenship was revoked in 1994. The answer the Taliban would give is that it is due to a combination of self-interest and revenge; self-interest centred on ensuring the continuity of the oil supplies from the former southern Soviet Republics and the Middle East, and revenge for the affront to America's sense of immunity from the world's ills. For the Americans it is a natural response to the sheer wickedness of the World Trade Center massacre.

I state the Taliban case not to justify it – the writer is, after all, a Western liberal conditioned by those values – but to try to understand it and to emphasize the dangers of any equally extreme and indiscriminate response. So why and how did the Taliban come to power in Afghanistan?

The origins of the movement have been obscured by myth, but in a sense they go back to the Deobandi school of Islamic thought founded in the Indian town of that name in 1867. The Deobandi studied how to reconcile Islamic texts with the Raj-ruled India in which they found themselves. The Deobandi urged their followers to throw off the rule of the British unbelievers. As the state is seen only as an embodiment of Islamic values, rather than being an end in itself, it becomes legitimate to overthrow any government, even one's own, whose concept of statehood departs from these values. The Taliban leaders felt justified in taking military action against the mujehadin Islamist parties because they failed to govern by what the Taliban saw as Islamic values.

The Deobandi placed a great emphasis on observing correct ritual, and, consequently, on modes of behaviour and scorned Shi'a Muslims, such as the Hazara,* as unbelievers. A significant part of the later Afghan ulema originated from this school, but Islam as practiced in Afghanistan until quite recently was tolerant of other faiths and of differing sects of Islam itself. Such extreme orthodoxy as that of the Wahabi was virtually unknown. Sadly, of the great faiths that were once widespread in Afghanistan, such as Buddhism, or which had originated there, like Zoroastrianism, there is scarcely a trace of either relic or practice today. The form of Islam espoused by the Taliban is that of the Wahabi school founded by Abd el Wahabi in the eighteenth century. This ultra-orthodox version of Islam draws a firm distinction between believers and unbelievers, and allows no deviation from Shari'at. Those who do so deviate "deserve severe punishment".

Wahabism claims the right to interpret the Koran according to circumstances, but in an excessively puritan way. My use of the adjective puritan suggests to me fascinating parallels to be drawn with seventeenth-century England and America, which there is no room to explore here. W.G. Palgrave (the Arabist not he of the *Golden Treasury*) wrote somewhat unkindly of one Wahabi in his 1865 account of his travels in Arabia that "he was a model of all the orthodox vices of his sect". It was the early twentieth-century Wahabi adherent Abdul Aziz in Saudi Arabia who created the first

---

*There are also some very small Pathan tribal groups who are Shi'a but live mostly in Pakistan.

Committee for the Promotion of Virtue and the Prevention of Vice (CPVPV) to punish those who did not observe Islamic rituals and prohibitions and which the Taliban so zealously adopted. In 1932 Abdul Aziz proclaimed himself King of Arabia and founded the dynasty that, ever since, has applied his rules in that country and publicly supported their Taliban adherents – until September 11 2001 at least. There may remain more covert support than diplomatic prudence can acknowledge.

In Pakistan, shortly before independence, the Deobandi also founded a political party, the Jamiat-ul-Ulema-e-Islami (JUI), under the leadership of Maulana Fazul Rahman. Both Deobandi and JUI were egalitarian in outlook and opposed the tribalized structure of Pakistan, believing that Islam should supersede national, ethnic and tribal loyalties. JUI always did well in elections in Baluchistan and the Pathan border areas, but had little political clout. The JUI can be confused with the Jamaat-i-Islami (JI) founded by the respected theologian Maulana Abdul Ala Maududi in India in 1941 which translated to Pakistan in 1947. The JUI, ultra-conservative and elitist, viewed the West as morally decadent and its ideas to be alien and superfluous to Islam. The JUI had little influence until it became junior partner in Benazir Bhutto's 1988 government. The Deobandi exercised ideological influence, however, through their madrasahs founded to teach their doctrines and these have much influenced the Taliban. These madrasahs, together with those set up by other Islamist parties, proliferated in Pakistan during Afghanistan's war with the Soviet Union.

The syllabus of the traditional madrasah was limited and all but the cleverest students usually absorbed one subject at a time. Lessons consisted of learning the Koran by heart, interpreting the Koran, Islamic law, including jurisprudence and philosophy, the life and sayings of Mohammed, Arabic and simple mathematics. Unfortunately, many of the newer madrasahs were run by semi-literate and bigoted mullahs who knew little of their founder's more flexible doctrine, but seized eagerly on the Wahabism of the Saudis, who by then were paying most of the bills. For example, in 1997 the mullahs of this persuasion threatened to kill all Americans in Pakistan if bin Laden were extradited to the United States. The orphans and fatherless children in the camps in the madrasahs saw their Taliban mullahs and military instructors as the father figures so important in patriarchal Afghanistan. From them the youngsters learned the absolute obedience that was to make them such formidable fighters.

It is also argued with some justice that the Taliban are as much a military organization as a religious sect. The origins of that aspect of the present Taliban are fairly recent. There is no scope in this book to follow the endless ebb and flow of the Taliban campaigns in detail,* so I shall confine myself to those military events that had the widest repercussions. As far as I can ascertain, the first use in the military context of the word Taliban, with a capital T, was in 1982\83. At that time the Pakistan Special Services Group (the counterpart of Britain's SAS) trained the first talibs from the refugee camps. These then joined the forces of Khalis and Harakat where they operated in subgroups already known to their commanders as Taliban.

What we now know as the Taliban first came to more general notice through a military exploit, but one that has become coloured by the mythmaking of subsequent propaganda. On October 12 1994 a small force of Taliban attacked the town of Spin Baldak on the Pakistan/Afghanistan

*For those interested there is an excellent blow-by-blow account in Anthony Davis's chapter in Fundamentalism Reborn – see reading list.

border and swiftly routed its Hizb-i-Islami garrison. Suspiciously, they arrived for the attack by bus still unwrapping their nice new Kalashnikovs. Shortly afterwards they moved on to capture a nearby arms depot just over the border in Afghanistan. There was some doubt at the time as to whether the Taliban had actually captured a depot that was said to have been looted already. Was the claim simply to provide cover for the source of those shiny new weapons and the many more that soon followed them?

Suspicion also attaches to the convenient sequence of events that followed. On October 29, as part of Pakistan's expressed desire to open trade routes through to Turkmenistan, General Nasrullah Babar, Benazir Bhutto's Minister of the Interior and therefore the head of the ISI, arranged for a 30-truck convoy, laden with food, medicine and consumer goods, to leave Quetta for that destination. Babar, himself a Pathan, had played a major part in shaping the Afghan policy of Benazir's father, Zulfikar Ali Bhutto. Accompanying the convoy for no obvious commercial reason were two fairly senior ISI officers with considerable experience of covert operations and a Taliban armed escort.

On November 2 men under the command of three local warlords held up the convoy at gunpoint 35 kilometres short of Kandahar. This time, however, they were not demanding the usual toll for passing through their patch but, rather, the right to permanent free transit of the Pakistan border and that the ISI should stop giving support (supposedly still secret!) to the Taliban. Next day, when negotiations failed, the impasse was broken by a conveniently nearby Taliban strike force which attacked from across the Pakistan border. The Taliban relief force then swept on to take Kandahar almost without a fight. There they captured six MiG 21s (only one airworthy as it happened), half-a-dozen transport helicopters, 20 tanks and a stack of small arms and ammunition. Mansur Achakzai, the most powerful of the local warlords who had plagued Kandahar with pillage, rape and gang warfare, now gave in without a fight. Bribery seems the likely explanation, but who paid the bribe? On whose orders was a rescue mission turned into a local coup d'état? Was it the ISI or the Taliban on the spot? Senior figures in the Pakistan military or government? Or a distant Taliban guiding hand employing for the first time the tactic that was to become their hallmark? What we do know is that, well equipped for the next stage and joined by reinforcements bussed across the border, they soon moved outwards from their city base to occupy the neighbouring provinces of Zabul and Uruzgan.

It seems clear that Pakistani foreign policy strategists had already decided to replace Hekmatyar with this hopefully more biddable instrument. What is more surprising is that at this stage Rabbani, to the astonishment of his local commander in Kandahar, also offered the Taliban cooperation and moral and financial support. Kabul saw the Taliban as a potential means of alleviating the pain caused by Hekmatyar's continual bombardment of the city. Rabbani was soon disabused about the friendliness and helpful intentions of his new protégé. The Afghan President had backed the Taliban counter-attack aimed at preventing Hekmatyar from occupying the key city of Gardez. Rabbani's air support and radio announcements that the Taliban were fighting for the government implied an agreement between the two. A brusque public rebuttal of the claim made it clear that the Taliban were taking sides with no one – they considered all the former mujehadin groups to be as corrupt and venal as each other. To the perceptive on both sides of the Durand Line border, it was a clear declaration of intent by the Taliban that they were out to take control of the whole of Afghanistan. The

Taliban's aim must have seemed absurdly ambitious in 1994, but it was worth an outside bet not just to the Pakistanis, who had been the first to get their money on, but also to the Americans eyeing the oil riches of the former Soviet Asian republics and fearful lest they pass through Iranian hands. The United States clearly believed that the Taliban could eventually clean up the drugs trade for which America provided the largest market, counter the influence of Russia and Iran, and restore order. This would enable the US/Saudi UNOCAL/Delta consortium to secure a pipeline from central Asia to the Pakistani port of Gwadar on the Baluchistan coast. It was anticipated that this would carry five million barrels a day.

In 1995, the Assistant Secretary of State for South Asia, Robin Raphael, described the Taliban as supporting a peaceful political process and in December 1996 the State Department was still talking about "making contact" with the new regime despite its treatment of women.

Long before the end of the decade the regime in Iran had changed, as had its attitude and that of the US towards the Taliban. The constituent republics of the former Soviet Union were no longer powerful or influential enough to cause Americans to lose sleep, alternative supply routes for oil appeared more likely and only the drug trade remained a problem to solve. The self-interested reasons for supporting the Taliban had almost evaporated, and positive incentives to turn on them in the shape of feminist pressure at home and the dangerous growth of terrorism promulgated and practiced by Afghanistan's "guest", bin Laden, were more than enough to bring about a reversal of policy. From lukewarm support, the State Department's efforts switched to bringing the Taliban down. That this constituted yet further interference in Afghanistan's internal affairs appeared not to trouble too many consciences.

Returning to the rise of the Taliban, the next step on their road to power was to drive Hekmatyar from much of the rest of his territory. This they did. Hekmatyar panicked, abandoned his major base at Charasyab and withdrew to his stronghold of Sarobi, leaving large stocks of artillery and munitions behind him. These were gratefully received by the government forces – still not at war with the Taliban themselves – that were immediately sent to occupy Charasyab.

By mid-February 1995 a Taliban army of some 10,000 men, with substantial reserves on tap from the camps and madrasahs of Pakistan and well equipped with tanks and artillery, was rapidly gaining a self-fulfilling reputation for invincibility. That reputation was instrumental in swelling its ranks with officers and men of the PDPA's former armed services and many armed Pathans who found it convenient to be considered part of the Taliban. How strong the loyalty of such expedient recruits will be when tested by foreign opposition as it is at the time of writing remains to be seen. That the inner core of the Taliban will remain steadfast should not be doubted.

By this time Taliban operations were gradually becoming technically more sophisticated in both command communications and weaponry. Apart from the defectors already mentioned, instruction in the necessary techniques almost certainly came from foreign mujehadin, mainly Arabs, who had decided to stay in Afghanistan and Pakistani officers from the ISI and North-West Frontier Force.

As unfounded as the myth of Taliban invincibility was their claim that they were freeing an oppressed populace from the tyranny and corruption of the former mujehadin warlords wherever they went. While this was true of their first success in and around Kandahar, it could not be applied in the case of many of the other places they attacked and over-ran. What opened the eyes of Afghans at least to the fact that the Taliban was just another warlord in religious disguise was its attack in 1995 on Herat, a Dari-speaking city with a large Shi'a population that had enjoyed three years of ordered government and relative prosperity under Ismail Khan. But first we must deal with the events that led to their open breach with the Rabbani/Masood government.

When the Taliban first appeared before his gates, as it were, Masood made conciliatory overtures, even to the extent of handing over to them Hekmatyar's former base at Charasyab. With both Wahdat and Hizb hostile forces in his suburbs, Masood was too astute to become avoidably entangled on a third front. In the course of his negotiations with Taliban leaders, it became evident not only that their outlook on life was completely at odds with that of the more sophisticated and liberal Kabulis and their government, but also that they were being used by Pakistan as its newly chosen means of trying to exercise control over events in Afghanistan. Moreover Masood's intelligence reports suggested that Muhammad Mazari, the leader of the Wahdat force holding the city's western suburbs, was persuading the Taliban to join him against the government. Masood launched a fierce pre-emptive attack on Wahdat on March 6. In response Mazari invited the Taliban to take over his front line. Perhaps mistaking them for Mazari's men, government troops fired on the advancing talibs, inflicting significant casualties.

A brief ceasefire followed, but at that very juncture the Akbari faction of the Wahdat changed sides and resumed the attack on their erstwhile Taliban allies. On March 11, Masood drove Taliban and Mazari Wahdat alike out of Kabul. By March 19 they had been driven back on all fronts as Masood established a new defence perimeter 32 kilometres south of Kabul. This put the city out of rocket range at last and gave the government control of the entire city for the first time. The unfortunate Mazari, unfairly held accountable for Akbari's defection, was "shot trying to escape". As a result of these events, the Taliban found themselves with two new enemies in the course of a few days – the Shi'a Muslims, whom they had previously avoided alienating, and the formidable forces of the Rabbani government under Masood.

By contrast, in the west of the country a series of victories enabled the Taliban to advance rapidly towards Herat. Masood airlifted 2,000 troops to help Ismail Khan's men, but the Taliban advance was only finally halted within sight of the Shindand airbase, a mere 95 kilometres south of the city. After fierce fighting, and hampered by poor logistical support that led to serious shortages of ammunition, the Taliban were driven back to just beyond Farah.

Many military commentators wrote them off at this point, but the Taliban were fired by too much zeal just to lick their wounds and lie down. Their leaders were fast learners and also made the most of the largesse they received from abroad. A gift from Saudi Arabia of 400 pick-up trucks and better planning and administration improved both their supply lines and their mobility. The ever-opportunistic Uzbeg warlord, Abdul Dostam, kept his options open by sending technicians to turn the Taliban's grounded MiG 21s into operational aircraft. Recruitment from the madrasahs over the border was stepped up and training intensified. Pakistani volunteers began to join up, as did key veteran mujehadin leaders such as Haqqani, the victor of Khost. Towards the end of 1995 the Taliban had a far better equipped, combat-ready army of 25,000 men – more than double their strength of the year before.

In August 1995 Ismail Khan had led a highly successful new attack from the West on the Taliban force already driven back from Farah. By the end of the month Ismail Khan had taken

Dilaram and threatened Kandahar itself. It was another of those crucial "if only" moments. Pakistan's ISI, shocked that its surrogate seemed on the point of defeat, bolstered the Taliban's feeble logistics and engineered another transfusion of well-trained reinforcements armed with the latest weapons.

Instead of pausing to consolidate, an overconfident Ismail Khan advanced on Girishk, thereby outstripping his logistic support. Instead of gaining another victory, his hungry and sometimes unreliable troops were defeated and their retreat was turned into a rout by the Taliban's use of rapidly deployed units of a couple of hundred men to cut off the road behind them. On September 3, Ismail Khan, calculating that his disorganized and demoralized troops could not hold the Shindand airbase to which they had retreated, abandoned it without a fight. The following day Dostam joined in on the side of the Taliban, bombing the military headquarters and airport at Herat itself. On the 5th Ismail Khan gave up the unequal struggle and retreated towards the Oxus, leaving the city to the not so tender mercies of the Taliban. At the time some accused Ismail Khan of cowardice or treachery. His courageous return to the fray at the first opportunity repudiates such slanders.

Encouraged by their success at Herat, the Taliban now launched an attack on Kabul. However, its initial advances were followed by corresponding retreats as it came up against better armed, better spirited, better led men holding strong positions. As winter descended, the protagonists settled into a stalemate. A cold and exhausted Taliban army of some 7,000 men camped uncomfortably in the hills overlooking the city and in frustration launched a daily dozen of rockets on its unfortunate citizens. The Taliban may have occupied the military high ground, but the moral high ground had clearly been abandoned! Meanwhile Masood sat tight with over

20,000 well-armed, well-fed men in good heart who had proved to their own satisfaction that a Tajik fighter was every inch the equal of a Pathan.

With hindsight that winter of 1995/96 may be seen as another missed opportunity to defeat a still fairly raw Taliban once and for all. The omission was compounded by a second mistake. Rabbani invited Hekmatyar to join his government as Prime Minister and also allowed him to appoint his own nominees to defence and the interior, but Masood remained commander in chief. Widely distrusted and disliked, the Ghilzai Pathan brought few adherents with him, undermined the confidence of the mainly Tajik garrison and brought down on the city the heaviest bombardment it had known for some time. More corrosively, he kept badgering Masood to extend his tight lines of defence to cover Hizb's outlying bases which were falling one after another to the Taliban. Rabanni endorsed Hekmatyar's importunity and, against his better judgement, Masood made his second strategic mistake and overstretched his defensive lines. It is, perhaps, worthy of note that all of Masood's military triumphs came when he was in sole command and all his disasters when following the dictate of politicians he was unable to resist or outmanoeuvre.

In a series of typical lightning attacks in the provinces of Paktya and Nangarhar on September 12 1996, the Taliban went on to take the town of Jalalabad on the highway between Peshawar and Kabul. Their next main objective was Hekmatyar's stronghold of Sarobi 75 kilometres east of Kabul and now the fulcrum of Masood's defences. Scarcely pausing in Jalalabad to refuel and rearm, the Taliban now caught the Sarobi garrison in a three-pronged attack. Nevertheless, it should not have fallen so easily. A vast ammunition dump explosion behind the government's lines, probably as a result of sabotage by Taliban infiltrators, caused panic and confusion. The majority of Hekmatyar's men deserted or defected almost as soon as the attack began. These factors and the speed and ferocity of the Taliban attack turned defeat into a rout of the men Masood had sent to reinforce the town and secure the surrounding countryside. On September 24 Sarobi was taken. On the September 25, Masood's disorganized men were pushed back to their last line of defence along the eastern edge of the Kabul plain where it meets the mountains.

At 3 p.m. on September 26, no longer confident of the support of the citizens or of his troops' ability to regroup in time, Masood gave the order for a general retreat. Surprisingly this was successfully achieved under cover of darkness with little loss of life or equipment to the enemy. So, on September 27 1996, Kabul fell to the Taliban in a blitzkrieg, or rather, a geltkrieg, for casualties on both sides were few and surrenders swift and numerous as key, well-greased palms were raised in salute to the swiftly advancing Taliban.

Rabbani, Hekmatyar, and Masood, despite having 30,000 troops between them, fled to their respective strongholds in Takhar, Kunduz and the Panshir Valley whence, for the time being, the Taliban were unable to dislodge them. The Russians, after ten mechanized and helicopter-borne major offensives against the Panshir, had learned that it was impossible to take. The ever-opportunistic Hekmatyar naturally began to negotiate with the Taliban. He protested that he had never really opposed them, a plausible claim in view of the flight of his men from Sarobi with scarcely a shot fired. Masood, his bitter antipathy for Hekmatyar justified, felt that it was Hekmatyar's failure to impede the Taliban at Sarobi that had led directly to the fall of Kabul. That the Taliban had been confident of victory all along was perhaps evident from the fact that only a week after they captured Kabul, the JUI delivered the draft radical Islamic constitution that Omar had already asked them to prepare. But the causes were more complex than that. As Anthony Davis, who was there at the time, wrote later:

> In 17 years of war no Afghan force, either government or opposition, had ever carried out such a swift and complex series of operations over such a wide area. This was mobile warfare at its most effective. To suggest that semi-literate Taliban commanders whose military experience had never extended beyond the hit-and-run attacks of guerrilla warfare could have risen to this level of planning and execution defies belief... In the short space of two years, their numbers multiplied rapidly from a force of less than 100 men... to one estimated in late 1996 to number at least 30,000 to 35,000 troops with a functioning brigade and divisional structure. It was equipped with armour, a notably effective artillery arm, a small airforce, an impressive communications network and an intelligence system. The organisational skills and logistical wherewithal required to assemble from scratch, expand and maintain such an integrated fighting machine during a period of continuous hostilities are simply not to be found in Pakistani madrassas or Afghan villages.

Following these developments, at the beginning of 1997 there were three major forces contending for power in Afghanistan:

- What eventually became the Northern Alliance led by Rabbani and Masood with some 35,000 men well supplied with ex-government weapons and munitions and backed by Iran, Russia and India;
- Dostam and his force of 25,000, mainly Uzbeg but with some Hazara units, with ample artillery, aircraft and armoured vehicles and still opposed to;

- The Taliban with the same number of men under their direct command and with the tacit support of many lesser mujehadin commanders. Although they had fewer aircraft and helicopters, the Taliban were backed both by the Pakistan military and the wealth of Saudi Arabia.

Two other significant, though much smaller, players were the Persian-speaking forces of Ismail Khan in Herat and its western environs and the undefeated fighters of the Wahdat in the Hazarajat. At this stage Hekmatyar was no longer a serious player, although he continued to hover around the fringes of the struggle.

At first things continued to go the Taliban's way, but instead of consolidating their position they became overstretched. The critical action centred on Mazar-i-Sharif, the power base of Dostam. On May 24 1997 his second in command, General Abdul Malik, ousted his leader, who fled to his comfortable retreat in Turkey, and invited the Taliban to take over Mazar. Malik also handed over to the Taliban the influential Ismaili leader Ismail Khan. The subsequent daring escape from a Taliban prison, flight to Iran and the return to the fray in 1999 of the "Lion of Herat" provides one of the more dramatic personal stories of the anti-Taliban resistance and makes him a strong claimant to play a role in any post-Taliban coalition government.

What happened next in Mazar-i-Sharif has been much argued about by those fascinated by the niceties of treachery and betrayal that epitomize any history of Afghanistan. The Hazara contingent in what was now Malik's force probably objected forcibly to being disarmed. They saw this as a breach of the terms of the surrender of Mazar. Small-scale sporadic exchanges of fire broke out between them and the Taliban. The latter, charging about the city in small groups trying to enforce their disarmament programme, provoked still fiercer Hazara resistance. Malik took the opportunity this provided to attack the rear of the Taliban forces and inflicted heavy casualties. The Taliban were forced to retreat well beyond the city boundary and bide their time, vengeance in their hearts. On August 8 1998 they recaptured the city and duly wreaked that vengeance.

Reports from Amnesty International suggest that both sides carried out wholesale and brutal executions. It is clear that whichever side controlled Mazar behaved with the cruelty and ruthlessness that has been so characteristic of virtually all participants in these civil wars. The Taliban also claimed that during their brief occupation of the city a document came to light showing that Masood planned to drive all Pathans out of northern Afghanistan. If true, this carries a health warning to those who plan to use the Northern Alliance as the keystone of a post-Taliban government.

In September Dostam returned and was temporarily reconciled to his disciple in treachery, and erstwhile second in command, Abdul Malik. Between them they drove the Taliban out of Mazar again by the end of October. Once Malik had helped his former commander back into the saddle he too found himself fleeing, in his case to Iran. Meanwhile on the Panshir front Masood also drove the Taliban back to their defensive lines only 25 miles north of Kabul.

However, Omar's forces were not to be resisted for long and when the snows melted the following spring they began to counter-attack. In the summer of 1998, following their usual preliminary financial bombardment of key opposition commanders, they drove Dostam and the Wahdat back several hundred miles and recaptured Mazar. One incident in that campaign threatened to upset their plans. Whether under command or acting independently, no one can be sure, a Taliban unit not only captured 50 Iranian truck-drivers but also killed eight Iranian diplomats and a journalist. Iran threatened military intervention and amassed more than 70,000 troops on its border with Afghanistan. The Taliban defied Iran to do its worst. The posturing over, the Taliban apologized and handed over the prisoners. Iran stood down its forces.

On August 12 1998, the Taliban seizure of the port town of Hairatan, with its bridge to the far bank of the Oxus, not only cut off a major supply route for the Northern Alliance, but also made the Russians even more nervous. They made it clear, as they had in May 1997 when they bombed Kunduz and Takhar, that there would be a prompt military response to any Taliban incursions across the river.

That September the key centre of Bamiyan in the Hazarajat also fell to the Taliban when a number of Wahdat contingents, including that of the previously very hostile Mohammad Akbari, crossed over to them. In the spring of 1999 Bamiyan was briefly back under Wahdat control, only for fortunes to change again a couple of weeks later as it fell for the final time to the Taliban. It may be that the "tit-for-tat" taking and retaking of Bamiyan was a contributory factor in the Taliban decision to destroy its famous Buddhist statues in March 2001.

The year 2000 and the first eight months of 2001 saw a stalemate, a kind of limbo in the Afghan crisis. On the military front the Northern Alliance was driven into an even tighter corner with the loss of the key town of Taliqan east of Faizabad and the interdiction of one of its main supply lines. On the other hand Masood's well-trained and well-led troops received enough logistical support from Russia and Iran to render their total defeat virtually impossible.

In May, June and December of 2000 the Organization of Islamic Conference (OIC) convened a series of peace talks that got precisely nowhere apart from the exchange of a handful of prisoners. In firm control of 85 per cent of the country and with opposition reduced to the Northern Alliance's 10,000 plus men in the far north-east. Kabul could see no reason to take any notice of the attempts of the UN, US, the OIC or anyone else to negotiate a broadly based political settlement when its government was not even accorded official recognition. In any case, Pakistan, Afghanistan's most important neighbour, its eye on the prospects for an oil pipeline from Turkmenistan through Afghanistan that required peace and stability to attract the necessary investment, seemed quite content with the status quo.

During this period the Taliban intensified its attacks on the Northern Alliance in pursuit of its goal of the total control of Afghanistan that would have made it hard for the world to continue to refuse to recognize its government. The Northern Alliance behaved no better, countenancing a major incursion into Uzbekistan and Kyrgizstan by a mixed force of Tajiks, Uzbegs and other Islamic radicals. The CIS states agreed to combine to resist terrorism but ruled out air strikes on independent states.

In October 2000 the Taliban's "guest", Osama bin Laden, followed up his bombing of the US embassies in Nairobi and Dar es Salaam in 1999 with an attack on the USS *Cole* in the Yemen which killed 17 American sailors. The furious US ambassador to Pakistan told his Afghan counterpart that America was considering missile strikes unless bin Laden was handed over. Nothing happened. The previous year Russia had made similar threats "to prevent the further de-stabilization of the region". Nothing happened. In November 2000 Pakistan once more made the fairly empty gesture of closing its border in the wake of its equally ineffectual announcement in June that it proposed to bring the 40,000 madrasahs in Pakistan under state control and "curb their networks of Islamic militants".

The UN ultimatum of December 2000 for the Taliban to hand over bin Laden or else... was inevitably ignored. Its toughest sanction was an embargo on arms for the Taliban, but not the Northern Alliance which the Taliban saw as typical of the UN's role as a Western stooge and no better than "an act of undeclared war against Afghanistan". Cynics, however, noticed that the proposed UN ban on acetic anhydride, the essential chemical for the manufacture of heroin, which would have hurt the drugs barons and the Northern Alliance even more than the Taliban, was quietly dropped. The Taliban's response to both UN blandishments and UN threats was progressively to close down its various activities, most damagingly, in May 2001, the Special Mission to Afghanistan which coordinated refugee relief efforts, and the 116 bakeries of the World Food Programme in June. A year later the foreign aid workers who remained were required to sign a declaration to the effect that they would be ruled by the Shari'at.

It almost seemed as if the Taliban were deliberately provoking the Western world. On March 8 2001, in the face of appeals from all round the world, including many from Muslims, they destroyed the Buddhas at Bamiyan. Although, in my opinion, aesthetically less pleasing these remarkable and awe-inspiring colossi were of worldwide religious, archaeological and historical importance. In the same month the hardliners in the Taliban government took over control of the military through defence minister Fazal Akhund. In May the CPVPV issued instructions that all foreigners were to wear yellow badges – reminiscent of those introduced against the Jews in Nazi Germany. Hindus also had to hang a piece of yellow cloth on their outer doors. Still nothing happened.

Thus things might have remained, but for bin Laden's obsessive hatred of America and the attack on the World Trade Center on 11 September 2001.

14

THE FOURTH HORSEMAN

Of the four horsemen of the apocalypse the first two, the white and the red, war and civil strife, have been amply described in the preceding pages. The third, upon the dark horse, is famine and he has ridden across our television screens and the pages of our newspapers often enough in the weeks since September 11 and has passed to and fro across the land of the Afghans for the past four years to terrible effect. As I write, the aid agencies plead in vain for a break in the militarily futile bombing to enable them to distribute food and clothing in the three or four weeks before winter makes their task well nigh impossible. This war will not "be over by Christmas". All the evidence points to the prospect of prolonged and stubborn resistance by the Taliban, both from its national troops and its foreign mercenaries. In such circumstances, to refuse to suspend the bombardment is an act of cold inhumanity not of military necessity. Will 100,000 Afghans dead of cold and hunger appease America's desire for revenge? Will a million?

Can anyone's conscience be soothed by claims that it is nothing to do with us, it is all the fault of the Taliban? They are stealing the aid; they are poisoning the food.

And there is the fourth horseman yet to be accounted for, Death on a pale horse.

And death can come in many forms and in many places. The intervention of foreign powers, not just the chief culprits, the Soviet Union and the United States, but the rest of us too, has unleashed death worldwide in two of its most terrifying manifestations – drugs and terrorism.

Right from the outset of the mujehadin resistance to the

Soviet invasion, it became apparent that the already substantial Afghan opium trade would flourish in the hothouse of war. For the mujehadin, particularly in the early days, it was seen as a quick way to raise the cash needed to buy arms and equipment. For the CIA, opium widely available in Afghanistan would be a potentially potent weapon with which to undermine the morale of the enemy.* The CIA was by no means the first in history to use drugs as a weapon of war, but it was among the first to do so since the Second World War. The thirteenth-century Persian Assassins who gave their name to that black trade were actually "hashisheen" because their zeal was sharpened and their consciences blunted by their founder's judicious application of hashish. It is strange that the United States had not learned the lesson of Vietnam where the weapon backfired badly and narcotics intended to undermine the enemy actually debilitated America's own troops and inflicted more casualties back home than on the enemy.

In the autumn of 1980 I suggested to a number of sympathetic Conservative MPs that the government should buy up all of the mujehadin's crop of opium at the going rate and destroy it. This would not only keep the drugs off the market but would also enable finance to reach the mujehadin by a means to which the Soviets could scarcely object. I subsequently discovered that a US academic who had disclosed CIA links to the Colombian cartels had suggested a similar "buy and burn" scheme and was similarly ignored. In a typical left hand/right hand contradiction, the Drugs Enforcement Agency found its efforts to curtail the supply of drugs from South Asia overwhelmed by the CIA's determination to expand the trade as an anti-Soviet weapon of

This operation has been detailed in Cooley, Unholy Wars. See the reading list.

war. As a result of that expansion, drug-related deaths soared in the United States and Western Europe. When Zbigniew Brzezinski, the US National Security Advisor of the time, was asked in Taliban times if he regretted these consequences he retorted that he regretted nothing that had led to "drawing the Russians into the Afghan trap". That may turn out to be a bitter irony now that America has jumped into the same trap feet first.

It has to be admitted that it was an effective, if totally immoral and eventually self-destructive, weapon against the Soviet army. Drug taking among scared and reluctant conscripts and also many regular officers and men was rife by the end of the war. Some units were repatriated after nine months in a vain attempt to combat the problem. Many Soviet servicemen took the drug habit back with them to Russia's already strained social structure.

By 1989 Soviet Intelligence estimated that 800 tons of opium was coming out of Afghanistan – more than twice the production of Iran and Pakistan combined. By 1994, when the Taliban first appeared on the scene, Afghanistan was the world's leading producer of opium. In 1997 Afghanistan and Pakistan were putting 500 tons of white heroin powder onto the market with a street value in the US alone of $50bn. In the seventeen years from the Soviet invasion to the Taliban capture of Kabul, world production rose tenfold.

The UN estimated that Afghanistan produced 4,600 tonnes of opium in 1999 – 75 per cent of the world's output. Afghan opium found its way to world markets across every one of Afghanistan's borders, including that with China. Certainly, its most devastating effects have been experienced by those same neighbours. There are now estimated to be as many as five million users in Pakistan, three million in Iran and a million in China. A quarter to a third of these could be classified as addicts.

The World Bank calculated that the value of this trade to Afghanistan was $2.5bn and that the smuggling of the foreign goods financed by the opium trade cost Pakistan $6bn in 1998.

A Soviet account of the drug problem in the 1980s accused Gailani and National Islamic Front (NIFA) of being the leading player in the drugs trade. Soviet Intelligence believed his financial resources to be larger than he could have accumulated through his own successful business activity and Western aid. I know of no evidence to substantiate this claim, which I personally think unlikely, but whether or not the NIFA was involved in a big way (everyone was involved in a small way), the trade as a whole grew rapidly. Both Hekmatyar and the Northern Alliance became major suppliers. Ayoub Afridi, head of the Afridi tribe, was probably the largest of the drug barons. He offered a deal to Benazir Bhutto – in return for immunity from prosecution he would kill off the greater part of the drug trade – but she could scarcely accept this publicly without undermining attempts to stamp out what had become a very serious problem in Pakistan. Ayoub then gave himself up to the US authorities, expecting to be let off lightly. In fact the judge in New York sentenced him to five years. The sentence was mysteriously reduced for unspecified reasons, possibly evidence against other Pathan drug barons.

It may be significant in determining the Taliban's initial ambivalent attitude to the drug trade that its leaders mostly come from the same Pathan tribes as the majority of the principal drug traders. Certainly within a few weeks of Taliban occupying Kandahar in 1994, the smuggling traffic, on which they levied zakat, a tax of 10 per cent, grew apace. But its growth was not fast enough for the big players in the transport and smuggling "mafia" who wanted the Taliban to attack Herat, then securely held by Ismail Khan, in order to open up additional routes. Against Pakistani military advice they did so, and incurred their first defeat in May 1995, as described earlier. The Taliban did not ban the trade in heroin, the drug of choice in the West, but they did outlaw hashish, the drug of choice within their own borders. If the infidel chose to dope themselves to death, so much the better. Besides, the heroin traffic zakat formed a major part of Taliban revenue. The change in this attitude has been remarkable.

Mullah Omar's edict in July 2000 banning the cultivation of poppy has since had an astonishing effect and should certainly be entered on the credit side of the Taliban's balance sheet. In 2000 the UN Drug Control Programme annual survey showed that a little over 82,000 hectares of poppy were cultivated. That still represented a marked fall of 28 per cent from 4,600 tonnes of actual opium in 1999 to 3,300 in 2000. How much of this was attributable to Omar's prohibition and how much to the sustained drought is hard to tell. In 2001 the area under cultivation had shrunk dramatically to a little over 7,500 hectares. Even allowing for some slight undetected clandestine production, a 91 per cent drop is astonishing. The latest figures from the UNDCP imply that no more than 300 to 350 tonnes of opium are now coming out of Afghanistan.

Sceptics can be reassured that the UNDCP survey is carried out comprehensively and thoroughly by trained Afghans. Interestingly, only areas under Northern Alliance control increased production and they now account for three-quarters of Afghan poppy growing. Nearly all of the farmers interviewed attributed the fall in cultivation to the drought as much as to the Taliban's strictly enforced ban. Sadly, the inference to be drawn is that the cultivation of food crops may have fallen by a similar proportion since most food crops require more water than poppies.

What is true is that the excuse of raising funds for the jihad provided the perfect umbrella under which professional smugglers and criminals were able to set up massive drug operations to their own long-term financial advantage and the peril of the world. What Cooley rightly calls the "unholy wars" tolerated the rise of the biggest drug empire ever seen east of the great Colombian cocaine cartels.

The other knock-on effects were also serious. Land growing poppies could not grow the food Afghanistan so badly needed and the crime and corruption connected with the drug trade affected every level of Afghan and Pakistani society, from the customs officer taking bribes to the much larger kickbacks the smugglers paid for protection right up to the highest level.

The second form of death spread by the Afghan wars, terrorism, may use the drugs trade to finance its activities but seldom uses narcotics as a direct weapon. Indeed, terror's chief contemporary protagonist, Osama bin Laden, has expressly condemned drug taking as being symptomatic of a corrupt Western culture.

America's obsession with Osama bin Laden is entirely understandable in the aftermath of September 11, but runs the risk of distorting its perception of worldwide terrorism. The story of the United States' changing relationship with bin Laden is indeed a cautionary tale about choosing one's friends wisely.

When the United States and Saudi Arabia wanted to augment the flow of funds to the mujehadin by securing and distributing large private contributions discreetly, bin Laden was chosen as one of the most highly favoured intermediaries. A pious and extremely wealthy Wahabi, in 1981 he had already been sent on missions to the mujehadin in Pakistan by Prince Turki, Saudi Arabia's head of Intelligence. While there he not only met Mullah Omar, but also began constructing for the mujehadin in Afghanistan itself the roads, secure bunkers and supply depots that would be equally useful to al Qaida, his terrorist organization, once the war with the Russians was over.

Bin Laden's companies throughout the Arab world, and even in London, all employed mujehadin veterans, or Afghansi, of all nationalities. At a moment's notice they could abandon their cover occupations in construction to pursue bin Laden's real business – terrorism. As Cooley wrote, bin Laden had "privatised world terrorism and made it a major private enterprise".

Immensely rich – he is at least a dollar billionaire – bin Laden was also able to tap the private sources he had drawn on to help the mujehadin for his new jihad against America.

When the Russians left Afghanistan he moved back to Saudi Arabia, only to find soon that he was not as welcome as he had once been. When his own government tried to curtail his movements, he moved to the Sudan in 1991. In 1994 Saudi Arabia deprived him of his citizenship at the insistence of President Mubarak of Egypt. In 1996 US pressure on the Sudanese government forced him to move again, this time back to his old friends in Afghanistan.

There is little point in speculating about the origin and cause of bin Laden's deep hatred of America. It may be that of a genuine zealot enraged by what he sees as American injustices towards Arabs throughout the world from Palestine to Iraq. Or it may simply be psychopathic. Either way it is not amenable to reason or to the restraints of normal human respect for the lives of the innocent. For bin Laden as for Bush, it is a case of "if you are not with us you are against us". Whatever the cause there can be no doubt about the intensity of his animosity which grew from threatening broadcasts and innumerable fatwa to the bombing of the US embassies in Nairobi and Dar es Salaam on August 8 1998 with more than 200 victims, mostly Africans.

The American response was pitched in the same violent vein once its demand to Afghanistan that Bin Laden should be handed over on suspicion of complicity was not met immediately. When the Taliban, not unreasonably, asked the US for proof of bin Laden's implication in the bombings, America replied with Tomahawk missiles on August 20, only twelve days later. The attack did little damage and casualties were few, but the wound to Afghan pride was deep. From that moment on Afghan nationalism and Islamic religious conviction alike made inevitable their protection of bin Laden – despite the fact that the Taliban had condemned his terrorist activities previously, as they were to do again tacitly in September 2001.

When in February 1999, following the attack on the USS *Cole* off the coast of bin Laden's native Yemen, in which 17 US sailors were killed, the US demanded that the Taliban hand over bin Laden or else. . . America never spelled out, publicly at least, of what or else consisted. Although the Saudi terrorist disappeared from Kandahar, where he had been lodged to try to keep a restraining eye on him, some senior Taliban began to see him as a liability. Possibly only his intimate friendship with Omar saved him from expulsion, as it almost certainly did again in September 2001. Had the US not acted so hastily and in such a heavy-handed way bin Laden might have been handed over or expelled in due course when loss of honour was less obviously involved. In October 1999 the UN invoked a strict trade embargo, particularly of weapons, if Afghanistan did not hand over its guest for trial in connection with the embassy and USS *Cole* bombings. Once more threats had the opposite effect to that intended. Bin Laden and al Qaida felt justified in brewing an even more wickedly devastating terrorist concoction.

Which brings us back to one purpose of this book, to try to trace the historical path in Afghanistan which led, albeit indirectly, to the events of September 11. The tracing back of cause and effect can go on for ever – (a) was caused by (b), caused by (c), caused by (d) and so on ad infinitum – but the two catalytic events that have led to the present turmoil in Afghanistan, and its breeding of international terrorism and a massive increase in international drugs traffic, were undoubtedly the Soviet Politburo decision of December 12 1979 to invade and the US decision a fortnight later to back the mujehadin. The habit of interference dies hard and the consequences of America's latest indulgence in it have yet to be seen.

15

INCONCLUSIVE CONCLUSIONS

Lord Curzon, not renowned for his modesty, once remarked that "no man who has ever read a page of Indian history will every prophesy about the frontier". Curzon was right. All one can sensibly do is offer a personal appraisal of the conflicting forces in that area and their motives and raise some of the questions facing us in the present crisis.

The United States – and Britain – had every right to seek retribution against the perpetrators of the September 11 massacre. But how is this retribution to be exacted? Upon whom? What form should it take? Should it be by due process of law in which bin Laden is brought before a court or even tried formally in absentia? Or will it be by those same terrorist methods, the hit squad, the political assassination, we have been quick to condemn elsewhere? Had we the right to launch an act of war against a government, however odious we might deem it, without any UN sanction, that had committed no legally recognized act of war against us? Is it for us to decide that the Taliban government is not legitimate? Does sheltering a person accused, but not publicly convicted, of terrorism justify attacking an entire country? Does what the US military choose so euphemistically to call collateral damage and destroying assets – by which we mean killing innocent civilians and destroying unrelated property – equate in the Western conscience to no more than the "regrettable" deaths and damage that sometimes ensue when a cop has a shoot-out with a suspect or a police car kills someone when in hot pursuit? Do we think a few hundred, or even a few thousand, sacks of wheat and woolly jumpers air-dropped fairly haphazardly over this vast landscape will prevent the wholesale death by starvation and hypothermia that might have been staved off by airlifts and truck convoys using the roads and airfields our attacks have rendered even more unusable than they were before?

The amount of aid needed to restore Afghanistan to even a moderate level of prosperity will dwarf the scale of any previous aid programme since Marshall Aid put Germany back on its feet in the late 1940s. Will the governments of richer nations in a world whose economy is in or near recession continue to allocate billions of dollars to Afghanistan once the current military campaign and its immediate humanitarian aftermath have passed? Or will they, as outside powers have done so often in the past, walk away from these desperate people once their short-term objectives have been achieved? Will the US, or US companies and consortia, be willing to meet the substantial extra cost of building a pipeline from Turkmenistan through Afghanistan to the Pakistan port of Gwadar simply to benefit the people of those two poor countries? Or will they use the shorter and more economic route through northern Iran?

What will have been achieved a few months from now as a result of the heavy handed attack on Afghanistan, is the recruitment of ten terrorists for every Afghan killed – it matters not whether Taliban or innocent child. For every three or four Muslim states cajoled or coerced into supporting Bush's "crusade", a "friendly" government in one or two will have been destabilized and ultimately toppled through popular uprising. It is very doubtful if Saudi Arabia, Pakistan and at least one of the CIS states will be under the same kind of rule in five years' time as they are now.

Plenty of questions and accusations you may say, but what about some answers? I readily admit there are no easy ones, but I do believe that there were better options which could have been pursued. The Taliban regime, despite semi-controlling nine-tenths of the country was – and this book has shown how tenuous central control has always been in Afghanistan – under considerable stress. It might have moderated its stance or even collapsed without outside interference. Tensions were growing between traditionalists and hard-line radicals. The economy was reaching a state of collapse in which outside aid, to which conditions could have been attached, would almost certainly have been called for. All of Afghanistan's neighbours, even those that helped put the Taliban in power, were becoming disillusioned with its government. By the nature of our assault we have done the one thing that will ease the Taliban's internal stresses and unite behind them the great majority of Afghans of all ethnic groups. Any Afghan, Pathan or Tajik, Hazara or Uzbeg resents one thing more than internal tyranny – and that is a foreign invasion of their land, as the Russians found to their cost and the Americans are also likely to find out.

I happen to believe it would have been possible to strike a bargain with the Taliban by patient and subtle negotiation, but it seems that in America patience means 26 days. President Bush would do well to be mindful of the Pathan saying " I took revenge after a hundred years and I took it too quickly."

It is all too easy simply to adopt an anti-American stance, which does not solve the problem. However, it has to be said that US judgement in foreign affairs, whether through ignorance or arrogance, has consistently been appalling. With the best possible intentions they have invariably backed the wrong side in internal conflicts for the wrong reasons with the worst possible results, so it is reasonable to ask whether they have not done the same again in Afghanistan, not once but three times: mujehadin, pro-Taliban and anti-Taliban.

All justice must contain an element of revenge to be generally acceptable, but once it consists of that element alone it ceases to be justice and that to many Muslims, and throughout the Third World, is what has happened in the case of bin Laden and the Afghans. So of what might a judicially balanced but effective approach have consisted?

Supposing Britain had taken the initiative, preferably clandestinely, to create an aid alliance that could put billions rather than millions on the bare Afghan table as part of a quid pro quo? It would have been no use simply offering an open trade – aid for bin Laden – for that would have offended too deeply against the Pathan code of Pushtunwali. However, a Muslim divine is as capable as any Jesuit of sophisticated casuistry and allowing a special forces snatch squad – tacitly pointed in the right direction – to go in and abduct him might not have been deemed dishonourable.

In order to persuade the Taliban government it would have been necessary for Britain to undertake convincingly that bin Laden would not be handed over for trial to the Americans, Satan incarnate, but to a fair trial before an International War Crimes Tribunal presided over by a Muslim judge and taking account of the Shari'at in its liberations. That may not have been acceptable to the Americans, whose thirst for vengeance might not have been appeased by such an approach, but surely it was worth attempting before embarking on the horrors of war. The World Trade Center massacre killed not only Americans, but also citizens of many other nations. The crime was not just against America, but against humanity and should still be tried as such if any verdict is to be endorsed as just by Muslims worldwide as well as the injured parties.

If this approach had worked it would have had many advantages, not least the eventual weakening of the Taliban in a more prosperous Afghanistan. It would probably also have been necessary to ensure that aid reached the destitute not the divines by channelling it through acceptable agencies such as the Red Cross and the Red Crescent. Western, and particularly Christian, aid agencies would not be acceptable nor, probably, would the UN itself, which is seen by many in Afghanistan, however unjustly, as an American stooge.

This strategy could have spared the lives of many innocents, prevented tens of thousands from being driven to flee their homes, alleviated suffering in one of the world's poorest countries, and diminished the despair that recruits many terrorists. It could have saved the United States from sinking to the level of the terrorists it condemns by resorting to the political assassination currently illegal under its constitution. Above all, it would have established that the writ of international law can run even to the most remote and inaccessible corner of the world. That opportunity has been missed by America's enraged ineptitude. Is it too late to create another?

Notwithstanding Lord Curzon's stricture cited at the start of this chapter, there are some lessons to be learned from the history of Afghanistan and the frontier.

1. There are no immutable loyalties or alliances in Afghanistan, whatever ethnic or religious umbrella they may be formed under and however fervent the oaths that seal them. In Afghanistan expediency rules, OK?
2. Afghans of all races will oppose, with or without external help, any foreign invader of their land and reject any "Afghan Solution" imposed from outside.
3. The control of government in Kabul does not mean the control of all Afghanistan – the central writ tends to run not much further than the suburbs.

4. Any outsider who sticks his finger in the Afghan pie finds it was a damn sight hotter than he thought and ruins the pie for the Afghans. Persia, Britain, Russia and now the United States have all found their goals unobtainable and the cost of seeking them unsustainable, but the greatest price has always been paid by the poor, bloodied people of Afghanistan.

There may be some prospect of avoiding yet another disastrous outcome if we confine ourselves to a single goal – the trial and, if convicted, the punishment of bin Laden. The first must be fair, and the second commensurate with the crime. The principles of international law and the Shari'at need to be reconciled so that people of all faiths and of none feel that justice has been done. If the evidence would endanger lives if made public – usually a pretty specious excuse for not having sufficient to stand scrutiny – then let the trial be in camera and also in absentia.

Let the trial be presided over by a Muslim judge and the bench consist of another six leading judges, one from the US, one from the Taliban and four from states who are neutral in this affair – India, China, South Africa and Brazil, for example. Let the verdict be by majority with the president having a casting vote. If the verdict is guilty, let the court demand from the Taliban (or its successor) the handing over of bin Laden with the clear proviso that if he is not surrendered then all available means, including military force, will be used to arrest him. Let his punishment be imposed in a neutral state where neither a lynch mob nor a convenient escape might thwart the course of justice.

But what about the Afghans when this high noon affair is done? How can we help them without doing more harm than good?

Massive aid, yes, as we have already said, but at village and district level where the historic patterns of cooperation and authority have always worked best.

We need to pay, without quibbling, ample "blood money" to the families of all civilians killed by US and allied action. That is a satisfaction in honour the Pathans in particular can understand and though no doubt there will be some fraudulent claims it would be better to accept them without too much scrutiny. Only thus can the age-old desire for vengeance be assuaged in the land of the blood feud.

We need under UN auspices a massive disarmament programme of all heavy weapons, from rocket launchers to heavy machine guns held by all contending factions. There is no point in trying to gather in personal arms other than on a voluntary basis with large financial incentives. The majority of Afghans, Pathans in particular, look on the possession of a gun as the symbol of their manhood.

As a corollary we need to provide any agreed central government with a UN peacekeeping force both to ensure its tenure of office and to supervise disarmament as well as can be. Moreover, any peacekeeping force should probably consist of a number of quite separate commands differently composed in each of the main ethnic areas of Afghanistan.

We need to buy in for destruction all opium poppy production for the next season at above the market price on condition that other crops (for which the seed, fertilizer and cultivation aids are provided free) are planted in their place. Half of the poppy purchase price to be paid on witnessed delivery or destruction, half on evidence of the new crop being planted and no poppies being grown. A fairly similar, but less generous and much smaller-scale scheme, has been successfully introduced in the past in some areas.

We need to give high priority to helping Afghans to restore

their irrigation and communication systems, their fertilizer plants and their electricity generating capacity.

If a multi-ethnic, multi-party system of government were deemed essential to the development of Afghanistan, then it should probably be bicameral. A new Shura would have to consist, as in Zahir Shah's reign, of a Wolasi Jirgah (lower house) related to population and a Meshrano Jirgah (upper house) on an equal regional representation basis. Nor is it much use talking about conventional elections in a country with such low levels of literacy (30 per cent at the last very optimistic count) and such high levels of suspicion of any activity that might conceivably give authority more control over the individual. The turnout figure quoted in chapter 8 is unlikely to be much improved upon.

What might work would be something more akin to the panchayat system briefly tried in Pakistan, with each village jirgah electing one or two representatives, according to population, to attend an annual Shura at which matters of general interest could be discussed and a proportion of those attending are then elected to form the membership of the Wolasi Jirgah.

Finally we have to leave the Afghans to work out their social systems for themselves whatever we may feel about women's rights, trial by jury, universal suffrage and many other Western concepts.

That was, I realize, a long catalogue of ifs and buts, yet without some hope for the future in the wake of our intervention in Afghanistan we may as well give the world up to anarchy here and now.

Our dilemma is sharpened by the fact that freedom from foreign interference and what Western liberals choose to call reform appear to be on opposite sides. The history of Afghanistan throughout the past hundred years has been of reformers – Abdur Rahman, Amanullah, the "democrat", even Daoud and the Marxists – being successfully defeated by the bigotry of the mullahs and the pugnacity of the Pathan tribes. Encouraging the present war against the Taliban would be to back men whose policy, if they were in unrestrained power, would probably be as much anathema to Western liberal principles as those of the regime we now seek to overthrow. It is arrogant to presume we know best what is best for the Afghans when we should be upholding the no less fundamental principle of a people's right to determine the pattern of their lives without external military interference. We have to recognize that once the bin Laden case is closed, the West's prime objective should not be revenge or even the nebulous "War on Terrorism", but to help the Afghan people to further their own interests in their own way.

Short Reading List

History (pre Soviet invasion)
Caroe, Sir Olaf, *The Pathans* (Macmillan, 1962)
Dupree, Louis, *Afghanistan* (Princeton, 1973)
Griffiths, John.C., *Afghanistan* (Pall Mall, 1967)
Fletcher, Arnold, *Afghanistan: Highway of Conquest* (Cornell, 1965)
Fraser-Tytler, Sir William, *Afghanistan* (Oxford University Press, 1953)
Newell, N. & R., *The Struggle for Afghanistan* (Cowell, 1981)

Historical accounts
Elphinstone, Mountstuart, *Account of the Kingdom of Caubul* (London, 1815)
Holdich, Sir Thomas, *The Indian Borderland* (London, 1901)

Ideology
Bradsher, Henry *Political Order in Post Communist Afghanistan*
  (Lynne Rienner Publications, 1992)
Cooley, John.K., *Unholy Wars* (Pluto, 2000)
Magnus, Ralph H. and Eden Naby *Afghanistan: Marx, Mullah and Mujahid*
  (Westview, 2000)

Military and General:
Rogers, Tom, *The Soviet Withdrawal from Afghanistan* (Greenwood Press, 1993)
Sarin and Dvoretsky, *The Afghan Syndrome* (Presidio, 1993)

The Taliban
Maley, William (ed) *Fundamentalism Reborn*, (New York University Press, 1998)
Marsden, Peter, *The Taliban* (Zed Books, 1998)
Rashid, Ahmed, *Taliban: Islam, Oil and the Great Game* (Yale University Press, 2001)

Sheer pleasure
Elliott, Jason, *An Unexpected Light* (Picador, 1999)
Michaud, Roland and Sabrina, *Afghanistan* (Thames and Hudson, 1980)
Newby, Eric, *A Short Walk in the Hindu Kush* (Secker and Warburg, 1958)

Articles
The journals covering Afghan affairs are too numerous to mention,
but these will be found generally useful:

Asian Survey
Foreign Affairs
Journal of the Royal Asiatic Society
Keesings
Review of International Studies

Index